Philip Kerr & Ceri Jones

Straightforward

Intermediate Student's Book

MACMILLAN

CONTENTS

Lesson	Grammar	Vocabulary	Functional language	Pronunciation
1A **Double lives** p6	Stative & dynamic verbs			
1B **Daily lives** p8	Present simple & present continuous	Verbs with two meanings		
1C **Britishness** p10	Subject & object questions	Self-image		
1D **First impressions** p12		Describing people	Describing people	Intonation (lists)
1 Language reference p14				
2A **Around the world** p16	Present perfect & past simple			
2B **Unusual journeys** p18		Phrasal verbs		Word linking
2C **Down under** p20	Present perfect for unfinished time			
2D **Getting around** p22		Verb collocations (travel)	Travelling	
2 Language reference p24				
3A **Dream homes** p26	Modals of obligation, permission & prohibition (present time)			
3B **Unusual homes** p28	*Make*, *let* & *allow*	Accommodation		
3C **Bedrooms** p30	Modals of obligation, permission & prohibition (past time)	Verb collocations (sleep)		
3D **Dinner invitation** p32			Requests	Intonation (requests)
3 Language reference p34				
4A **Luck of the draw** p36	Past simple & past continuous	Idioms (taking risks)		*Was* & *were*
4B **Twists of fate** p38	Past perfect simple	Injuries		
4C **Bad luck stories** p40		Time linkers		
4D **Fancy that!** p42		*Both* & *neither*	Talking about similarities & differences	
4 Language reference p44				
5A **Hard sell** p46	Comparisons 1	Adjectives (advertising)		
5B **Cold calling** p48	Comparisons 2	Adjectives (negative prefixes)		/s/, /z/ & /ʃ/
5C **The office** p50	Comparing nouns	Office activities		
5D **Paperwork** p52		Office supplies	On the phone	
5 Language reference p54				
6A **Summer holiday** p56	Future 1 (future plans)	Holidays 1		
6B **Getting away** p58	Future 2 (predictions)	Holidays 2		
6C **Perfect day** p60	Present tenses in future time clauses			
6D **Travel plans** p62		Collocations with *sound*	Indirect questions	Word stress
6 Language reference p64				

		Reading & Listening	Speaking	Writing (in the Workbook)
1A	R	Liars! (Mad Men)	Discussing what people are most likely to lie about Talking about yourself	A description of a best friend
1B	L	Radio review of TV programme: How Michael Portillo Became a Single Mum	Describing daily routines **Did you know?** British political parties	
1C	R	Are you British enough?	Discussing answers to a British culture quiz Devising a quiz about culture in your country	
1D	L	Dialogue about a new flatmate	Talking about first impressions Discussing making a good impression	
2A	R	Lawyer gives up job to cycle around the world	Discussing travelling	A description of a town or city
2B	L/R	Three unusual journeys	Talking about a film or book of a long journey	
2C	R	Excerpt from a blog about a trip around Australia	Talking about Australia Planning a journey across your country	
2D	L	Three dialogues about trying to get somewhere	Talking about daily transport in a city you know well **Did you know?** New York & London taxis	
3A	R	Paradise Ridge	Discussing where you live	Advantages and disadvantages
	L	Interviews with residents talking about disadvantages of living in Paradise Ridge		
3B	L	Three interviews with people who live in unusual homes	Designing a luxury holiday home	
3C	R	Six things you probably didn't know about beds and bedrooms	Talking about sleeping & dreaming	
3D	L	Dinner party	Describing a recent dinner party Roleplay: dinner party **Did you know?** Food in Britain	
4A	R	Lottery winners and losers	Inventing a story about a lottery winner	A narrative: lottery winner
4B	L	The world's luckiest man		
	R	Lucky Luciano		
4C	R	Three bad luck stories	Inventing a bad luck story **Did you know?** Superstitions in Britain	
4D	L	Dialogue at work: discussing things in common	Identifying & discussing coincidences	
5A	R	Catch them young	Planning & presenting an advertisement for a mineral water	An advertisement
5B	L	Phone call: credit card telesales	Carrying out a market research survey	
5C	R	Office stereotypes	Planning an office party	
5D	L	Ordering office supplies over the phone	Roleplay: phone dialogue ordering office supplies **Did you know?** London's Mayfair and Park Lane districts	
6A	R	Questionnaire: What kind of holiday person are you?	Making plans with other holiday makers	An extract from a holiday brochure
6B	L	Six short interviews at the airport	Planning a holiday for a family group	
6C	R	Emerald Tours	Discussing the perfect day out **Did you know?** Cork – European capital of culture	
6D	L	Enquiring about flights over the phone	Discussing the advantages of booking a holiday online or through a travel agent's	

Lesson	Grammar	Vocabulary	Functional language	Pronunciation
7A **Moving** p66	Present perfect continuous 1	Phrasal verbs with *live*		
7B **Life changes** p68		Metaphor		
7C **Happy birthday** p70	Present perfect continuous 2	Life stages		
7D **Dilemmas** p72		Exclamations with *what*	Giving advice	Intonation (feelings)
7 Language reference p74				
8A **Breaking news** p76	*Would*	Newspapers		
8B **Protests** p78	Unreal conditions (type 2)			/u/ & /uː/
8C **Bank robbers** p80	Unreal conditions (type 3)	Law & order		
8D **Driving** p82		Compound nouns (driving)	Offers	
8 Language reference p84				
9A **The shopping basket** p86	Articles & determiners	Containers		*of*
9B **Shoppers** p88	Quantifiers 1	Shopping		
9C **E-shopping** p90	Quantifiers 2	Collocations with *take*		
9D **Phone calls** p92		Prepositional phrases	Complaints	
9 Language reference p94				
10A **Secrets** p96	Modals of speculation 1 (present time)	Illusions		Sentence stress
10B **Fact or fiction?** p98	Modals of speculation 2 (present time)	Word families		
10C **Mysteries** p100	Modals of speculation (past time)	Verbs followed by infinitive		
10D **Strictly confidential** p102		Idioms	Advantages & disadvantages	
10 Language reference p104				
11A **Total sport** p106	Passive	Sport		
11B **Olympic® dreams** p108	Verbs with two objects	Nouns and adjectives (describing people)		
11C **Strange sports** p110	Causative	Services		/ɪə/ & /eə/
11D **Sport relief** p112		*Make* & *do*	Question tags (checking)	
11 Language reference p114				
12A **Basic needs** p116	Reported speech & thought			
12B **Money** p118	Reported questions	Verb collocations (money)		
12C **Sue!** p120	*Tell* & *ask* with infinitive	Reporting verbs		
12D **Golden moments** p122			Social expressions	Intonation (social expressions)
12 Language reference p124				
Communication activities p126	Audioscripts p135	Irregular verb list p147	Unit reviews p148	

		Reading & Listening	Speaking	Writing (in the Workbook)
7A	R	*Redundancy was the best thing that ever happened to me*		A letter of advice
7B	L	Interview with a house husband	Discussing important life events *Did you know?* Legal ages in England & Wales	
7C	R	*Florrie prepares to celebrate her 113th birthday*	Discussing different stages of life Talking about changes in students' lifetimes	
7D	L	Dialogue about a dilemma at work	Discussing personal dilemmas Giving advice about a problem	
8A	L	Interview with an investigative journalist	Planning the front page for a newspaper *Did you know?* Rupert Murdoch	A funny crime story
8B	R	Five newspaper reports about protests	Discussing three related newspaper articles	
8C	R	Newspaper article about idiot robbers	Talking about films with robberies Continuing a dialogue from a film	
8D	L	Two dialogues involving driving problems	Discussing the advantages and disadvantages of cars Discussing the seriousness of driving offences	
9A	R	*Checking out the check out*		A letter of complaint
9B	L	Interview with a shopaholic	Planning a shopping centre	
9C	R	*Eezeemall.com*	Devising a quiz to test whether classmates are technophobes or cybernauts	
9D	L	Two dialogues about problems with phones	Discussing mobile phones and their features Roleplay: a complaint *Did you know?* The red phone box	
0A	R	*The tricks of the trade*	Performing a magic trick	A narrative
0B	L	Radio phone-in: *The Da Vinci Code*	Discussing conspiracy theories *Did you know?* Glastonbury	
0C	R	John Darwin	Solving a mystery	
0D	L	Dialogue about the installation of spy software at work	Discussing confidential information Debate about installing CCTV cameras in secondary schools	
1A	R	Chrissie Wellington	Talking about sports & how to play them	A description of a sporting event
1B	L	Interview with a psychologist about child sports stars	Planning & presenting an Olympic bid	
1C	R	Strange sports	Interviewing each other about services	
1D	L	Five dialogues about a sponsored bike ride	Discussing ways to raise money for charity *Did you know?* British royal family & charity	
2A	R	*I never thought it would happen to me*	Ordering important things in life	Writing a report
2B	R	A money survey		
	L	Dialogue about the results of the money survey		
2C	R	Five newspaper articles	Discussing how much compensation someone should receive	
2D	L	Two dialogues about important news	Choosing presents for special occasions *Did you know?* The US Congressional Gold Medal	

1A | Double lives

SPEAKING

1 Work in small groups. Look at the list and decide which things are the most important when you are describing who you are.

- name
- age
- job
- nationality
- marital status
- qualifications
- friends
- salary

2 Discuss these questions with your group.

- Which information in exercise 1 are you most interested in when you meet someone for the first time?
- Which of these things do you think people are most likely to lie about?
- Talk about the most honest person you know.

3 Put the following in order of seriousness (1 = most serious ➔ 6 = least serious).

- ☐ lying about why you are late for work/ school
- ☐ lying about your age to get into a nightclub
- ☐ lying about your qualifications to get a job
- ☐ lying to your partner about another person
- ☐ lying to a friend about their new hairstyle
- ☐ lying to a member of your family about a present that you didn't like

READING

1 Look at the headlines on the web page. Which of the following pieces of information do you expect to find?

1 what people do when they lie
2 why people lie
3 who lies more, men or women
4 examples of famous liars
5 examples of liars in films and on television
6 examples of favourite lies

2 Read the web page to check your answers.

Liars!

How to spot them

He thinks he's getting away with it, but his body and his voice are giving him away. He's stumbling over his words. He's fidgeting and nervous. His hands won't stay still and his palms are probably sweaty as well. He seems to be smiling, but there's a little bit of tension around his lips and his nose. Although the bottom half of his face is forming a smile, it hasn't reached his eyes. He's looking at you straight in the eyes and he appears to be 100% sincere, but the tone of his voice has dropped and the rhythm of his speech has slowed down. There's no doubt about it: he's lying.

Learn to spot the telltale signs.

Screen liars

It's 1960s New York. Don Draper is a successful advertising executive, a happily married man with a beautiful wife. But all of this is built on a lie, or better said, a series of lies. Even his name is a lie. He 'stole' it from an officer who was killed fighting in Korea. He returned to the States and turned his back on his past. With no experience and no qualifications he lied his way into a job with a successful advertising agency, where his talent in lying and selling lies makes him a big success. Everything seems to be going really well. Everybody respects and looks up to him, no one knows about his past. Until one day that is, when Don's half-brother suddenly appears …

Read more about screen liars.

The world's top ten lies

1 I love you.
2 You look great.
3 I'll call you tomorrow.
4 We never got the letter.
5 I'm not feeling very well.
6 I had no choice.
7 We had a lovely time.
8 I missed you.
9 It wasn't me.
10 I won't be long.

Read **the top 100** lies.

Glossary
fidget *v* make small movements because you are nervous or bored
stumble *v* fall or almost fall

3 Read the texts again and say if the sentences are true (T) or false (F). Correct the false sentences.

1 It is possible to spot a liar because of his body language.
2 Liars sometimes speak more quickly.
3 Don Draper is good at his job.
4 Don Draper is not his real name.
5 He is proud of his past.
6 Most of the world's top ten lies are about money.

4 Work in pairs. Discuss these questions.

- What other sentences would you expect to see in the top 100 lies?
- Do you know of any other films where a liar is the central character? Tell your partner.

GRAMMAR: stative & dynamic verbs

1 Look at the verbs in italics. Circle the stative verbs and underline the dynamic verbs.

1 Every morning Gerald *puts on* a suit and tie, *kisses* his wife goodbye and *goes* to work.
2 Or, at least, that's what his wife *thinks,* and that's what Gerald *wants* his wife to believe.
3 In fact, Gerald *feeds* pigeons in the park or *does* crosswords in the local library.
4 His wife *goes* shopping every Saturday and *buys* new furniture for the house with her credit card.
5 She *doesn't know* that they *don't have* any more money.

> Use dynamic verbs …
> - in either the simple or the continuous form.
> - to describe an action.
>   *He's **looking** at you.*
>
> Use stative verbs …
> - in the simple form, not usually in the continuous form.
> - to describe emotions, opinions, the senses and states that do not change.
>   *He **loves** his kids.* Not ~~He's loving his kids~~.
>   *Everything **seems** to be going well.* Not ~~Everything is seeming to be going well.~~
>
> **Common stative verbs:**
> agree   appear   be   believe   belong   cost
> dislike   forget   hate   have   know   like   love
> matter   mean   need   own   prefer   realize
> remember   seem   think   understand   want

⊙ SEE LANGUAGE REFERENCE PAGE 14

2 Walter Mitty is the hero of a short story by James Thurber. His life is sad and ordinary, but most of the time he lives in a dream world, as the heroic Captain Mitty. Correct three mistakes with stative or dynamic verbs in the two paragraphs from the story.

1 The weather is getting worse and the plane is not having enough fuel to return to base. But, Captain Mitty, who is sitting at the controls, is not knowing the meaning of the word *fear*. He is understanding that there is only one way to save everyone's life. 'We're going through,' he announces.

2 'I am being accurate at 100 metres. I never miss.' Mitty is holding a heavy automatic and the crowd believe him. The courtroom is in chaos. Mitty is needing to find a way out, but he is not wanting to use the gun.

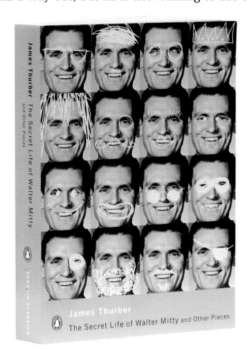

James Thurber
The Secret Life of Walter Mitty and Other Pieces

3 Work in pairs, A and B. You are going to describe a moment of Mitty's real and imaginary life using both dynamic and stative verbs.

A: Turn to page 126 and describe what is happening.
B: Turn to page 134 and describe what is happening in Mitty's imagination.

SPEAKING

1 Turn to page 126. Choose one sentence and complete it so that it is true for you. Complete the other sentences so that they are **not** true for you.

2 Work in pairs. Tell your partner your sentences from exercise 1. Can he/she guess which sentence is true?

1B | Daily lives

LISTENING & SPEAKING

1 Work in pairs. Discuss these questions.

- What do you think the following people do on a typical working day?
  a) a mother of four small children
  b) a member of parliament
- Whose lifestyle is more similar to yours? In what ways?

2 Work in pairs. Read the TV review. What do you think the main differences between Michael Portillo and Jenny Miner's lifestyles will be?

TONIGHT • BBC2 9PM

In tonight's *How Michael Portillo Became a Single Mum*, a classic example of reality TV at its best, former politician, Michael Portillo, adds new skills to his CV. The son of a Spanish political refugee, Michael Portillo has had a long career in politics. He has been Secretary of State for Defence and he has stood for leadership of the Tory party, but in tonight's programme he takes on a whole new challenge. In his first appearance in the wonderful world of reality TV, he volunteers to look after Jenny Miner's four children for a week. It's a rare chance to see a politician at work in the real world.

3 🔘 1.1 Listen to the first part of a review of the TV programme. Check the answers you gave in exercise 2.

4 🔘 1.2 Listen to the second part of the review and answer the questions.

1 What did the reviewer think of Michael Portillo before the programme?
2 What did the reviewer think of him after the programme?
3 What was Tasha and her friends' reaction to him?
4 Which did he find more difficult: working in the supermarket or working as a classroom assistant? Why?
5 What was the biggest challenge Portillo faced on the programme?
6 Who was the reviewer's favourite character?

5 🔘 1.1–1.2 Listen again and complete the sentences.

1 Michael Portillo volunteered **to step into single mum Jenny Miner's** _____ for a week.
2 Life as a single mum is going to be **a real** _____-**opener**.
3 It is one of **the high** _____ of his week.
4 It looks as if **he's** _____ **off more than he can chew**.
5 All his people skills and lessons in political diplomacy **will get him** _____.

6 Work in pairs. Explain the meaning of the phrases in bold in exercise 5.

7 Which politician in your country would you like to see in a similar TV programme? Why?

GRAMMAR: present simple & present continuous

1 Choose the correct phrases to complete the rules below. Then choose examples from the sentences highlighted in audioscripts 1.1–1.2 on page 135.

Use the *present simple / present continuous* ...
- to talk about facts (things that are always true) and permanent situations.
  Example _____
- to talk about habits and actions that happen regularly.
  Example _____

Use the *present simple / present continuous* ...
- to talk about actions that are happening at the moment of speaking.
  Example _____
- to talk about temporary situations and activities.
  Example _____

We usually use stative verbs in the *present simple / present continuous*.
  Example _____ Not *is wanting to*

> ⊙ FOR THE PRESENT SIMPLE AND THE PRESENT CONTINUOUS WITH FUTURE MEANINGS, SEE PAGE 64
> ⊙ SEE LANGUAGE REFERENCE PAGE 14

2 Choose the correct verb forms to complete the article.

FAKING IT • BBC2 9PM

Faking it is the hit TV series where people learn a new job in just a few weeks and then try to persuade experts that it's their real job! In this week's episode, a volunteer (1) *has / is having* four weeks to learn a new skill. This week's volunteer, Tim Hutch, usually (2) *works / is working* as a music teacher in a secondary school. In *Faking it*, he becomes a rock star. When you see him in the programme, he (3) *plays / is playing* live on stage in a rock band! In his real job as a music teacher, he (4) *teaches / is teaching* kids to play classical guitar. That's the only instrument he can play. But in *Faking it* he (5) *learns / is learning* to play the bass guitar. Tim Hutch has many challenges to face, but the thing he most (6) *wants / is wanting* to learn is how to dance in time. Don't miss it!

3 Write six sentences about yourself using these time expressions.

| now | usually | once a week |
| this week | never | at the moment |

VOCABULARY: verbs with two meanings

Some verbs can be both stative and dynamic, but the meaning changes. You can use the verbs *think*, *see* and *have* in the simple and continuous forms, but with different meanings.

*I **see** what the problem is now.*
(= I understand what the problem is now.)
*I**'m seeing** a TV reviewer at ten tomorrow.*
(= I have arranged to meet her.)

> SEE LANGUAGE REFERENCE PAGE 14

1 Choose the correct verb to complete the sentences.

1 I *think / am thinking* this is probably the best programme I've seen all year.
2 I don't know if Portillo *thinks / is thinking* about starting a new career.
3 I *see / am seeing* what you mean.
4 I *am seeing / see* two politicians for a meeting tomorrow.
5 Jenny Miner *has / is having* four children.
6 Look at Portillo. He *has / is having* a really good time at the party.

2 Work in pairs. Explain the meaning of each use of the verbs in exercise 1.

3 Complete the sentences with *see, have* or *think* in the present simple or present continuous.

see
1 He _____ his doctor next week.
2 She _____ why he lied to her, but she isn't going to forgive him.

have
3 He _____ £5 in his pocket.
4 She _____ a party at her flat on Saturday.

think
5 He _____ about getting his hair cut this weekend.
6 She _____ reality TV shows should be banned.

4 Work in pairs. Use the three verbs from exercise 3 to make sentences that are true for you. Then tell your partner about yourself.

I think a lot of programmes on TV are very funny.
I'm thinking of going on holiday to Greece next year.

DID YOU KNOW?

1 Work in pairs. Read about British political parties and discuss the questions.

For nearly one hundred years, only two British political parties had governed Britain: the Labour Party, a socialist party whose leaders have included Tony Blair and Harold Wilson, and the Conservatives (also known as the Tories), traditionally a more right-wing party. Winston Churchill and Margaret Thatcher are perhaps the most famous leaders of the Tory Party. In the general elections in 2010 a third party, the Liberal Democrats, came into power for the first time, forming a coalition government with the Tory Party. The first Liberal Democrat leader to serve in government was the Deputy Prime Minister, Nick Clegg.

- What are the main political parties in your country?
- What are the differences between them?
- What other political parties are there?
- Who are the most famous members of those political parties?

1c | Britishness

SPEAKING & VOCABULARY: self-image

1 Complete the sentences in column A with a phrase from column B.

A	B
1 I think of myself as *a Scot,*	a *an old-age pensioner – I'm too busy for that.*
2 I would describe myself	b as *quite fit for my age.*
3 I don't see myself as	c but *I've lived in England for 25 years.*
4 I'm proud to be the	d *grandmother of two very clever girls.*
5 *My family* is the most	e important thing to me.
6 My neighbours probably see	f *live in such a nice house.*
7 I consider myself lucky to	g me *as a very friendly person.*

2 Change the words in italics in exercise 1 to make sentences that are true for you. Compare your sentences with a partner.

I think of myself as a European, but I've lived in the US for the last ten years.

READING

1 Read the article about a test for people who want to become British citizens. Which of the people 1–8 think the test is a good idea?

2 Read the article again and answer the questions.

1 What does Clive Morgan want the government to spend money on?
2 What does James Radcliffe think is dead?
3 What has become a dirty word?
4 What do British people like doing in bars?
5 Who came from Uganda?
6 Who thinks that the test is unfair?
7 How many Britons would pass the test?
8 Where does Jayne Godfrey come from?

3 Do you think the test is a good idea? Why or why not?

Are you British enough?

All people who want to become British citizens or apply for permanent residence in the UK must pass a British Citizenship test. Some people say the test is too hard, others that it is impossible to test 'Britishness'. Here are some reactions:

1 I once read that the rock star Malcolm McLaren described being British as 'singing karaoke in bars, eating Chinese noodles, wearing Prada and Nike, holidaying in Ibiza ...' Why do we need to test that?
(Jared Steele, London nightclub owner)

2 What is the point in the test if only one in seven Britons can answer? Surely to make this a real test more than half of Britons should be able to answer. In my opinion it's totally unfair – and a waste of taxpayers' money.
(Mina, administrative assistant)

3 I don't think anyone thinks of themselves as 'British'. You ask people where they come from and they say London, or Scotland, or Kent. They never say Britain! If you ask me where I come from, I'll say I'm a Londoner. If you ask me what nationality I am, I'm European.
(Jayne Godfrey, actor)

4 I don't think 'Britishness' exists anymore. Figures like Winston Churchill, bull dogs and Beefeaters are all irrelevant now. The only place you see them is on postcards for tourists.
(James Radcliffe, advertising executive)

5 Why do we need a test? Most people that I know would fail it. Why don't we welcome immigrants with open arms?
(Penny Porter, Church of England priest)

6 My family is very proud to be British. We came here from Uganda in the 1970s. In those days, they didn't have a test, but I think it's a good idea. People are always asking: What does this country do for me? But a better question is: What can I do for my country?
(Amina Patel, shopkeeper)

7 When I think of Britain, I think of the royal family, cricket, warm beer, cheese and cucumber sandwiches and wet weather. Who cares about these things? Why is the government wasting its time and money on this? They should spend the money on making better schools and decent hospitals.
(Clive Morgan, rugby player)

8 People forget that Britain used to be great. There was a time when we were proud to wear the Union Jack. What happened to all the good old-fashioned patriotism? It's become a dirty word now, but the true British qualities are still important. Of course we should test them.
(S Sullivan, MBE)

GRAMMAR: subject & object questions

Questions

This is the usual word order in questions:

question word	auxiliary	subject	infinitive
What	does	this country	do for me?
Why	do	we	need a test?

Subject questions

When the question word (*who, what, which* or *how many*) is the subject of the question, you do not need an auxiliary verb (*do, does* or *did*) with the present simple and past simple.

subject	verb
Who	cares about these things?
How many people	describe themselves as British?
What	happened to patriotism?

Object questions

If the question word is the object of a question, you use normal question word order with *do, does* or *did*.

object	auxiliary	subject	infinitive
Who	does	he	work for?
What	did	he	say?

⊙ SEE LANGUAGE REFERENCE PAGE 14

1 Look at the questions in Reading exercise 2. Find four subject questions and four object questions.

2 Correct the grammatical mistakes in four of these questions.

1 How many people do live in Scotland?
2 What did happen in 1066?
3 When can the British police arrest you without a reason?
4 What CRE stands for?
5 What number you do dial for the emergency services?
6 Who speaks Cornish?

3 Use the prompts to make questions.

1 *Who became Britain's first woman prime minister in 1979?*

1 Who / become / Britain's first woman prime minister / in 1979?
2 Which British political party / use / blue / as its official colour?
3 Why / the policeman / stand / outside the house / in the photo above?
4 What / happen / on Guy Fawkes' Day?
5 When / women in Britain / vote / in political elections / for the first time?
6 Which / English king / have / six wives?

SPEAKING

1 Work in pairs. Turn to page 126. Choose the correct answer to the questions in Grammar exercises 2 and 3. If you do not know the answer, guess!

2 Now work with a new partner. You are each going to see the answers for one exercise. Tell your partner if his/her answers are correct.

A: Turn to page 130. B: Turn to page 129.

3 Work in groups. Prepare six questions that test knowledge of your own national culture. Use the examples in Grammar exercises 2 and 3 and these topics to help you.

everyday life   famous people   history
important places   law   multiculturalism
politics   regions

4 Work with students from another group. Ask them your test questions.

1D | First impressions

Police officer

DJ

Student

Accountant

SPEAKING

1 Work in pairs. Look at the photos and the labels. What link is there between the photos and the title of this lesson? Discuss these questions.

- When and where was the last time you met someone new?
- Who was it?
- What was your first impression of them?
- Were your first impressions accurate?

2 Think of five situations when it is important to look good and make a good impression.

3 Explain the meaning of the saying below. Do you agree or disagree? Give examples to explain your opinion.

You can't judge a book by its cover.

LISTENING

1 Look at the photo. What are the people doing? What do you think is the relationship between them? What do you think they're talking about?

2 🔘 1.3 Listen to their dialogue. Check your answers to exercise 1.

3 🔘 1.3 Listen again. Correct the mistakes in the sentences below.

1 Both girls have met the girl who might be their new flatmate.
2 She's the same age as them.
3 She's a businesswoman.
4 She really liked the bedroom.
5 She has already decided to take the room.

4 Look at the photos of the three women below. Which photo do you think shows the new flatmate?

5 Read the information and answer the questions.

There are more than two million foreign students studying at universities in the UK. More than 50,000 come from China. More than any other one country.

- Do foreign students come to study in your country?
- If yes, where do they usually come from?
- Do you know any foreign students studying in your town?

VOCABULARY: describing people

1 Work in pairs. How many parts of the body can you name?

2 Match the groups of adjectives in column A to the nouns in column B.

A		**B**
1 average/muscular/slim	a	eyes
2 bald/round/shaved	b	hair
3 blond/shiny/wavy	c	head
4 dark/narrow/wide	d	nose
5 healthy/pale/tanned	e	complexion
6 pointed/prominent/straight	f	build

3 Make a list of eight famous people with your partner. Choose one of the people from your list and describe his/her appearance. Your partner must guess who you are describing.

FUNCTIONAL LANGUAGE: describing people

1 Match the questions 1–3 to the answers a–f.

1 What is she like?
2 What does she look like?
3 What does she like?

a I think she's into Italian fashion.
b She seems very nice, relaxed and chatty.
c She's got long dark hair and dark eyes.
d She's young and wears really trendy clothes.
e She's very friendly.
f Rock music.

2 Work in pairs. Write the names of four people you know. Use the questions in exercise 1 to find out more about the people whose names your partner has written.

A: Who's Mark?
B: He's my brother.
A: What's he like?
B: He's cheerful and funny.

3 Complete the sentences in column A with a phrase from column B.

A		**B**
1 She looks	a	a film star. (+ noun)
2 She looks like	b	quite friendly. (+ adjective)
3 She looks as if	c	she's going to a wedding. (+ phrase)

4 Complete the sentences with *like*, *as if* or –.

1 He doesn't look _____ very happy.
2 He looks _____ a doctor.
3 He looks _____ about 55.
4 He looks _____ he's just woken up.
5 He looks _____ he wants to be somewhere else.
6 He looks _____ the prime minister.

PRONUNCIATION: intonation (lists)

1 🔘 1.4 Listen to this extract from the dialogue in Listening exercise 2.

… the kitchen, the living room, the bathroom, her bedroom and the bedrooms.

Notice how the voice goes up for each item of the list and then down at the end of the list.

2 Practise reading these lists in the same way.

1 Monday, Tuesday, Wednesday and Thursday
2 who, what, where, when and why
3 Sue, Nick, Beth, John and me

3 🔘 1.5 Listen to the recording to check your pronunciation.

4 Work in pairs. Take it in turns to add one more item to the lists below. Repeat the whole list each time.

1 A: Britain, America, Australia and Canada
B: Britain, America, Australia, Canada and Ireland

1 Britain, America, Australia, …
2 eyes, ears, nose, …
3 intelligent, good-looking, kind, …
4 mother, cousin, grandfather, …
5 red, blue, yellow, …

Self-assessment (✓)

☐ I can talk about first impressions.
☐ I can describe someone's appearance.
☐ I can understand descriptions of people's characteristics.
☐ I can describe similarities.

GRAMMAR
Stative & dynamic verbs

Some verbs can only be used in the simple form. These are called stative verbs. They often describe emotions, opinions, the senses and states that do not change.

I love you. Not *I am loving you.*
He seems friendly. Not *He is seeming friendly.*

Here are some common stative verbs:

agree	*appear*	*be*	*believe*	*belong*	*contain*
dislike	*fit*	*forget*	*hate*	*know*	*last*	*like*
love	*matter*	*mean*	*need*	*own*	*prefer*
realize	*remember*	*seem*	*understand*	*want*	

We can use most verbs in both the simple and the continuous forms. These are called dynamic verbs.

> *The weather is getting worse.*
> *It often snows in January.*

It is possible for some verbs to be both dynamic and stative if they have two different meanings.

> *He has a house in north London.* (have = own)
> *She's having a few problems.* (have = experience)

Other common verbs that can be dynamic or stative (with different meanings) include:

be	*feel*	*see*	*smell*	*think*

Present simple & present continuous

We use the present simple …
● to talk about facts (things that are always true) and permanent situations.
She lives in a small flat.
● to talk about habits and actions that happen regularly.
She drives the kids to school every day.

We use the present continuous …
● to talk about actions that are happening at the moment of speaking.
He's trying to explain a problem to them.
● to talk about temporary situations and activities.
She's going through a very rebellious phase.

We can sometimes use both the present simple and the present continuous. Our choice depends on how we see the action.

> *I live in Madrid.* (= I think this is permanent.)
> *I'm living in Madrid.* (= I think this is temporary.)

See page 64 for information about the present tenses with future meaning.

Subject & object questions

The usual word order in questions is:

	auxiliary verb	subject	verb
Who	*does*	*he*	*work for?*
What	*do*	*you*	*do on New Year's Eve?*
Which party	*did*	*you*	*vote for?*

These questions are called object questions because the question words (*who, what, which party*) are the object of the verb.

In some *Wh-* questions, the question word (*who, what, which* or *how many*) is the subject of the verb. These are called subject questions. With a subject question, we do not need an auxiliary verb (*do, does* or *did*) with the present simple and the past simple.

subject (question word)	verb
Who	*thinks the test is a good idea?*
What	*happens on New Year's Eve?*
Which party	*won the last election?*
How many people	*voted for the government?*

FUNCTIONAL LANGUAGE
Describing people

What is *she* **like?**
(= We are asking for a general description of the person.)

What does *she* **look like?**
(= We are asking for a description of the person's appearance.)

What does *she* **like?**
(= We are asking about the person's preferences or interests.)

She looks	+ adjective *intelligent.*
	like + noun *like a doctor.*
	as if/as though + phrase *as if she needs a holiday.*

Some English speakers use *like* instead of *as if/as though*. Many people, however, think this is incorrect.

> *She looks **like** she needs a holiday.*

Word list

Self-image

consider (sb) + *adj*	/kən'sɪdə(r)/
consider (sb) to be...	/kən'sɪdə(r) tə ˌbiː/
describe (sb) as ...	/dɪ'skraɪb ˌəz/
proud to + *infinitive*	/'praʊd ˌtuː/
see (sb) as ...	/'siː ˌəz/
think of (sb) as ...	/'θɪŋk əv ˌəz/

Describing people

average *adj* ***	/'æv(ə)rɪdʒ/
bald *adj* *	/bɔːld/
blond *adj* *	/blɒnd/
build *n C* *	/bɪld/
complexion *n C* *	/kəm'plekʃ(ə)n/
dark *adj* ***	/dɑː(r)k/
healthy *adj* ***	/'helθi/
muscular *adj*	/'mʌskjʊlə(r)/
narrow *adj* ***	/'nærəʊ/
pale *adj* ***	/peɪl/
pointed *adj* *	/'pɔɪntɪd/
prominent *adj* **	/'prɒmɪnənt/
round *adj* ***	/raʊnd/
shaved *adj*	/ʃeɪvd/
shiny *adj* *	/'ʃaɪni/
slim *adj* **	/slɪm/
straight *adj* **	/streɪt/
tanned *adj*	/tænd/
wavy *adj*	/'weɪvi/
wide *adj* ***	/waɪd/

Other words & phrases

agency *n C* **	/'eɪdʒ(ə)nsi/
analyst *n C* **	/'ænəlɪst/
arrest *v* **	/ə'rest/
arrogant *adj* *	/'ærəgənt/
automatic *n C/adj* **	/ˌɔːtə'mætɪk/
ban *v* **	/bæn/
base *n C* ***	/beɪs/
Beefeater *n C*	/'biːfˌiːtə(r)/
bite *v* **	/baɪt/
bottom *n C/adj* ***	/'bɒtəm/
career *n C* ***	/kə'rɪə(r)/
cashier *n C*	/kæ'ʃɪə(r)/
challenge *n C* ***	/'tʃælɪndʒ/
chaos *n U* **	/'keɪɒs/
chew *v* **	/tʃuː/
citizen *n C* ***	/'sɪtɪz(ə)n/
clever *adj* **	/'klevə(r)/
clip *n C* *	/klɪp/
coalition *n C* **	/ˌkəʊə'lɪʃ(ə)n/
courtroom *n C*	/'kɔː(r)tˌruːm/
crossword *n C* *	/'krɒsˌwɜː(r)d/
cucumber *n C*	/'kjuːˌkʌmbə(r)/
decent *adj* **	/'diːs(ə)nt/
deputy *adj/n C* ***	/'depjʊti/
dial *v* *	/'daɪəl/
diplomacy *n U*	/dɪ'pləʊməsi/
election *n C* ***	/ɪ'lekʃ(ə)n/
emergency services *n pl*	/ɪ'mɜː(r)dʒənsi ˌsɜːvɪsɪz/
episode *n C* **	/'epɪsəʊd/
executive *n C/adj* **	/ɪg'zekjʊtɪv/
expert *n C* ***	/'ekspɜː(r)t/
eye-opener *n C*	/'aɪ ˌəʊp(ə)nə(r)/
face *v* ***	/feɪs/
fake *v/adj/n C*	/feɪk/
fidget *v*	/'fɪdʒɪt/
fireworks *n pl*	/'faɪə(r)ˌwɜː(r)ks/
fit *adj* **	/fɪt/
flatly *adv*	/'flætli/
fuel *n U* ***	/'fjuːəl/
get away with (sth) *v*	/get ə'weɪ wɪð/
give (sb) away *v*	/ˌgɪv ə'weɪ/
govern *v* **	/'gʌvə(r)n/
headquarters *n pl* **	/hed'kwɔː(r)tə(r)z/
hero *n C* **	/'hɪərəʊ/
honest *adj* **	/'ɒnɪst/
imaginary *adj* *	/ɪ'mædʒɪnəri/
immigrant *n C* *	/'ɪmɪgrənt/
impress *v* **	/ɪm'pres/
impression *n C* ***	/ɪm'preʃ(ə)n/
instrument *n C* ***	/'ɪnstrʊmənt/
invade *v* *	/ɪn'veɪd/
invasion *n C* **	/ɪn'veɪʒ(ə)n/
irrelevant *adj* **	/ɪ'reləvənt/
karaoke *n U*	/ˌkæri'əʊki/
kid *n C* ***	/kɪd/
landlord *n C* **	/'læn(d)ˌlɔː(r)d/
liar *n C*	/'laɪə(r)/
lie *v/n C* ***	/laɪ/
lifestyle *n C* **	/'laɪfˌstaɪl/
likeable *adj*	/'laɪkəb(ə)l/
lip *n C* ***	/lɪp/
live off (sth/sb) *v*	/'lɪv ɒf/
look up to *v*	/lʊk 'ʌp tʊ/
marital *adj*	/'mærɪt(ə)l/
modest *adj* **	/'mɒdɪst/
multiculturalism *n U*	/ˌmʌlti'kʌltʃərəˌlɪz(ə)m/
mum *n C* **	/mʌm/
noodle *n C*	/'nuːd(ə)l/
old-age pensioner *n C*	/ˌəʊld eɪdʒ 'penʃ(ə)nə(r)/
palm *n C* **	/pɑːm/
parliament *n C* ***	/'pɑː(r)ləmənt/
patiently *adv*	/'peɪʃ(ə)ntli/
patriotism *n U*	/'pætriəˌtɪz(ə)m; 'peɪtriəˌtɪz(ə)m/
phase *n C* ***	/feɪz/
pigeon *n C* *	/'pɪdʒ(ə)n/
political *adj* ***	/pə'lɪtɪk(ə)l/
politician *n C* ***	/ˌpɒlə'tɪʃ(ə)n/
pretend *v* **	/prɪ'tend/
racism *n U* *	/'reɪˌsɪz(ə)m/
rare *adj* ***	/reə(r)/
reality TV *n U*	/rɪˌæləti tiː 'viː/
reaction *n C* ***	/ri'ækʃ(ə)n/
rebellious *adj*	/rɪ'beljəs/
refugee *n C* **	/ˌrefjʊ'dʒiː/
reviewer *n C*	/rɪ'vjuːə(r)/
rhythm *n C* **	/'rɪðəm/
right-wing *adj* *	/ˌraɪt'wɪŋ/
salary *n C* **	/'sæləri/
self-important *adj*	/ˌselfɪm'pɔː(r)t(ə)nt/
series *n C* ***	/'sɪəriːz/
sincere *adj* *	/sɪn'sɪə(r)/
single parent *n C*	/ˌsɪŋg(ə)l 'peərənt/
socialist *adj/n C*	/'səʊʃəlɪst/
spot *v* **	/spɒt/
stage *n C* ***	/steɪdʒ/
stand for *v*	/'stænd ˌfɔː/
status *n U* ***	/'steɪtəs/
stubborn *adj* *	/'stʌbə(r)n/
sweaty *adj*	/'sweti/
stumble *v* *	/'stʌmb(ə)l/
talent *n C/U* **	/'tælənt/
telltale *adj*	/'telˌteɪl/
tension *n U* ***	/'tenʃ(ə)n/
till *n C*	/tɪl/
traditionally *adv*	/trə'dɪʃ(ə)nəli/
typical *adj* ***	/'tɪpɪk(ə)l/
unfair *adj* **	/ʌn'feə(r)/
volunteer *n C/v* **	/ˌvɒlən'tɪə(r)/

Abbreviations

n	noun	*sth*	something
v	verb	*C*	countable
adj	adjective	*U*	uncountable
adv	adverb	*pl*	plural
prep	preposition	*s*	singular
sb	somebody		

*** the most common and basic words
** very common words
* fairly common words

2A | Around the world

SPEAKING

1 Work in pairs. Discuss these questions.

- What do you like and dislike about travelling?
- Who is the most widely-travelled person that you know? Where has he/she been? Why did he/she go there?
- According to an English saying, *travel broadens the mind.* Do you agree? In what ways has travel broadened your mind?

READING

1 Work in pairs. You are going to read an article about a long journey. Look at the photos and headline. Think of two possible answers for each of the questions.

1 Why did the lawyer decide to cycle around South America?
2 Why is he dressed as a clown in the second photo?

Now read the article and find out if you were right.

2 Read the article again. What do the numbers in the box refer to?

100,000	more than 60	three
30,000	ten	more than five	60

3 Match the highlighted phrasal verbs in the article to the words and phrases 1–6.

1 meets by chance
2 left
3 managing to survive
4 stayed
5 combining
6 started (a journey)

4 Work in pairs. Discuss these questions.

- Would you consider giving up your job or studies to do something like Alvaro did? Why or why not?
- Have you ever wanted to go on a long trip like Alvaro's? Where would you like to go?

LAWYER
GIVES UP JOB TO CYCLE AROUND THE WORLD

More than ten years ago, a Spanish lawyer gave up a good job and left a comfortable life to cycle around the world. Ten years and almost 100,000 kilometres later, he's still very happy with his decision, 'You
5 only live once and life in an office just isn't a life,' he says.

He began his journey in South America. The first country he visited was Bolivia. Since he first set out on his adventure he has visited more than 60 countries. The journey has already taken him to three continents and most of Asia still
10 lies ahead. He is currently cycling through Mongolia and Japan is the next country on his route.

He spends two or three months in each country, but he has never stopped off for more than five days in any one place. Alvaro is getting by on a budget of three dollars a day,
15 and has slept in fire stations, police stations and churches, in the mountains of Nepal and the dry Atacama desert of Chile.

He has given 60 performances to more than 30,000 people. 'My show
20 includes juggling, music, magic, acrobatics and theatre. I perform to the poorest people and my sole purpose is to bring them a little happiness,' says Alvaro.

25 He explains that the trip is a way of bringing together the three things he loves most in life: 'Cycling's in my blood, I'm a born clown and I enjoy helping other people.' He is sponsored by his fans and his mission is to
30 bring a smile into the lives of the people he runs into on his travels.

GRAMMAR: present perfect & past simple

1 Look at the first three paragraphs of the article on page 16 again. Underline all the examples of the present perfect and past simple. Then answer the questions.

1 Which verb form do you use when the time is known?
2 Which verb form do you use when the time is not stated?

2 Choose the correct verb forms to complete the newspaper article.

From our Dublin Correspondent

The well-known writer and comedian, Tony Hawks, (1) *has accepted / accepted* a bet to hitchhike around Ireland with a fridge. He (2) *has begun / began* his journey in Dublin last week. He (3) *has almost given up / almost gave up* on the first day when his first lift (4) *has taken / took* him only three miles. But since then he (5) *has had / had* better luck. He (6) *has had / had* lifts in vans, cars and trucks, and yesterday he and his fridge (7) *has taken / took* a fishing boat to Tory Island. So if you're driving around in the Sligo area and see a man hitchhiking with a fridge – stop and give him a lift!

3 Complete the questions. Put the verbs in brackets into the present perfect or the past simple.

1 How many countries _____ you _____ (*visit*)?
2 What's the most interesting place you _____ (*be*) to?
3 How many times _____ you _____ (*go*) away last year?
4 Where _____ you _____ (*go*) for your last holiday?
5 What's the furthest you _____ ever _____ (*fly*)?
6 When _____ you _____ (*fly*) for the first time?
7 What's the strangest form of transport you _____ ever _____ (*use*)?
8 _____ you ever _____ (*travel*) on your own?

4 Work in pairs. Ask and answer the questions in exercise 3.

Use the past simple ...
* with questions that ask about the time of an event.
  *When **did** you last **catch** a taxi?*
* to talk about past actions when you know when the event happened.
  *He **caught** a taxi to the airport yesterday to meet a friend.*
* with certain time expressions, eg *yesterday, last week, one night, the last time, when.*

Use the present perfect ...
* to talk about past actions when the time is not stated. The event happened in the past, but the time is not important.
  ***Have** you ever **travelled** alone?*
  *I've **travelled** alone on business, but I've never **been** on holiday on my own.*
* with certain time expressions, eg *ever, never, already, yet, since, just.*
  *I've **just** come back from Dublin.*

⊙ FOR OTHER USES OF THE PRESENT PERFECT, SEE PAGE 74
⊙ SEE LANGUAGE REFERENCE PAGE 24

2B | Unusual journeys

LISTENING & READING

1 🔘 **1.6–1.8** Listen to three stories about unusual journeys. Match each journey to two of the photos A–F.

A

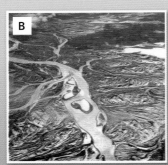
B

C

D

E

F

2 🔘 **1.6–1.8** Listen again and answer the questions.

Journey 1
1 Where did he finish his journey?
2 Who rescued him in the Alps? Why?

Journey 2
3 How long did their journey last?
4 What were they looking for?

Journey 3
5 How many people took part in the trip?
6 How long did it take the winners to complete the trip?

3 Read these texts about the three journeys. Find two mistakes in each text and correct them.

4 🔘 **1.6–1.8** Listen again to check your answers.

5 Which journey sounds the most interesting or enjoyable? Why?

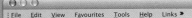
File   Edit   View   Favourites   Tools   Help   Links ➤

1
YOUR NEWS!

Swedish student wins web competition
21-year-old Tommy Kallstrom has won this month's Web Travel Site of the Month competition. His winning website contains details of his four-month trip through fifteen European countries on a Vespa that he used to deliver pizzas in his home town of Uppsala.

2 HUNTING THE TIGER • CHANNEL 6, 9PM

Tonight's documentary in the *Wildlife on 6* series takes a fascinating look at the animals of Siberia. Award-winning filmmakers, Chiara and Luca Colucci, spent six months in the far east of Russia looking for the rare Siberian tiger. There are only about 300 of these beautiful animals in the wild. With the help of a baby fox cub they found early on the trip, the Coluccis explore the beautiful River Amur region in their search for the tiger. An unforgettable journey and an unforgettable film.

3 University teachers hitchhike for charity

A group of teachers have hitchhiked the length of Britain to raise money for the charity, Oxfam International. The teachers had to get from Land's End to John O'Groats in less than two days. Only four of the teachers completed the trip in time.

VOCABULARY: phrasal verbs

> Phrasal verbs have two parts: a verb and a particle, eg *get by, set out, stop off.*
>
> **Separable phrasal verbs**
> With some phrasal verbs, the object can come either before or after the particle.
> *He **sorted out** the problem.*
> *He **sorted** the problem **out**.*
>
> If the object is a pronoun, eg *him, her, it,* the object always comes before the particle.
> *He sorted **it out**. Not He sorted out it.*
>
> **Inseparable phrasal verbs**
> With some phrasal verbs, the verb and the particle always come together, so the object always comes after the particle.
> *They looked after **the bear cub**.*
> *They looked after **it**.*
>
> ❯ SEE LANGUAGE REFERENCE PAGE 24

1 Match the phrasal verbs in bold in 1–6 to the definitions a–f.

1 He was able to **sort** the problem **out**.
2 They **came across** the bear near a river.
3 Tizio **got over** his injury.
4 Their friends and families **saw** them **off**.
5 A van **picked** her **up** after only five minutes.
6 The van **dropped** her **off** near the finishing line.

a felt well or happy again after something bad
b found an answer to a problem
c took someone or something in a car
d let someone get out of your car
e met or found by chance
f said goodbye to someone who was going on a journey

2 Which two phrasal verbs in exercise 1 are inseparable?

3 Put *it* in the correct place in the sentences.

*1 I sorted **it** out before I left work.*

1 I sorted out before I left work.
2 I'm sure you'll get over soon.
3 I've never come across before.
4 I've tried to give up many times.
5 Why don't you pick up on your way home?

4 Now think of a noun to replace *it* in each sentence.

1 I sorted the problem out before I left work.

5 Work in pairs. You are going to ask and answer questions using the phrasal verbs in exercise 1.

A: Turn to page 126.   B: Turn to page 129.

PRONUNCIATION: word linking

1 🔊 1.9 We often join two words when an initial vowel sound follows a final consonant sound. Look at these examples from the listening exercise, then listen and repeat.

1 arrived‿in‿Athens
2 gave‿it‿all‿up
3 film‿of‿another‿incredible
4 still‿exist‿in
5 it's‿Alex‿and‿Isabelle
6 part‿of‿a‿group

2 Practise saying the phrases in exercise 1 quickly.

3 🔊 1.10 Listen and write the four phrases.

4 Practise saying the phrases. Remember to link the words.

SPEAKING

1 Think of a film or book you have seen or read recently that described a long journey. Prepare to tell a partner about it. Use the questions below to help you.

● Where was the film/book set?
● Who was going on the journey and why?
● What were the main events?
● Would you like to go on the same journey? Why or why not?
● Would you recommend the film/book to your partner? Why or why not?

2 Work in pairs. Tell your partner about the film/book.

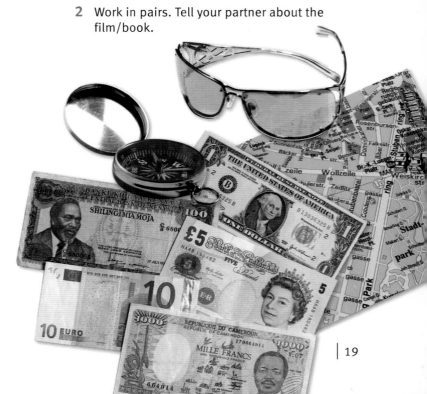

2c | Down under

SPEAKING

1 Work in groups. Look at the photos on the blog below and share all that you know about Australia. Use the ideas in the box to help you.

> sports, film and music personalities
> climate   history   cities   things to do
> animals   well-known sights and landmarks

2 Now prepare a short quiz about Australia. Use your questions to test students from another group.

3 Work in pairs. Turn to page 133 and read about Uluru (Ayer's rock), one of the most famous landmarks in Australia. Discuss these questions.

1 Where is it?
2 What does it represent for the local people?

READING

1 Read the first part of a blog about a trip around Australia and answer the questions.

1 Who is the author? What does she do?
2 What is she going to do?
3 What is the purpose of her blog?

2 Share your ideas with the class.

3 Find the adjectives in the blog that Nerina uses to describe these things.

1 the people that she has met   *incredible*
2 her experiences during the trip
3 the Rock at the start of the day
4 the Anangu caves and sacred art
5 the way that the Rock changes colour

: File   Edit   View   Favourites   Tools   Help   Links ➤

Nerina Klein's
travel blog

: File   Edit   View   Favourites   Tools   Help   Links ➤

During my 35 years as a travel writer, I've visited more countries than I can count. I've backpacked
5 through Asia, cycled through Europe, driven across Africa, but I've never explored my own home, Australia. So the time has come to put
10 this right. Over the next six weeks, I'm planning to cover as much of the outback as I possibly can in a second-hand four-wheel drive, and I'll
15 be accompanied by my two grandchildren. They, unlike me, want to get to know their own country before they start exploring the rest of the
20 world. What follows is a diary of our travels and adventures. I hope it inspires people to leave the coast and find out what the real Australia is all
25 about.

Day 33 We camped out last night near the best place to watch the sunrise. After a few drinks and an hour or two of looking at the stars, we turned in and got some sleep before the climax of our six week trip: our first glimpse of Uluru (Ayers Rock).

30 In the last five and a half weeks we've seen and done some amazing things. We've been blinded by the salt lakes of Curara Soak, we've relived history in the goldfields of Kalgoorlie-Boulder, we've been guests at the campfires of Aboriginal communities. But nothing compares to the spectacular sight of the famous Uluru, shining purple in the light of dawn. Over the years I've heard
35 plenty of people talk about the wonderful changing colours of the Rock, but until you see it yourself, it's impossible to imagine. We were absolutely spellbound.

We spent a good part of the day walking the 9.4 kilometres around the base of the Rock. It's well worth it. The caves and rock art are fascinating. If you get a
40 chance to join one of the tours given by the Anangu guides, do it. They explain everything about Uluru and all its sacred sites.

At sunset, we settled down to watch the Rock turn red against the darkening sky and planned the last leg of our trip – 450 kilometres across the desert to the modern town of Alice Springs.
45 We talked about all the incredible friends we've made during our trip and about the things we're going to miss once we leave the bush behind.

> **Glossary**
> turned in *v* went to bed
> glimpse *n* quick sight
> spellbound *adj* really fascinated

GRAMMAR: present perfect for unfinished time

1 Look at the highlighted phrases in the blog. Choose the correct phrases to complete the notes.

* They are all expressions that refer to a (1) *specific time in the past / period of time that hasn't finished*.
* The verb form that we use with them is the (2) *present perfect / past simple*.

2 Mark the phrases finished time (F) or unfinished time (U).

in the last few days	last month
last year	up till now
two days ago	during the last two weeks
over the past year	yesterday

3 Complete the text. Put the verbs in brackets into the present perfect or the past simple.

We (1) _____ (*arrive*) in Alice Springs yesterday. It's the biggest town we (2) _____ (*see*) over the last two months. Up till now, we (3) _____ (*camp*) under the stars. Last night, we (4) _____ (*sleep*) in a four-star hotel. We (5) _____ (*have*) a hot bath before we went to bed. We (6) _____ (*not / watch*) TV in the last six weeks.

4 Use the time expressions in exercise 2 and these verbs to make five sentences that are true for you.

do	eat	go to	have	make	see

I haven't been to a café in the last few days.

5 Make questions from your sentences in exercise 4. Then work in pairs. Ask and answer the questions.

Have you been to a café in the last few days?
No, I haven't. Have you …?

Use the past simple to talk about actions in the past that happened at a finished time.
*We **camped** out last night.*
*At sunset, we **settled** down to watch the Rock turn red.*

Use the present perfect to talk about actions in the past that happened in a period of time which is unfinished.
During my 35 years as a travel writer, I've visited more countries than I can count.
(= She is still a travel writer now.)
*In the last five and a half weeks we've seen and **done** some amazing things.*
(= The last five and a half weeks includes now.)

Here are some common expressions to describe unfinished time:

during		
in	the last	*few months/two years*, etc.
over		

> ❯ FOR OTHER USES OF THE PRESENT PERFECT, SEE PAGE 74
> ❯ SEE LANGUAGE REFERENCE PAGE 24

SPEAKING

1 Work in pairs. You are going to plan a journey across your own country. Discuss these topics and prepare your route.

* from where to where?
* transport: motorbike/car/train/bicycle?
* how long?
* how many stops?
* places to stay?
* things to see/do?

2 Describe your route to the class. Who has the most interesting route?

Useful language

Our route begins in …
We travel by …
Our first stop is in …
In … we visit the …

2D | Getting around

SPEAKING & VOCABULARY: verb collocations (travel)

1 Work in pairs. Think about transport in your town/city and discuss these questions.

- What's the quickest way of travelling around your town/city?
- What's the most popular form of transport for people going to work?
- What's the best way for a tourist to travel around your town/city to see the sights?

2 Choose the correct verbs to complete the information from a tourist guide about Edinburgh.

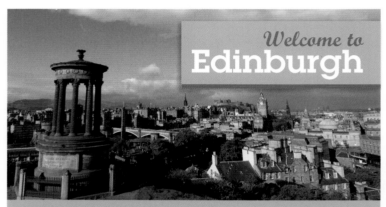

Welcome to Edinburgh

Getting there ...

By air
From the airport, you can (1) *catch / get out of* the Airlink 100 bus, which (2) *runs / takes* 25 minutes to the city centre. Alternatively, you can (3) *miss / take* a taxi. The advantage of this is that the taxi driver can (4) *drop / arrive* you off wherever you like, but of course it is more expensive than public transport.

By rail
If you (5) *arrive / catch* by train, (6) *drop / get off* at Waverley Station, which is right in the city centre. From there, you can (7) *walk / get on* to most of the major sights.

Getting around
A good way to get to know the city is with a city bus tour. You can buy special tickets for the double-decker buses which allow you to (8) *get in / get on* and off when and where you want. In the evenings, the buses (9) *run / take* late, but if you (10) *get out of / miss* the last one, you can always take a taxi.

3 Work in pairs. Change the information in exercise 2 so that it is true for a city you both know well.

From the airport you can take the metro into the city centre. It takes 40 minutes.

LISTENING

1 Look at the photos. Where are the people? What are they doing?

2 🔘 1.11–1.13 Listen and match the dialogues 1–3 to the photos A–C.

3 🔘 1.11–1.13 Listen again. Decide if the sentences are true (T) or false (F). Correct the false sentences.

Dialogue 1
1 The passenger doesn't have the right money.
2 She doesn't know where to get off.

Dialogue 2
3 The man is taking a taxi because his car has broken down.
4 He is going to take the taxi alone.

Dialogue 3
5 The woman's train has already left.
6 The woman will have to get a taxi.

FUNCTIONAL LANGUAGE: travelling

1 Match the phrases 1–8 to the photos A–C in Listening exercise 1.

1 Can I get a *taxi* anywhere *round here*?
2 Can you tell me the time of the next *train* to *North Park*?
3 Has the *11.40* for *North Park* left yet?
4 Could you tell me when we get to the *bridge*, please?
5 Does this *bus* go to the *town centre*?
6 Have you got change for a *ten-pound note*?
7 I'd like a cab for the *Pizzeria Roma*, please.
8 A *single* to the *town centre*, please.

2 Match the responses a–h to the phrases 1–8 in exercise 1.

a That'll be one twenty, please.
b Certainly, sir. We'll send one right away.
c Yeah, we go there.
d No, sorry, exact change only.
e I'll let you know.
f Not if you hurry, it's still at the platform.
g Yes, madam. There's a taxi rank at the front of the station.
h The next one's at 2.35, madam.

3 Replace the words in italics in exercise 1 with alternative words and phrases.

1 *Can I get a bus anywhere near the airport?*

4 Work in pairs. Prepare then practise short dialogues for the following situations.

- You're in a city centre. Ask a passerby for the nearest taxi rank.
- You are at home. Phone for a cab to take you to the station tomorrow morning.
- You are a stranger in the town. You are getting on a bus. Ask the driver for tickets to the town centre. You are going to the theatre. You don't know where to get off.
- You are getting off the bus. Ask the driver when the last bus leaves to get home.
- You are on a train. Ask if you can sit in an empty seat.

DID YOU KNOW?

1 Work in pairs. Read about taxis in New York and London and discuss the questions.

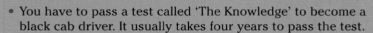

- There are over 12,000 yellow cabs in New York City.
- There are 21,000 black cabs in London.
- Yellow cabs are the only taxis that can pick up passengers on the streets of New York.
- Black cabs are the only taxis that can pick up passengers on the streets of London.
- You have to pass an English language test to become a yellow cab driver.
- You have to pass a test called 'The Knowledge' to become a black cab driver. It usually takes four years to pass the test.
- Robert de Niro was nominated for an Oscar® for his role as a New York taxi driver.
- Not all black cabs are black!

- Are taxis expensive in your town?
- Are they easy to find?
- Do they operate 24 hours a day?
- How often do you take a taxi?
- When was the last time you caught a taxi? Where were you going?
- Do you usually chat to the driver?

Self-assessment (✓)

☐ I can describe how to get around my town or city.
☐ I can ask for a taxi over the phone.
☐ I can ask for information about transport options.

GRAMMAR
Present perfect & past simple

When we talk about past actions, we can sometimes choose between the past simple and the present perfect.
We use the past simple …
- when we ask when the event happened (with *when*).
  *When **did** she **arrive** at Alice Springs?*
- when we say when the event happened (with time expressions like *yesterday, last week, one night,* that indicate a finished time).
  *She got there **two weeks ago**.*
  *He gave up his job **last year**.*

We use the present perfect …
- when the time is not stated. The event happened in the past, but the time is not important. We often use the present perfect to talk about general experience.
  ***Have** you ever **been** to Australia?*
  ***They've visited** many interesting places.*
- with time expressions that do not specify the exact time (eg *ever, never, already, yet, since, just, recently*).
  *He**'s just** begun his journey.*
  *He**'s already** visited six different countries.*
- when we talk about actions in the past that happened in a period of time which is unfinished.
  *She's made a lot of friends **in the last few weeks**.*
  (*in the last few weeks* includes present time)

Common expressions that refer to unfinished time are:

during	
in	the last few days/weeks/months/years
over	

Some time expressions can refer to both finished time and unfinished time.

> *Have you done anything interesting **this morning**?*
> (= It is still the morning.)
> *Did you do anything interesting **this morning**?*
> (= The morning is now finished.)

Other expressions that we can use with both tenses include *today, this week, this month,* etc.

Present perfect

affirmative	subject + *have/has* + past participle
negative	subject + *haven't/hasn't* + past participle
question	*have/has* + subject + past participle

Past simple

affirmative	Regular verbs: infinitive + *-ed* Irregular verbs: see list of irregular verbs on page 147
negative	Regular and irregular verbs: subject + *didn't* + infinitive
question	Regular and irregular verbs: *did* + subject + infinitive

See page 74 for more information about the present perfect.

Phrasal verbs

Phrasal verbs contain a verb and a particle (eg *get by, set out, stop off*). With some phrasal verbs, the particle is in two parts (eg *run out of, look forward to*). Phrasal verbs are either separable or inseparable.

With an inseparable phrasal verb, we cannot separate the verb and the particle.

> *He finally **got over** his illness.*
> Not *He finally got his illness over.*

With a separable phrasal verb, the object can come either before or after the particle.

> *She **dropped off** her husband at the airport.*
> *She **dropped** her husband **off** at the airport.*

If the object is a pronoun (eg *him, her, it*) the object always comes before the particle.

> *Will you see **us** off?* Not *Will you see off us?*

FUNCTIONAL LANGUAGE
Travelling

Can I get a bus anywhere near/round here?
Could you tell me the time of the next train?
Could you tell us when we get to the station, please?
Does this bus go to the airport?
Has the 11.40 for North Park left yet?
Have you got change for a ten-pound note?
I'd like a cab for the Pizzeria Roma, please.
One single/A return to the town centre, please.

WORD LIST

Phrasal verbs

bring together	/ˌbrɪŋ təˈɡeðə(r)/
break down	/ˌbreɪk ˈdaʊn/
come across	/ˌkʌm əˈkrɒs/
drop (sb) off	/ˌdrɒp ˈɒf/
get by	/ˌget ˈbaɪ/
get over (sth)	/ˌget ˈəʊvə(r)/
give (sth) up	/ˌgɪv ˈʌp/
look after (sb)	/ˌlʊk ˈɑːftə(r)/
pick (sb) up	/ˌpɪk ˈʌp/
pull out	/ˌpʊl ˈaʊt/
run into (sb)	/ˌrʌn ˈɪntuː/
see (sb) off	/ˌsiː ˈɒf/
set out	/ˌset ˈaʊt/
settle down	/ˌset(ə)l ˈdaʊn/
sort out	/ˌsɔː(r)t ˈaʊt/
stand up for (sth)	/stænd ˈʌp ˌfɔː(r)/
stop off	/ˌstɒp ˈɒf/
turn in	/ˌtɜː(r)n ˈɪn/

Travel

catch a bus /plane/train	/ˌkætʃ ə ˈbʌs /ˈpleɪn/ˈtreɪn/
get in a bus/car/taxi	/get ˌɪn ə ˈbʌs/ ˈkɑː(r)/ˈtæksi/
get out of a bus /car/taxi	/get ˌaʊt əv ə ˈbʌs /ˈkɑː(r)/ˈtæksi/
get off a bus /plane/train	/get ˌɒf ə ˈbʌs /ˈpleɪn/ˈtreɪn/
get on a bus /plane/train	/get ˌɒn ə ˈbʌs /ˈpleɪn/ˈtreɪn/
miss a bus/plane /train	/ˌmɪs ə ˈbʌs/ˈpleɪn /ˈtreɪn/
take a bus/taxi/train	/ˌteɪk ə ˈbʌs/ ˈtæksi/ˈtreɪn/
take (time) to + *infinitive*	/ˈteɪk (taɪm) ˌtuː/

Other words & phrases

acrobatics n pl	/ˌækrəˈbætɪks/
act n C ***	/ækt/
adventure n C **	/ədˈventʃə(r)/
alternatively adv **	/ɔːlˈtɜː(r)nətɪvli/
amazing adj *	/əˈmeɪzɪŋ/
apparently adv ***	/əˈpærəntli/
award n C/v ***	/əˈwɔː(r)d/
backpack n C	/ˈbækˌpæk/
bear n C **	/beə(r)/
bet n C/v **	/bet/
blind adj/v **	/blaɪnd/
blood n U ***	/blʌd/
broaden v *	/ˈbrɔːd(ə)n/
budget n C ***	/ˈbʌdʒɪt/
bush n U **	/bʊʃ/
cab n C	/kæb/
campfire n C	/ˈkæmpˌfaɪə(r)/
cave n C **	/keɪv/
celebrate v ***	/ˈseləˌbreɪt/
charity n C/U ***	/ˈtʃærəti/
climate n C **	/ˈklaɪmət/
climax n C *	/ˈklaɪmæks/
clown n C	/klaʊn/
coast n C ***	/kəʊst/
comedian n C	/kəˈmiːdiən/
comfortable adj ***	/ˈkʌmftəb(ə)l/
competition n C ***	/ˌkɒmpəˈtɪʃ(ə)n/
continent n C **	/ˈkɒntɪnənt/
cub n C	/kʌb/
currently adv ***	/ˈkʌrəntli/
darken v	/ˈdɑː(r)kən/
dawn n C **	/dɔːn/
declare v ***	/dɪˈkleə(r)/
desert n C **	/ˈdezə(r)t/
double-decker adj/n C	/ˌdʌb(ə)l ˈdekə(r)/
eventually adv ***	/ɪˈventʃuəli/
exist v ***	/ɪɡˈzɪst/
explore v ***	/ɪkˈsplɔː(r)/
extraordinarily adv *	/ɪkˈstrɔː(r)d(ə)nərəli/
fascinating adj **	/ˈfæsɪneɪtɪŋ/
fire station n C	/ˈfaɪə(r) ˌsteɪʃ(ə)n/
formation n C ***	/fɔː(r)ˈmeɪʃ(ə)n/
four-wheel drive n C	/ˌfɔː(r)wiːl ˈdraɪv/
fox n C **	/fɒks/
fridge n C *	/frɪdʒ/
glimpse v/n C *	/ɡlɪmps/
goldfield n C	/ˈɡəʊldˌfiːld/
headline n C **	/ˈhedˌlaɪn/
helicopter n C **	/ˈheliˌkɒptə(r)/
heritage n U **	/ˈherɪtɪdʒ/
hire v **	/ˈhaɪə(r)/
hitchhike v	/ˈhɪtʃˌhaɪk/
home town n C	/ˌhəʊmˈtaʊn/
in the wild adv	/ˌɪn ðə ˈwaɪld/
incredible adj *	/ɪnˈkredəb(ə)l/
injure v **	/ˈɪndʒə(r)/
injury n C/U ***	/ˈɪndʒəri/
inspire v **	/ɪnˈspaɪə(r)/
juggling n U	/ˈdʒʌɡ(ə)lɪŋ/
landmark n C	/ˈlæn(d)ˌmɑː(r)k/
lawyer n C ***	/ˈlɔːjə(r)/
length n C ***	/leŋθ/
lie ahead v	/ˌlaɪ əˈhed/
lift n C **	/lɪft/
local adj ***	/ˈləʊk(ə)l/
magic n U **	/ˈmædʒɪk/
mechanical adj **	/mɪˈkænɪk(ə)l/
mission n C **	/ˈmɪʃ(ə)n/
outback n U	/ˈaʊtˌbæk/
passerby n C	/ˌpɑːsə(r)ˈbaɪ/
perform v ***	/pə(r)ˈfɔː(r)m/
platform n C **	/ˈplætˌfɔː(r)m/
post v **	/pəʊst/
principality n C	/ˌprɪnsəˈpæləti/
purple adj *	/ˈpɜː(r)p(ə)l/
purpose n C ***	/ˈpɜː(r)pəs/
put (sth) right v	/ˌpʊt ˈraɪt/
raise v ***	/reɪz/
represent v ***	/ˌreprɪˈzent/
rescue v **	/ˈreskjuː/
rock n U/C ***	/rɒk/
sacred adj **	/ˈseɪkrɪd/
salt n U **	/sɔːlt/
search n C/v ***	/sɜː(r)tʃ/
second-hand adj *	/ˌsekəndˈhænd/
sight n C/U ***	/saɪt/
site n C **	/saɪt/
sole adj **	/səʊl/
solo adj / adv *	/ˈsəʊləʊ/
spectacular adj **	/spekˈtækjʊlə(r)/
spellbound adj	/ˈspelˌbaʊnd/
sponsor v **	/ˈspɒnsə(r)/
storm n C **	/stɔː(r)m/
stranger n C **	/ˈstreɪndʒə(r)/
taxi rank n C	/ˈtæksi ˌræŋk/
tiger n C *	/ˈtaɪɡə(r)/
time limit n C	/ˈtaɪm ˌlɪmɪt/
tractor n C	/ˈtræktə(r)/
truck n C **	/trʌk/
unforgettable adj	/ˌʌnfə(r)ˈɡetəb(ə)l/
van n C **	/væn/
widely-travelled adj	/ˌwaɪdli ˈtræv(ə)ld/
wildlife n U	/ˈwaɪldˌlaɪf/

3A | Dream homes

SPEAKING

1 Do any of these phrases describe where you live?

- It's really convenient for the shops.
- It gets quite noisy at night.
- It can be a bit dull at times.
- The neighbours are really friendly.
- It's a bit small and we need more space.
- It's quite a long way from where I work/study.
- There's loads of space and plenty of light.

2 Work in pairs. Compare your answers in exercise 1 and discuss these questions.

- What are the advantages and disadvantages of living where you live?
- Would you like to live somewhere completely different? If yes, where?

READING

1 Read the magazine article on page 27. Which section of the magazine does it come from?

a Advice for home buyers
b Alternative lifestyles
c Home improvements

2 Read the article again and tick the information that is mentioned.

1 Paradise Ridge opened over 20 years ago.
2 A lot of people want to live there.
3 It is very near a primary school and community college.
4 You are not allowed to drive your car in the cabin park.
5 Most of the residents work in Vancouver.
6 Everybody helps with the work of the community.
7 Meetings of the residents take place every month.
8 They grow vegetables in a community garden.

3 Work in pairs. List three advantages of living in Paradise Ridge. Then think of three possible disadvantages.

4 🔊 1.14–1.18 Listen to five residents of Paradise Ridge. Do they mention any of the disadvantages you listed in exercise 3?

5 🔊 1.14–1.18 Listen again and say who mentioned which topics. Match the residents 1–5 to the topics a–e.

a kids   c meetings   e isolation
b food   d shared work

6 Would you like to live in Paradise Ridge? Why or why not?

GRAMMAR: modals of obligation, permission & prohibition (present time)

1 Complete the rules with words and phrases 1–4.

> To talk about permission, you use …
> To talk about prohibition, you use …
> To talk about obligation, you use …
> To talk about a lack of obligation, you use …
>
> 1 *don't have to* and *don't need to*.
> 2 *must* and *have to*.
> 3 *can* and *be allowed to*.
> 4 *mustn't, can't* and *not be allowed to*.
>
> ❯ SEE LANGUAGE REFERENCE PAGE 34

2 Find one example in the article about Paradise Ridge for each of the rules in exercise 1.

3 Complete the house rules with words or phrases from exercise 1. Use your own ideas.

HOUSE RULES

1 You *don't have to* pay electricity and gas bills.
2 You _____ pay the rent on the first day of the month.
3 You _____ pay for phone calls.
4 You _____ smoke in the kitchen and lounge.
5 You _____ switch off the TV and CD player in the lounge at midnight.
6 You _____ have pets in the house.
7 You _____ do the housework.
8 You _____ have small parties on Saturday nights.
9 Visitors who stay the night _____ help with the housework.
10 Visitors _____ stay for more than three days.

4 Compare your rules with a partner. Whose rules are stricter?

5 Choose a place from the box and write four sentences about it using the words and phrases from exercise 1. Do not mention the name of the place.

church   hospital   library   museum
plane   prison   school   theatre

You aren't allowed to touch anything.
You don't have to go there, but it's usually interesting.
You often have to buy a ticket.
You have to leave your bag outside.

6 Work in pairs. Read your sentences to your partner. He/She must decide which place you are talking about.

7 Do you have to follow any rules where you live? Tell a partner about them.

We aren't allowed to put the rubbish out before 8pm. We have to pay a monthly charge for the lift and the lights on the stairs.

Paradise Ridge

About 70 miles north-east of Vancouver is one of Canada's most beautiful tourist regions. Visitors come to enjoy fishing and water sports in the region's many lakes and rivers, to go skiing in
5 **the winter or simply to enjoy the spectacular mountain scenery.**

But while most people come for a short break, promising to return the following year, many people have decided to stay for good. One such visitor was a
10 Vancouver businesswoman, Kirsty Bourne, who first came to the region on a skiing trip.

Kirsty was looking for a place to live with her young family. 'Vancouver is fine for work,' she said, 'but, like all big cities, it's not a great place to live. I wanted
15 somewhere where everybody knows everybody else, where your neighbours are also your friends and all your problems are shared. Where parents don't have to worry about their kids when they're playing in the street and you don't need to lock your door at night.'

20 Just over twenty years ago, Kirsty founded Paradise Ridge, a cabin park in the heart of the Columbia Mountains, which is now home to 25 families. Each family owns their own small cabin, but they share ownership of the park and the common facilities. 'This
25 is a real, living community,' insists Kirsty, 'so residents aren't allowed to use their cabins as a holiday home. They can't come here just for their vacations.'

The heart of the Paradise Ridge community is a large wooden house that stands at the centre of the
30 25 cabins. Shared meals take place there three times a week and once a month there is a meeting when important decisions are made. 'Residents mustn't miss these meetings,' explains Kirsty, 'because it's important that we all share in the decision-making.' The most
35 important decisions usually concern new residents. Families can sell their homes if they want to leave, but the whole community must vote on new families before they are allowed to join.

'Keeping the community together is hard work,' says
40 Kirsty. 'Everybody has to lend a helping hand and take responsibility for the day-to-day running of the community. That includes doing repairs, looking after the kids, cooking the communal meals or leading one of the monthly meetings.' But it seems that there is no
45 shortage of families who want to join. There are more than 70 on the waiting list.

Glossary
for good *adv* permanently
lend a helping hand *v* share the work
running *n* management

3B | Unusual homes

VOCABULARY: accommodation

1 Look at the photos. Which countries do you think these are? Why? What does your town look like from the air?

2 Complete the sentences in column A with a phrase from column B.

A	B
1 Most people in Britain own their homes, but about 30% live	a a house or a **flat** with their friends.
2 Accommodation in British town centres is usually	b in France.
3 It is quite common for young people to share	c in detached or **semi-detached** houses with gardens.
4 British families often prefer to live in the **suburbs**	d in **rented accommodation**.
5 About half a million British people own **holiday homes**	e in **apartment blocks** or rows of old **terraced** houses.

3 Match the words in bold in exercise 2 to the definitions 1–7.

1 two houses joined together
2 houses that are joined together in a line
3 homes that you live in for only part of the year
4 a home that is usually on one floor of a larger building
5 buildings that contain a number of separate flats
6 lived in by someone who pays money to the owner
7 parts of a town that are away from the town centre

4 Change the sentences in exercise 2 so that they are true for your country.

LISTENING

1 Work in pairs. Match the words in the box to the photos A–F. Would you like to live in any of them? Why or why not?

cave   houseboat   lighthouse
mobile home   tree house   windmill

2 🔊 1.19–1.21 Listen to three people talking about their unusual homes. Where do they live? Choose your answers from the box in exercise 1.

3 🔊 1.19–1.21 Listen again and make a note of the best and the worst things about where they live.

4 Match the sentences 1–8 to the three unusual homes in exercise 2. Then check your answers in audioscripts 1.19–1.21 on page 136.

1 We make dog owners leave their pets in the garden.
2 The local authorities make us move on.
3 We don't let little kids come up on their own.
4 They let us keep pets.
5 The farmers are happy to let us stay on their land.
6 The local people don't let us stay.
7 They don't allow us to have visitors.
8 We don't allow smoking.

GRAMMAR: *make, let & allow*

We can use the verbs *make*, *let* and *allow* to talk about obligation and permission.

Obligation *make* + object + infinitive without *to*
*Our teacher **makes us do** a lot of homework.*
(= We must do a lot of homework.)

Permission *let* + object + infinitive without *to*
*The farmer **lets us stay** on his land.*
(= We can stay on his land.)

allow + object + *to* + infinitive
*They usually **allow us to stay** overnight.*
(= We can usually stay overnight.)

allow + noun/verb + *-ing*
*They **don't allow smoking** in the living room.*
(= You can't smoke in the living room.)

❯ SEE LANGUAGE REFERENCE PAGE 34

1 Choose the correct verb to complete the sentences.

1 They *let / allow* us to put up our tent wherever we want.
2 They *make / allow* us park our cars in the car park.
3 They *let / allow* us use the washing machine in their kitchen.
4 They *make / let* us come and go when we want.
5 They *make / let* us pay £3 a night.

2 What is being described in exercise 1?

a) a hotel   b) a campsite   c) a holiday flat

3 Use the prompts to make sentences which are true for you.

My	teacher parents boss wife husband boyfriend girlfriend	(doesn't) (don't)	make(s) let(s) allow(s)	me us	(to) …

My boss makes us work late on Fridays.
My girlfriend doesn't let me smoke in her car.

SPEAKING

1 Work in pairs. Discuss these questions.

- Is it common for people to have holiday homes in your country?
- Where are the most popular places to buy a holiday home? Why?
- Do people from abroad buy holiday homes in your country? Which countries do they usually come from?

2 Work in pairs. You are going to design a luxury holiday home. Discuss these questions.

- Where exactly is your holiday home?
- Is it a flat or a house?
- Is it old or new?
- How big is it?
- What facilities has it got? (eg garden, swimming pool, private beach …)

3 Talk to other pairs of students. Describe your holiday home and try to persuade them to book a holiday there.

Useful language

I think you'll really like it because …
It's just the thing you're looking for.
It's great for (families/couples/singles).
It's in the most fantastic spot …

3c | Bedrooms

SPEAKING & VOCABULARY: verb collocations (sleep)

1 Complete the sentences with a verb from the box.

fall	feel	go	have	make
remember	set	wake		

1 I often find it difficult to _____ up in the morning.
2 I always _____ the bed first thing in the morning.
3 I sometimes _____ a nap after lunch.
4 I sometimes _____ asleep in front of the TV.
5 I often _____ sleepy in the middle of the day.
6 I never _____ to sleep before ten o'clock.
7 I sometimes forget to _____ my alarm clock.
8 I can never _____ my dreams.

2 Change the sentences in exercise 1 so that they are true for you. Compare your sentences with a partner.

3 Work in pairs. Discuss these questions.

- Do you find it easy to get to sleep?
- What do you do when you can't get to sleep?
- Are you a heavy or a light sleeper?
- Do you usually remember your dreams the next morning?
- Can you remember a recent dream?

READING

1 Look at the photos on page 31. What do you know about the people?

2 Read the articles 1–6 and match them to the headings a–f.

a A week in bed
b Going nowhere
c Sleeping on the moon
d Rules for healthy bedrooms
e Sleeping with strangers
f A king's office

3 Read the articles again and match the phrases a–f to the end of each article.

a and it was never full!
b so he stayed where he was.
c because the green contained arsenic, a poisonous chemical.
d and they all suffered the physical effects of lack of sleep.
e where they recorded 'Give Peace a Chance'.
f with one hundred people in the room.

4 Find words in the article which match the definitions.

1 a decision by a court of law that someone is guilty of a crime
2 a man who looks after another man's clothes
3 a person who has to leave their country because it is dangerous for them to stay
4 a small hotel
5 a strong complaint or disagreement
6 a substance that gives a strong smell when it is burned
7 a bed made of rope or material that hangs between two posts or trees
8 an adjective used to describe things associated with the moon

GRAMMAR: modals of obligation, permission & prohibition (past time)

1 Read the sentences from the articles below. Then put the headings in the box in gaps 1–4.

obligation	permission	prohibition	no obligation

1 _____
*Important friends **were allowed to** come into his room.*

2 _____
*You **had to** keep cooking smells away from bedrooms.*

3 _____
*Poorer travellers **didn't need to** get out of bed.*
*Louis XIV **didn't have to** worry about getting up in the morning.*

4 _____
*You **couldn't** put green wallpaper in bedrooms.*
*Mehran **wasn't allowed to** go through passport control.*

> SEE LANGUAGE REFERENCE PAGE 34

2 Complete the text with modals from the grammar box.

A law of 1834 in Britain said that people (1) *couldn't* give money to the poor, unless they were old or ill. The government's solution to the problem of poverty was the building of workhouses around the country. Living conditions in the workhouses were very hard and you (2) _____ leave the building without special permission. Children under seven (3) _____ work, but everyone else (4) _____ do twelve hours a day. You (5) _____ have your own possessions and everyone (6) _____ wear a special uniform. You (7) _____ wash or shave only once a week. Husbands and wives (8) _____ speak to each other and they (9) _____ sleep in separate dormitories. The poor (10) _____ live in these workhouses, but, for many, there was not much choice.

Six things you probably didn't know about beds and bedrooms

1 In 19th century Britain, the Ladies' Sanitary Association published a list of rules for bedrooms. Bedrooms had to be fresh and airy, but not too airy in case people caught a cold. You had to keep cooking smells away from bedrooms, or burn incense to hide the smell. You couldn't put green wallpaper in bedrooms ...

2 Louis XIV of France was a busy man, but he didn't have to worry about getting up in the morning. His valet woke him up at 8.30 and important friends were then allowed to come into his room, where they could watch him wash and have breakfast. On some days when Louis was feeling sleepy, he didn't get up at all and he conducted the day's business from his bed ...

3 Astronauts on the first lunar missions in the 1960s and 1970s had big problems getting a good night's sleep. They had no hammocks in the lunar module and they had to sleep on the hard floor. They weren't allowed to take off their space suits because they took too long to get them back on. It was very difficult to get into a comfortable position ...

4 When people in Shakespeare's time stayed at an inn, they had to share their beds with complete strangers. When a rich traveller arrived at a busy hostel, he could take the place in bed of a poorer person. However, there was one inn in the small town of Ware where poorer travellers didn't need to get out of bed. The inn had a huge bed for eight people ...

5 After their wedding in 1969, John Lennon and Yoko Ono spent a week in bed at the Amsterdam Hilton hotel as a protest against the war in Vietnam. They wanted to repeat the protest two months later in the US, but Lennon couldn't get an American visa because he had a conviction for drugs. As a result, the couple had to go to Montreal ...

6 Political refugee, Alfred Mehran, lost his travel documents in Paris when he was on his way to London. Mehran wasn't allowed to go through passport control at Charles de Gaulle airport, so he made his bed on a plastic bench in the departure lounge and stayed there for eleven years until new documents finally arrived. When the documents arrived, Mehran wasn't sure he wanted to go home after all ...

3 Work in pairs. Look at the photo of a child's bedroom and discuss these questions.

- Did you sleep in a bed like this when you were younger?
- What was your bedroom like?
- What time did you have to go to bed?
- Were there any other rules that you had to follow as a child?

4 What were the rules in your home when you were a young child?

3D | Dinner invitation

SPEAKING

1 Think of the last time you had a meal at someone else's home and prepare answers to the questions.

- Whose home was it?
- How long ago was it?
- Was it a special occasion?
- Who was at the meal?
- What did you eat?
- What was the food like?
- What did you talk about during the meal?

2 Work in pairs. Describe the meal to your partner.

LISTENING

1 Work in pairs. Look at the pictures and describe what is happening in each one. What do you think the people are saying to each other?

2 🔘 1.22–1.25 Listen and match the dialogues 1–4 to the pictures A–D.

3 🔘 1.22–1.25 Listen again. Decide if the sentences are true (T) or false (F). Correct the false sentences.

1 The woman is doing something in the kitchen when the man arrives.
2 They go straight out to the garden.
3 The man hasn't been to the woman's house before.
4 The man likes sitting in the sun.
5 The woman doesn't want to go to the cinema.
6 The man's going to sit in the garden while the woman works.

Check your answers in audioscripts 1.22–1.25 on page 136–137.

4 Imagine that you have invited a new friend for dinner in your home. What preparations will you make?

FUNCTIONAL LANGUAGE: requests
PRONUNCIATION: intonation (requests)

1 Look at audioscripts 1.22–1.25 on pages 136–137 again and underline examples of the phrases 1–8.

1 Can you …
2 Could I …
3 Could you …
4 Would you mind if I …
5 Do you think I could …
6 Do you think you could …
7 Is it all right/OK if I …
8 Would you mind + -ing …

2 Complete the table with the phrases in exercise 1.

asking someone to do something	asking for permission to do something
Could you possibly … Do you mind + -ing … _____ _____ _____ _____	Can I … Could I possibly … I wonder if I could … _____ _____ _____

Which of the phrases are the most polite?

3 ● **1.26** Listen to these short exchanges. What is the problem with the responses?

1 A: I've got to do some work. Do you think I could do that first?
B: Yes.

2 A: Is it OK if I go out into the garden?
B: Yes.

3 A: Do you mind waiting? It'll only take me an hour or so.
B: No.

4 A: Would you mind if I moved the sunshade a little?
B: No.

4 Match the alternative responses a–d to questions 1–4 in exercise 3.

a Sure thing, be my guest. I thought we'd eat out there, actually.

b No worries, that's fine, could I wait out here?

c … feel free, do you need any help?

d … that's fine, do whatever you need to do.

● **1.27** Listen to the recording to check your answers.

5 You can make requests more polite in two ways: (a) say *please* (b) use friendly intonation.

● **1.28** Listen and repeat the example.

Could you take these plates out for me, please?

6 Work in pairs. Look at the requests in exercise 3 and the responses in exercise 4. Practise the dialogues, concentrating on making your intonation as polite as possible.

7 Work in pairs, A and B. You are going to act out a dinner party dialogue.

A: A friend has invited you for dinner in his/her home. Turn to page 126 for more information.

B: You have invited a friend for dinner in your home. Turn to page 131 for more information.

DID YOU KNOW?

1 Work in pairs. Read about British food and discuss the questions.

Although in the past, Britain had a bad reputation for food, in the last ten years things have definitely changed for the better and this reputation is no longer deserved. There are over 30,000 restaurants in the country. In many cities, and even small towns, you can choose from Indian, Chinese, Italian, Japanese, Thai, French, Mexican, Turkish, Greek and Spanish food. There has even been a growth in new restaurants serving high quality traditional British food.

Cooking programmes on TV are incredibly popular and TV chefs like Jamie Oliver are well-known celebrities. Recipe books are often at the top of the best-seller list. Health food shops are everywhere and more and more people are eating organic food.

- Does your country have a good reputation for food? Is the reputation deserved?
- How often do you go to a restaurant or have a meal with friends?
- What are the most popular food books and TV programmes in your country?

Self-assessment (✓)

☐ I can make polite requests.
☐ I can respond politely to requests.
☐ I can describe a meal I ate at someone's home.

GRAMMAR
Modals of obligation, permission & prohibition (present & past time)

Permission

We use *can* + infinitive and *is/are allowed to* + infinitive to talk about permission in the present.

> You **can drive** in the UK when you are 17.
> The children **are allowed to watch** TV until ten o'clock.

We use *could* + infinitive and *was/were allowed to* + infinitive to talk about permission in the past.

> Many years ago people **could smoke** anywhere.
> She **was allowed to stay out** until twelve o'clock.

Obligation

We use *must* + infinitive and *has/have to* + infinitive to talk about obligation in the present.

> You **must arrive** 30 minutes before your flight.
> We **have to leave** soon.

We use *had to* + infinitive to talk about obligation in the past.

> He **had to pay** a lot of tax last year.

No obligation

We use *don't/doesn't have to* + infinitive and *don't/doesn't need to* + infinitive to talk about something that is not necessary (but it is allowed).

> You **don't have to come** if you don't want to.
> I **don't need to wear** a tie to work.

We use *didn't have to* + infinitive and *didn't need to* + infinitive to talk about an absence of obligation in the past.

> She knew the restaurant manager so she **didn't have to pay** for her meal.
> They **didn't need to get up** early because it was a holiday.

Prohibition

We use *can't* + infinitive, *mustn't* + infinitive and *isn't/aren't allowed to* + infinitive to talk about something that is not allowed.

> You **can't enter** the US without a passport.
> You **mustn't open** your papers before the exam begins.
> The students **aren't allowed to take** mobile phones to school.

We use *couldn't* + infinitive and *wasn't/weren't allowed to* + infinitive to talk about prohibition in the past.

> British schoolchildren **couldn't have** long hair in the 1950s.
> The monks **were not allowed to speak**.

Make, let & allow

Permission

We can use *let* + object + infinitive (without *to*) and *allow* + object + *to* + infinitive to talk about permission.

> She **lets her children do** anything they want.
> My father **let me use** his car.
> The teacher **allowed the students to ask** questions.

Obligation

We can use *make/made* + object + infinitive (without *to*) to talk about obligation.

> The company **makes the staff work** very hard.
> She **made me do** it again.

Prohibition

We can use *doesn't/didn't let* + object + infinitive (without *to*) and *doesn't/didn't allow* + object + *to* + infinitive to talk about prohibition.

> They **don't let me leave** until five o'clock.
> He **didn't let me speak**.
> They **don't allow animals to come** into the house.

FUNCTIONAL LANGUAGE
Requests: asking for permission

Requests

Can I (possibly) + infinitive …?
Could I (possibly) + infinitive …?
Do you think I could + infinitive …?
Is it all right/OK if I + present tense …?
I wonder if I could + infinitive …?

Responses

Yes, sure/of course/certainly/no problem/go ahead.
I'm sorry, but …
I'm afraid that …
If we want to refuse permission, we usually give an explanation.

Requests: asking someone to do something

Requests

Can you (possibly) + infinitive ...?
Could you (possibly) + infinitive ...?
Do you think you could + infinitive ...?

Responses

Yes, sure/of course/certainly/no problem.
If we want to refuse the request, we usually give an explanation.

WORD LIST

Accommodation

apartment block *n C*	/ə'pɑ:(r)tmənt ˌblɒk/
cabin *n C* **	/'kæbɪn/
campsite *n C*	/'kæmpˌsaɪt/
cave *n C* **	/keɪv/
communal *adj* *	/'kɒmjʊn(ə)l/
community *n C* ***	/kə'mju:nəti/
detached *adj* *	/dɪ'tætʃt/
dormitory *n C*	/'dɔ:(r)mɪtri/
facilities *n pl* ***	/fə'sɪlətiz/
flat *n C* ***	/flæt/
holiday home *n C*	/'hɒlɪdeɪ ˌhəʊm/
houseboat *n C*	/'haʊsˌbəʊt/
lighthouse *n C*	/'laɪtˌhaʊs/
local authority *n C*	/ˌləʊk(ə)l ɔ:'θɒrəti/
lock *v* ***	/lɒk/
mobile home *n C*	/ˌməʊbaɪl 'həʊm/
monthly charge *n C*	/'mʌnθli 'tʃɑ:(r)dʒ/
ownership *n U* **	/'əʊnə(r)ʃɪp/
rent *v/n U* ***	/rent/
resident *n C* ***	/'rezɪd(ə)nt/
semi-detached *adj*	/ˌsemidɪ'tætʃt/
suburb *n C* *	/'sʌbɜ:(r)b/
tent *n C* **	/tent/
terraced *adj*	/'terəst/
tree house *n C*	/'tri:ˌhaʊs/
wallpaper *n U* *	/'wɔ:lˌpeɪpə(r)/
windmill *n C*	/'wɪn(d)ˌmɪl/

Sleep

fall asleep	/'fɔ:l ə'sli:p/
feel sleepy	/ˌfi:l 'sli:pi/
get to sleep	/ˌget tə 'sli:p/
go to sleep	/ˌgəʊ tə 'sli:p/
have a nap	/ˌhæv ə 'næp/
heavy sleeper *n C*	/ˌhevi 'sli:pə(r)/
light sleeper *n C*	/ˌlaɪt 'sli:pə(r)/
make the bed	/ˌmeɪk ðə 'bed/
set the alarm clock	/ˌset ði: ə'lɑ:(r)m ˌklɒk/
wake up *v* *	/'weɪk 'ʌp/

Other words & phrases

airy *adj*	/'eəri/
arsenic *n U*	/'ɑ:(r)s(ə)nɪk/
bench *n C* **	/bentʃ/
best-seller *n C*	/ˌbest'selə(r)/
big deal *n C*	/ˌbɪg 'di:l/
bill *n C* ***	/bɪl/
candle *n C* **	/'kænd(ə)l/
chef *n C* *	/ʃef/
chemical *n C/adj* ***	/'kemɪk(ə)l/
conduct *v* ***	/kən'dʌkt/
convenient *adj* **	/kən'vi:niənt/
conviction *n C* **	/kən'vɪkʃ(ə)n/
crash *v* **	/kræʃ/
day-to-day *adj* *	/ˌdeɪtə'deɪ/
deserved *adj*	/dɪ'zɜ:(r)vd/
dramatic *adj* ***	/drə'mætɪk/
drawback *n C*	/'drɔ:ˌbæk/
dull *adj* **	/dʌl/
effect *n C* ***	/ɪ'fekt/
enormous *adj* ***	/ɪ'nɔ:(r)məs/
feel free	/ˌfi:l 'fri:/
for good *adv*	/fə(r) 'gʊd/
found *v* ***	/faʊnd/
growth *n U* ***	/grəʊθ/
half-way *adj/adv* *	/ˌhɑ:f'weɪ/
hammock *n C*	/'hæmək/
a helping hand	/ə ˌhelpɪŋ 'hænd/
hostel *n C*	/'hɒst(ə)l/
incense *n U*	/'ɪnsens/
inn *n C* *	/ɪn/
isolated *adj* *	/'aɪsəˌleɪtɪd/
isolation *n U* **	/ˌaɪsə'leɪʃ(ə)n/
keep (sb) company *v*	/ˌki:p 'kʌmp(ə)ni/
living conditions *n pl*	/'lɪvɪŋ kənˌdɪʃ(ə)nz/
loads of **	/'ləʊdz əv/
lounge *n C* *	/laʊndʒ/
lunar *adj*	/'lu:nə(r)/
module *n C* ***	/'mɒdju:l/
noisy *adj* *	/'nɔɪzi/
obviously *adv* ***	/'ɒbviəsli/
organic *adj* *	/ɔ:(r)'gænɪk/

owner *n C* ***	/'əʊnə(r)/
paradise *n C/U* *	/'pærədaɪs/
poisonous *adj* *	/'pɔɪz(ə)nəs/
poverty *n U* **	/'pɒvə(r)ti/
refugee *adj* **	/ˌrefjʊ'dʒi:/
reputation *n C/U* ***	/ˌrepjʊ'teɪʃ(ə)n/
responsibility *n U/C* ***	/rɪˌspɒnsə'bɪləti/
ridge *n C* **	/rɪdʒ/
rubbish *n U* **	/'rʌbɪʃ/
sanitary *adj*	/'sænət(ə)ri/
scenery *n U* *	/'si:nəri/
shortage *n C* **	/'ʃɔ:(r)tɪdʒ/
substance *n C* ***	/'sʌbstəns/
sunshade *n C*	/'sʌnˌʃeɪd/
task *n C* ***	/tɑ:sk/
uniform *n C* **	/'ju:nɪfɔ:(r)m/
vacation *n C*	/və'keɪʃ(ə)n/
valet *n C*	/'vælɪt/ /'væleɪ/
waiting list *n C*	/'weɪtɪŋ ˌlɪst/
wave *n C* ***	/weɪv/
wooden *adj* ***	/'wʊd(ə)n/
workhouse *n C*	/'wɜ:(r)kˌhaʊs/

4A | Luck of the draw

Vocabulary: idioms (taking risks)

1 Match the phrases in bold in sentences 1–6 to the definitions a–f.

1 **It's a bit of a gamble**, but I think we should give it a go.
2 **There's a lot at stake** here, I really don't think it's a good idea.
3 **It's against the odds**, but you never know – maybe we'll win. What do you think?
4 Well, I'm not sure. We could take a risk and win a million or we could **play safe** and keep what we have.
5 I never **try my luck** because I always lose.
6 **It's a lottery** – but if we don't play, we'll never win anything.

a you probably won't win
b take a risk
c there's a risk here, but it's only a small one
d if you lose, you could lose a lot
e it's a question of luck – anyone could win
f decide not to take a risk

2 Work in pairs. Discuss these questions.

- What are the risks involved in the following situations?
  a) asking your boss for a pay rise
  b) playing the lottery
  c) walking home alone in the dark
- Do you usually play it safe or do you like to try your luck?
- What was the last big risk that you took?

Reading

1 Look at the title of the article. Which of these words do you think you will find in the article?

| addicts celebrate charities |
| governments jackpot low income |
| millionaires schoolchildren |

2 Read the article and choose the best ending, 1 or 2.

1 But when a ticket only costs a handful of small change, there is not much at stake. Why not try your luck?
2 The lottery clearly isn't the quick-fix solution to life's problems. It solves some; it causes others. But that isn't going to stop me buying my weekly ticket!

3 Explain in your own words who the lottery winners and losers are.

4   Saturday 6th August

Lottery winners and losers

Feeling lucky and want to try your luck on the lottery? The chances of becoming a millionaire are definitely well against the odds (1) _____. But millions of ordinary people, like you or me – or John Goodman*, this week's lottery millionaire – regularly buy
5 our tickets, just in case. Maybe, we too will join the hundreds of people who win jackpots on national lotteries every week.

John Goodman, 42, an unemployed father of two from Swindon, is the latest to join the jet set. John was having a quiet drink (2) _____ when his winning numbers came up on the TV and he found out he'd won £17 million. According to locals, John is
10 already planning to buy the pub.

But people like John and his fellow lottery millionaires aren't the only winners. The turnover for the gambling industry in the UK alone is over £42 billion per year – (3) _____. And over £1.5
15 billion of this goes to the government in taxes.

The lottery has always been popular with politicians as a way of raising money. When the British government was looking for ways to spend more on sport and the arts in the 1990s, it turned to the lottery. (4) _____, lotteries helped pay for the building of more
20 than 50 universities, including Harvard and Yale. And over 2,000 years ago in China, the Great Wall was partly paid for with lottery money.

But where there are winners, there are also losers. It is well-known that the poor play the lottery more often than the rich and some
25 critics of the lottery call it a tax on the poor. People on low incomes can end up spending hundreds of pounds a year on lottery tickets and some will become lottery addicts. Meanwhile, the rich play it safe by investing their money in less risky ways – (5) _____.

Large sums of government money go to charities every year and the
30 charities certainly welcome it. But at the same time, when lottery money starts coming in, governments usually reduce the amount that they normally spend on good causes. This means that many charities, (6) _____, can suddenly find themselves with a lot less money.

35 So who actually wins in the end? It's something to think about next time you find yourself tempted to buy a ticket.

* For legal reasons, this is not his real name.

4 Put the phrases a–f into the gaps 1–6 in the article.

a and especially the low profile ones
b (in fact you're more likely to be struck by lightning)
c buying stocks and shares, for instance
d in his local pub with his mates
e When America was recovering from the Civil War
f that's over £115 million a day

5 How do lotteries work in your country? Do you think that lotteries are a good way to raise money?

GRAMMAR: past simple & past continuous

1 Work in pairs. Look at the sentence from the article below. Then complete the rules with *past simple* or *past continuous*.

> *John **was having** a quiet drink in his local pub when his winning numbers **came up** on the TV.*

Use the _____ for completed past actions.
Use the _____ for actions that were in progress at a particular time in the past.

You often use the past continuous with the past simple. Use the _____ for longer activities. Use the _____ for shorter, completed actions.

> *When America **was recovering** from the Civil War, lotteries **helped** pay for more than 50 universities.*

❯ SEE LANGUAGE REFERENCE PAGE 44

2 Complete the two true stories. Put the verbs in brackets into the past simple or the past continuous.

Three friends (1) _____ (*spend*) the weekend in London when they were refused entry at a nightclub because they (2) _____ (*not / wear*) shirts and ties. They (3) _____ (*go*) to an all-night supermarket and (4) _____ (*buy*) some new shirts. While they (5) _____ (*pay*) for the shirts, they (6) _____ (*decide*) to buy a scratchcard and (7) _____ (*win*) £20,000. They (8) _____ (*spend*) the whole night celebrating in the nightclub!

A man (9) _____ (*walk*) under a tree when some bird droppings (10) _____ (*fall*) on his head. As this is supposed to be lucky, he (11) _____ (*decide*) to buy an instant lottery ticket and he (12) _____ (*win*) £24. The following week he (13) _____ (*stand*) under the same tree when the same thing (14) _____ (*happen*) again! So he (15) _____ (*buy*) another lottery ticket and won £444. He now spends time every week standing under that lucky tree, waiting for that little bird.

SPEAKING

1 Work in pairs. Make up a story about a lottery winner by answering the questions below. Then practise telling the story to another pair of students.

● Where and when did he/she buy the ticket(s)?
● How did he/she choose the numbers?
● Where and when did he/she hear about his/her lottery win?
● What was he/she doing at the time?
● What did he/she do next?

PRONUNCIATION: *was* & *were*

1 🔊 1.29 Listen to the dialogue. Are the underlined words pronounced in their strong or weak forms? When do we use the strong forms of these words?

	strong	weak
was	/wɒz/	/wəz/
were	/wɜː/	/wə/

A: (1) <u>Was</u> that man standing under the tree again?
B: Yes, he (2) <u>was</u>. He (3) <u>was</u> with a friend this time.
A: What do you think they (4) <u>were</u> doing?
B: I asked them. They said they (5) <u>were</u> waiting for a bird.
A: A bird! I find that hard to believe.
B: They (6) <u>were</u>! They said it (7) <u>was</u> a lucky bird.
A: I knew he (8) <u>was</u> a bit crazy!

2 Work in pairs. Practise the dialogue with your partner.

4B | Twists of fate

VOCABULARY: injuries

1 Match the injuries 1–8 to the pictures A–H.

1 He's bleeding.
2 He's got a big bruise.
3 He's got a black eye.
4 He's got a few scratches.
5 He's sprained his wrist.
6 He's suffering from shock.
7 He's twisted his ankle.
8 He's unconscious.

2 Work in pairs. Put the injuries in exercise 1 in order of seriousness (1 = most serious → 8 = least serious).

3 Work in pairs, A and B.

A: Choose an injury from exercise 1 and explain how it happened.
He was running for the bus when he fell over.

B: Listen to your partner's explanation and decide which injury he/she is talking about.

Then exchange roles.

The world's luckiest man?

Frane Selak, a retired Croatian music teacher, may well be one the luckiest people alive.

Click here for the full story. >>

LISTENING

1 Work in pairs. Discuss these questions.

• Do you know anyone who is particularly unlucky?
• When was the last time that you were unlucky?

2 Work in pairs. Look at the photo and headline to a news story. What do you think has happened to the man to make him 'the world's luckiest man'?

3 🔘 1.30 Listen to the first part of a radio news story about Frane Selak and answer the questions.

1 What did he win?
2 What did he buy?

4 🔊 **1.31** Listen to the rest of the story. What other things have happened to him to make him the world's luckiest man?

5 🔊 **1.30–1.31** Listen again to the whole story and put the events in the correct order. Then answer the questions below.

- ☐ He bought a new house.
- ☐ He had a car accident in the mountains.
- ☐ He was burnt at a petrol station.
- ☐ He was hit by a bus.
- ☐ He was in a plane crash.
- ☐ He won the lottery.
- ☐ His bus fell into a river.
- ☐ His train fell into a river.

1   How many accidents was Selak involved in?
2   In what way is his latest piece of good luck different to all the other good luck stories?

6 Find the highlighted words and phrases in audioscripts 1.30–1.31 on page 137 and match them to the definitions 1–6.

ploughed into	exploded	rails
corpses	haystack	sprayed

1   crashed into
2   suddenly caught fire with a loud noise
3   threw liquid over something
4   dead bodies
5   the lines that a train runs on
6   large pile of dried grass

GRAMMAR: past perfect simple

Use the past perfect to talk about completed actions in the past that happened *before* other actions in the past.
*He won the lottery with the first ticket he **had bought** for forty years.*
(= He bought a ticket and then he won the lottery.)

Make the past perfect with ***had/hadn't*** + past participle.

Look at the difference between the past perfect and the past simple.
*He was in hospital again. He **had had** another accident.*
(= He had an accident and so he went to hospital.)
*He was in hospital again where he **had** another accident.*
(= He had the accident when he was in hospital.)

❯ SEE LANGUAGE REFERENCE PAGE 44

1 Complete the text. Put the verbs in brackets into the past simple or the past perfect.

In the late 1940s, the members of a church choir in Nebraska (1) _____ (*meet*) every Wednesday at 7.20 to practise their singing. But one day in 1950, it was already 7.25 and the choir (2) _____ (*not / arrive*). They (3) _____ (*be*) fortunate because at that moment a gas explosion (4) _____ (*destroy*) the church. The fifteen members of the choir (5) _____ (*have*) different reasons for being late. Two people (6) _____ (*break*) down in their car. Others (7) _____ (*decide*) to finish some work and another person (8) _____ (*fall*) asleep.

2 Read the short text. Use your imagination to answer the questions. Begin your answers with *Because he had ...*

Lucky Luciano, an American gangster, was both famous and feared. Everybody recognized him because he had an injured eye and everybody wanted to be his friend. When America went to war in the 1940s, he didn't have to join the forces, but after the war finished he was forced to leave the country. He lived in Italy until his death in 1962.

1   Why was he called Lucky?
2   Why did he have a problem with his eye?
3   Why did he become famous?
4   Why were people frightened of him?
5   Why did he not have to join the army?
6   Why did he leave America?

🔊 **1.32** Listen to the recording to check your answers.

4c | Bad luck stories

A	**MUM LEFT OUT IN THE COLD**
B	*Mum pays for expensive joke*
C	**Man loses job after mountain top adventure**

READING

1 Read the news stories and match the stories 1–3 to the headlines A–C.

2 Read the stories again and answer these questions.

Story 1
1 How long was the man stuck on the mountain?
2 How did he survive?
3 Who found him?

Story 2
4 How long did the woman have to wait on the balcony?
5 Why did the woman go out onto the balcony?
6 How old was the little boy?

Story 3
7 How much will the mother have to pay?
8 How did the egg get on the roof of the car?
9 How long did it stay there before it was discovered?

3 Have you heard any bad luck stories in the news recently? If so, what were they?

1

A German man has lost his job because he was late for work. Thomas Milnik had survived five days in the Alps in freezing temperatures. But he lost his job because he had missed four days at work.

Thomas received a letter telling him that he'd lost his job while he was still in hospital. At the same time that he was reading his letter, the doctors were deciding whether to cut off six of his frostbitten toes!

The 41-year-old hiker was climbing in the Alps last Saturday when it suddenly started to snow. He was eventually rescued five days later when workers at a nearby research station heard his cries for help and called the mountain rescue services.

2

A local woman had to be rescued by police yesterday after her toddler son locked her out on the balcony.

The woman had gone outside on the balcony to hang out some clothes to dry. But her son, aged eighteen months, had pushed the door shut from the inside. The mother could only watch as her son walked to the sofa, climbed up on to it and then fell asleep!

After two hours of shouting for help, neighbours heard the woman's screams and called the police.

3

A mother will have to pay £675 because her teenage son fried an egg on the roof of his teacher's car. The boy, aged 14, had met up with friends at school one afternoon when the teachers were meeting inside to discuss their pupils' end of term reports. The three boys threw several eggs at the school windows of the conference room. One egg missed the window and landed on the roof of a teacher's Ford Mondeo.

Because of the summer sun, the roof was so hot the egg was immediately fried. And it continued to cook until the owner of the car discovered it two hours later. By the time he found it, the fried egg had burned into the paint.

VOCABULARY: time linkers

Use *while*, *as* and *when* to show that two actions happen at the same time.
  *A black cat crossed my path **while/as/when** I was walking down the street.*

Use *the moment*, *as soon as* and *when* to show that one action happens immediately after another action.
  *I crossed the road **the moment/as soon as/when** I saw the black cat.*

Use *by the time* to show that one action has happened before another.
  *I'd had three different accidents **by the time** I got home.*

⊙ SEE LANGUAGE REFERENCE
PAGE 44

1 Look at the sentences below. One of the three time linkers in italics in each sentence is wrong. Underline it. Then explain why it is wrong.

1 Thomas Milnik found out that he'd lost his job *while / as / after* doctors at the hospital were deciding whether to cut off six of his toes.
2 The 41-year-old hiker was climbing in the Alps *as soon as / when / as* it suddenly started to snow.
3 He was eventually rescued five days later *the moment / after / when* workers at a research station heard his cries for help.
4 A woman had to be rescued by police yesterday *when / after / as soon as* her son locked her out on the balcony.
5 The mother could only watch *as / while / after* her son walked to the sofa, climbed up on to it and then fell asleep.
6 The egg continued to cook until the owner of the car discovered it two hours later. *By the time / When / The moment* he found it, the fried egg had burned into the paint.

2 Complete the article with appropriate time linkers from the grammar box.

Police arrested two burglars last night (1) _____ they jumped into a police car thinking it was their getaway car.

Police say that the two men had planned to break into two houses on the same street that night. They had arranged to meet a third man on the corner of the street (2) _____ they had finished in the second house.

The policeman who was driving the car said: 'They only realized it was the wrong car (3) _____ they were actually sitting in the back of it. But (4) _____ they realized it was a police car, it was too late. I'd locked the doors, and they couldn't get out.'

SPEAKING

1 Work in groups. Look at the pictures. They show another bad luck story. What's happening in each picture? What do you think happened in between?

2 Look at the words in the box and imagine five unlucky things that happened to the girl in the story.

broken glass	car	mobile phone
bus	rain	puddle	wrong address

3 Work as a class. Take it in turns to tell the story one sentence at a time.

A: *Jane was getting ready for an important date.*

B: *She was putting her make-up on when suddenly the cat jumped onto the table.*

C: *Unfortunately, when the cat jumped onto the table, it smashed the mirror.*

DID YOU KNOW?

1 Work in pairs. Read about superstitions and discuss the questions.

Superstitions in Britain

In Britain, there are many superstitions connected with cats. Black cats are good-luck animals, and you should welcome them into your house. A black cat sitting outside your front door means that you will be rich, and you will be very lucky if you see a cat sneeze. However, if a black cat crosses your path, you will have bad luck. The bad luck will go away if you walk backwards or spit on the ground in front of you.

- Which birds or animals in your country are considered to be lucky or unlucky?
- What other superstitions are common?
- How superstitious are you?

4D | Fancy that!

VOCABULARY: *both* & *neither*

> Use *both* and *neither* to compare two people or things.
> *We both have brown hair.*
> *Neither of us has a car.*
> *Jenny and Zoe both live in London.*
> *Neither Jenny nor Zoe has a boyfriend.*

Arnold Schwarzenegger
Actor and politician

Penélope Cruz
Hollywood actress

1 Look at the photos. Complete the sentences below with *both* or *neither*.

1 _____ are very successful.
2 They _____ have brown hair.
3 _____ of them live in the United States.
4 _____ of them is American.
5 _____ Arnold Schwarzenegger nor Penélope Cruz have university degrees.
6 _____ Schwarzenegger and Cruz look very serious in the photos.

2 Look at sentences 5 and 6 in exercise 1 again. Choose the correct words to complete the rules below.

> We use a *plural / singular* verb and *and / nor* with **both**.
> We use a *plural / singular* verb and *and / nor* with **neither**.

> ❯ SEE LANGUAGE REFERENCE PAGE 44

3 Work in pairs. Ask your partner questions and find six things you have in common. Then tell the rest of the class about the things you have in common. Use *both* or *neither* with *we* or *us* in your sentences.

We both have a brother.
Neither of us has visited London.

LISTENING

1 🔘 1.33 Listen to two colleagues chatting at work. Put the topics below in the order in which they are discussed. Two of the topics are not discussed.

☐ sport
☐ food
☐ TV programmes
☐ what they're doing tomorrow evening
☐ where they live
☐ where they were born

2 🔘 1.33 Listen again. Make a note of five things they have in common.

3 What did they say about the following things?

1 The White Rose
2 squash lessons
3 Harlech Crescent
4 Chinese takeaway

4 Find these expressions in audioscript 1.33 on pages 137–138 and explain them in your own words.

1 it's worth it
2 it's a bit out of your way
3 you're kidding
4 small world
5 no rest for the wicked

FUNCTIONAL LANGUAGE: talking about similarities & differences

Similarities

So/Neither + auxiliary verb + subject

Use *so* after a positive sentence and *neither* after a negative.
> *I'm very busy at the moment.* **So am I.**
> *I can't understand.* **Neither can I.**

Use *do/does/did* if there's no auxiliary.
> *I study English on Thursdays.* **So do I.**
> *I started two years ago.* **So did I.**

Use *Me, too* and *Me, neither.*
> *I like pizzas.* **Me, too.**
> *I'm not very good at squash.* **Me, neither.**

Differences

Use subject + auxiliary verb, not *so* or *neither.*
> *I'm very busy at the moment.* **I'm not.**
> *I can't understand Chinese.* **I can.**

Use *do/does/did* if there's no auxiliary.
> *I went to the meeting yesterday.* **I didn't.**

> SEE LANGUAGE REFERENCE PAGE 44

1 Find and underline five examples of *so/neither* + auxiliary verb + subject in audioscript 1.33 on pages 137–138. For each example, find the verb that corresponds to the auxiliary verb in the response.

So am I. – I'm going tomorrow.

2 Choose the best response to complete the exchanges.

1   A: I didn't like the concert much.
    B: *Neither did I. / Neither didn't I. / Neither I did.*
2   A: I love Beethoven's 5th Symphony.
    B: *I do. / I don't. / Neither do I.*
3   A: I wasn't feeling too well yesterday.
    B: *Neither I was. / Neither was I. / So was I.*
4   A: I work in an office.
    B: *So am I. / So can I. / So do I.*
5   A: I'll have a pepperoni pizza, please.
    B: *So do I. / So have I. / So will I.*
6   A: I'm a very good squash player.
    B: *I'm not. / Neither am I. / So I'm not.*
7   A: I'm sure we've met before.
    B: *I am. / Neither am I. / So am I.*
8   A: I haven't been to the park for ages.
    B: *Me, neither. / Me, too. / Neither I have.*

3 Work in small groups. Take it in turns to respond to the sentences.

1   I like hip-hop and rap music.
2   I haven't been on a date for ages.
3   I'm going to be famous one day.
4   I'll probably write a novel when I'm older.
5   I'm never late for anything.
6   I've got several unusual pets, including a snake.
7   I didn't understand maths when I was a kid.
8   I was very popular in my last job/at my last school.

1   A: *I like hip hop and rap music.*
    B: *I don't!*
    C: *Neither do I!*

SPEAKING

1 Work in pairs, A and B. You are going to read a text about two American presidents and find out about the things they have in common.

A: Turn to page 127.
B: Turn to page 130.

2 Work in pairs. Without looking back at the text about the two presidents, how many coincidences can you remember?

3 Do you know any other stories about coincidences?

Yes? Spend a few minutes preparing your story.
No? Spend a few minutes inventing a story about a coincidence.

4 Now tell your story to the rest of the class. They must decide if your story is true or if you invented it.

Self-assessment (✓)

☐ I can discuss similarities and differences.
☐ I can use both *neither* and *both* to compare people.
☐ I can recognize the main topics discussed in informal dialogues.

GRAMMAR
Past simple & past continuous

We use the past continuous for actions in progress at a particular time in the past. These actions are incomplete.

At nine o'clock last night, he was watching TV.

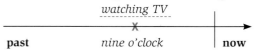

We use the past simple for completed past actions.

*He **decided** to buy a lottery ticket.*

We often use the past continuous and the past simple together. We use the past continuous for longer, 'background' actions and we use the past simple for shorter, completed actions.

*Three friends **were spending** a weekend in London and they **decided** to go to a nightclub.*

Past continuous

affirmative
subject + *was/were* + verb + *-ing* ...
negative
subject + *was/were* + *not* + verb + *-ing* ...
question
Was/Were + subject + verb + *-ing*?

Past perfect simple

We use the past perfect to talk about completed actions in the past that happened before other actions in the past.

*Rescuers arrived, but Selak **had swum** to safety.*
(= Selak swam to safety and then rescuers arrived.)

We often use the past perfect and the past simple together to show the order in which two actions took place.

Compare the following pair of sentences:

*He **had married** her when he **won** the lottery.*
(= He married her and then he won the lottery.)

*He **married** her when he **had won** the lottery.*
(= He won the lottery and then he married her.)

affirmative & negative			
I/You/He/She/We/They	had hadn't	broken	a leg.
question			
What	*had*	*I/you/he/she/we/they*	*done?*

Time linkers

We can use *while*, *as* and *when* to show that two actions happen at the same time.

*He was reading a letter **while/as/when** the doctors were deciding what to do next.*
***While/As/When** the doctors were deciding what to do next, he was reading a letter.*

We can use *the moment*, *as soon as* and *when* to show that one action happens immediately after another one.

*The boy fell asleep **the moment/as soon as/when** he climbed onto the sofa.*
***The moment/As soon as/When** the boy climbed onto the sofa, he fell asleep.*

We can use *by the time* to show that one action has happened before another.

*The party had finished **by the time** we arrived.*
***By the time** we arrived, the party had finished.*

FUNCTIONAL LANGUAGE
Talking about similarities & differences

Similarities
We can make short statements that begin with *so* and *neither* to show a similarity or agreement between what we think and a statement made by another person.

We use *so* after an affirmative statement, and we use *neither* after a negative statement.

I'm feeling tired. **So** *am I.*
She's got a cold. **So** *have I.*
They won't be happy. **Neither** *will you.*
He hasn't finished. **Neither** *has she.*

The auxiliary verb in the first statement is repeated in the statement that begins with *so* or *neither*.
If the first statement is in the present simple, the second statement will include *do/don't/does/doesn't*. If the first statement is in the past simple, the second statement will include *did/didn't*.

I like this place. *So **do** I.*
I didn't understand. *Neither **did** I.*

It is also possible to use *too* and *neither* after a pronoun.

He's Canadian. *Me, **too.***
She's not well. *Me, **neither.***

Differences

When we want to say the opposite of another statement, we do not use *so* or *neither*. We use a pronoun followed by an auxiliary verb. We stress both the pronoun and the auxiliary verb.

> I can't swim.   **I can.**
> I'm not hungry.   **I am.**

If the first statement is in the present simple or the past simple, the second statement will include *do/don't/does/ doesn't/did/didn't*.

> I don't like hamburgers.   I **do**!
> He wants a divorce.   She **doesn't**.
> They arrived early.   You **didn't**!

Both & neither

We use *both* and *neither* to compare two people or things. The meaning of *both* is positive and the meaning of *neither* is negative.

> **Both** of them have a good job.
> (= He has a good job and she has a good job.)

> **Neither** of them has a good job.
> (= He doesn't have a good job and she doesn't have a good job.)

We use a plural verb when *both* is the subject of the sentence. We normally use a singular verb when *neither* is the subject of a sentence.

When we name the two subjects, *both* is used with *and*. *Neither* is used with *nor*.

> Both Ceri and Philip **speak** Spanish.
> Neither Ceri nor Philip **speaks** Slovenian.

Both can be used in two positions in a sentence.

> **Both** of them have children.
> They **both** have children.

WORD LIST

Idioms (taking risks)

a bit of a gamble	/ə ˌbɪt əv ə ˈgæmb(ə)l/
a lot at stake	/ə ˌlɒt ət ˈsteɪk/
against the odds	/əˌgenst ði: ˈɒdz/
give (sth) a go	/ˌgɪv ə ˈgəʊ/
it's a lottery	/ˌɪts ə ˈlɒtəri/
play safe	/ˌpleɪ ˈseɪf/
try your luck	/ˌtraɪ jə(r) ˈlʊk/

Injuries

ankle *n C* **	/ˈæŋk(ə)l/
black eye *n C*	/ˌblæk ˈaɪ/
bleed *v* *	/bli:d/
bruise *v/n C* *	/bru:z/
burn *v/n C* ***	/bɜː(r)n/
frostbitten *adj*	/ˈfrɒs(t)ˌbɪt(ə)n/
scratch *n C/v* *	/skrætʃ/
shock *n C/v* ***	/ʃɒk/
sprain *n C/v*	/spreɪn/
wrist *n C* **	/rɪst/
suffer from *v* ***	/ˈsʌfə(r) ˌfrɒm/
twist *v* **	/twɪst/
unconscious *adj* *	/ʌnˈkɒnʃəs/

Other words & phrases

according to *prep* ***	/əˈkɔː(r)dɪŋ ˌtu:/
addict *n C* *	/ˈædɪkt/
all-night *adj*	/ˌɔ:l ˈnaɪt/
balcony *n C* *	/ˈbælkəni/
billion *n C* **	/ˈbɪljən/
burglar *n C* *	/ˈbɜː(r)glə(r)/
catch fire *v*	/ˌkætʃ ˈfaɪə(r)/
choir *n C* *	/kwaɪə(r)/
coincidence *n C* *	/kəʊˈɪnsɪd(ə)ns/
corpse *n C* *	/kɔː(r)ps/
critic *n C* ***	/ˈkrɪtɪk/
destroy *v* ***	/dɪˈstrɔɪ/
droppings *n pl*	/ˈdrɒpɪŋz/
end up *v*	/ˌend ˈʌp/
explode *v* **	/ɪkˈspləʊd/
explosion *n C* **	/ɪkˈspləʊʒ(ə)n/
fancy *v* **	/ˈfænsi/
fry *v* *	/fraɪ/
gamble *v* *	/ˈgæmb(ə)l/
gangster *n C*	/ˈgæŋstə(r)/
good cause *n C*	/ˌgʊd ˈkɔːz/
handful *n C* **	/ˈhæn(d)fʊl/
have (sth) in common	/ˌhæv ɪn ˈkɒmən/
haystack *n C*	/ˈheɪˌstæk/
hiker *n C*	/ˈhaɪkə(r)/
icy *adj* *	/ˈaɪsi/

income *n C/U* ***	/ˈɪnkʌm/
industry *n C* ***	/ˈɪndəstri/
it's (not) worth it	/ˌɪts nɒt ˈwɜːθ ɪt/
jackpot *n C*	/ˈdʒækˌpɒt/
jet set *n C*	/ˈdʒet ˌset/
jump *v* ***	/dʒʌmp/
kidnap *v* *	/ˈkɪdnæp/
knock *v* ***	/nɒk/
legal *adj* ***	/ˈli:g(ə)l/
leisure club *n C*	/ˈleʒə(r) ˌklʌb/
lightning *n U* *	/ˈlaɪtnɪŋ/
liquid *n C/U* ***	/ˈlɪkwɪd/
local *adj/n C* ***	/ˈləʊk(ə)l/
make-up *n U* *	/ˈmeɪk ˌʌp/
nearby *adj/adv* **	/ˌnɪə(r)ˈbaɪ/
partly *adv* ***	/ˈpɑː(r)tli/
pepperoni *n U*	/ˌpepəˈrəʊni/
petrol station *n C*	/ˈpetrəl ˌsteɪʃ(ə)n/
pile *n C* **	/paɪl/
plough into *v*	/ˌplaʊ ˈɪntu:/
profile *n C* **	/ˈprəʊfaɪl/
puddle *n C*	/ˈpʌd(ə)l/
pupil *n C* ***	/ˈpju:p(ə)l/
quick-fix *adj*	/ˌkwɪk ˈfɪks/
rail *n C* ***	/reɪl/
reduce *v* ***	/rɪˈdju:s/
regularly *adv* ***	/ˈregjʊlə(r)li/
rescue *v/n C* **	/ˈreskju:/
scream *v/n C* **	/skri:m/
smash *v* **	/smæʃ/
snake *n C* *	/sneɪk/
sneeze *v*	/sni:z/
solution *n C* ***	/səˈlu:ʃ(ə)n/
solve *v* ***	/sɒlv/
speedboat *n C*	/ˈspi:dˌbəʊt/
spit *v* *	/spɪt/
spray *v/n C/U* *	/spreɪ/
squash *n U*	/skwɒʃ/
stuck *adj*	/stʌk/
sum *n C* ***	/sʌm/
superstition *n C*	/ˌsu:pə(r)ˈstɪʃ(ə)n/
survive *v* ***	/sə(r)ˈvaɪv/
symphony *n C* *	/ˈsɪmfəni/
tempt *v* **	/tempt/
toddler *n C* *	/ˈtɒdlə(r)/
toe *n C* **	/təʊ/
turnover *n U* **	/ˈtɜː(r)nˌəʊvə(r)/
twist of fate	/ˌtwɪst əv ˈfeɪt/
warehouse *n C* **	/ˈweə(r)ˌhaʊs/
wave *v* **	/weɪv/
wicked *adj* *	/ˈwɪkɪd/
you're kidding	/ˌjɔː(r) ˈkɪdɪŋ/

5A Hard sell

VOCABULARY: adjectives (advertising)

1 Think of three different brand names that you know for each of the products below.

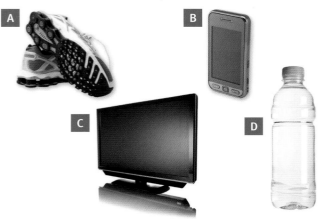

Which are your favourite brands for these products? Why?

2 Match the adjectives in the box to the products in exercise 1. Can you think of any other adjectives to describe them?

comfortable	delicious	efficient	fashionable
healthy	popular	reliable	strong	stylish

3 Think of another product and write six adjectives to describe it. Read your adjectives to the class. Can they guess what the product is?

READING

1 Look at this list of products that are often advertised with children in mind. How many more items can you add to it?

breakfast cereals, computer games, fast food, sweets …

Can you remember seeing any advertisements for these products? How did the advertisements appeal to children?

2 Read the article and answer the questions.

1 What is more important for American advertisers – the money that children spend now, or in the future?

2 How many different ways of catching children's attention are mentioned in the text?

3 Why is classroom advertising 'here to stay'?

CATCH THEM *young*

You want children to learn languages, compute skills, play the piano or become good, honest citize Any educationalist will tell you the simple answe catch them young. You want children to buy your produc
5 and to develop brand loyalty? The answer is the same.

In 1997, children in America spent or influenced the spendi of $500 billion and the figure is certainly much higher now. But far more important to the advertisers is what they will spend when they are adults. 'The kids we're reaching
10 are consumers in training,' said Joseph Fenton of Donnelly Marketing.

Kids spend 20% of their lives in school, so it is no surprise to find advertisers turning their attention to the classroom. What is rather more surprising is to learn how far advertisers
15 have already gone.

- Over half of American students receive free covers for their text books with adverts for snacks and breakfast cereals.
- Many teachers use educational materials that are paid for
20 by big business – mathematics worksheets with Disney characters, for example.
- Students who do better than others in their studies are given vouchers for free pizzas, burgers and French fries.
- Many school cafeterias serve and advertise brand name
25 food. Schools also sell advertising space in school corridors and toilets, on the side of the school bus and school websites.
- Probably the least popular form of classroom advertising is Channel One. Eight million American teenagers have
30 to watch a twelve-minute programme every day. This contains ten minutes of news and two minutes of commercials.

Not everyone is happy with the growth of classroom advertising, but it is almost certainly here to stay. The biggest
35 problem facing most schools in America is a shortage of cash. Taxpayers don't want to pay more and other fund-raising programmes don't raise enough money. 'Advertising is not just the best way to raise money,' said one school head. 'It's the only way.'

3 Read the first two paragraphs of the article again and complete the end of each line where it has been torn.

4 Is it right to advertise to young children? Why or why not?

GRAMMAR: comparisons 1

Use comparatives to compare two things or people.
The figure is **higher than** *ever before.*
Advertisers have **bigger** *budgets* **than** *they used to have.*
Brand names are **more expensive than** *other products.*

Make negative comparisons with *less* + adjective + *than*.
Classroom advertising is **less common** *in Europe* **than** *in the States.*

Make the difference between the two things bigger or smaller with a modifier before the comparative adjective. For big differences, use *much, a lot, far*. For small differences, use *a little, slightly, a bit*.
The figure is **much higher** *now* **than** *it used to be.*
Advertisements are **slightly longer** *than they used to be.*

Use superlatives to compare more than two things or people.
The biggest *problem for schools is cash.*
Children are one of **the most important** *markets for advertisers.*

Make negative comparisons with *the least* + adjective.
The least popular *form of advertising is Channel One.*

> SEE LANGUAGE REFERENCE PAGE 54

1 Write the comparative and superlative forms of the adjectives in the box.

bad	big	good	happy
healthy	strong	surprising	

2 Complete the sentences. Put the words in brackets into positive or negative comparative or superlative forms. Remember that you may also need to include *than* or *the*.

1 I usually buy famous brand names because they are a lot _____ (*reliable*) other brands.
2 I always do my shopping at _____ (*cheap*) shops in town.
3 I prefer to go shopping during the week when it is _____ (*busy*) the weekend.
4 I think that _____ (*good*) time to go shopping is during the sales.
5 Small shops are often a bit _____ (*expensive*) big supermarkets, but they are much _____ (*interesting*).

3 Work in pairs. Think of three shops in your town. Make comparative and superlative sentences about them using the prompts.

cheap/expensive	stylish/old-fashioned
popular/crowded	bad/good quality
bad/good service	wide range of goods
friendly staff	easy to get to

4 Compare your ideas with another pair of students.

SPEAKING

1 Work in small groups. Read the information.

You work for an advertising agency. A company that produces a fizzy mineral water called *Life* has hired you to create an advertisement. It wants to sell the water to young people (16–25) as an alternative to cola and other fizzy drinks. It has decided to advertise on TV. The advertising slogan will be 'Natural and Healthy'.

2 Plan your advertisement. Follow the steps below.

● Make a list of seven images you associate with the words 'natural' and 'healthy'.
● Choose one image from your list that is fashionable and will appeal to young people.
● Choose the kind of music you want to use.
● Decide whether you want to use a famous personality.
● Decide when would be the best time to show the advert on TV (before or after which programme).

3 Present your advertisement to the class.

5B | Cold calling

The all-new
Spark Platinum card

Spark Platinum

40009 9908 4443 1234

VALID FROM
01 11
MR A N OTHER
EXPIRES END
01 15
VISA

Mr Thomas Jones
491 Western Avenue
Greenford

Low interest rate – only 5.5%
High credit limit – borrow up to £15,000
Six months' free credit
Reward points for every £500 you spend

Apply for
your card now

The
red seal
of
approval

LISTENING

1 Work in pairs. Discuss these questions.

- Do you ever get emails, letters or phone calls from people who want to sell you something? If yes, do you ever reply? Why or why not?
- Do you think this kind of selling is a good idea? Explain your reasons.

2 Look at the advertising envelope. Find words or phrases which match the definitions 1–3.

1 a period of time when you don't pay extra for borrowing money
2 the maximum amount of money that you can borrow
3 the money (percentage) that you pay when you borrow money from a bank

3 🌐 **1.34** Listen to a telephone dialogue and say if the sentences below are true (T) or false (F). Correct the false sentences. Explain your answers.

1 The people on the phone know each other.
2 The caller is rude and aggressive.
3 The person at the other end is not really interested.
4 The caller eventually persuades the person on the other end to try the new card.

4 🌐 **1.34** Listen to the dialogue again. Find five differences between the credit card that the salesman describes and the credit card on the envelope.

5 Work in pairs. Repeat the dialogue. Use the information on the envelope to help you.

A: You are the salesperson. Be as persuasive as you can.
B: You are interested in finding out more about the card. Ask as many questions as possible.

6 Work in pairs. Repeat the dialogue.

A: You are very busy and you are not at all happy that a salesperson has called you at home. Ask the caller how they got your name and number.
B: Be as polite as possible, try to calm the other person down and continue with the call.

GRAMMAR: comparisons 2

Use *the same as, as* + adjective + *as* … or *similar to* to say that two things are the same, or almost the same.
 *This credit card is **the same as** that one.*
 *This credit card is **as good as** that one.*
 *His name is **similar to** mine.*

Use *different from* or *not as* + adjective + *as* … to talk about the differences between two things.
 *This credit card is **different from** that one.*
 *The Platinum Card is **not as good as** the Gold Card.*
 (= The Gold Card is better.)

> ❱ SEE LANGUAGE REFERENCE PAGE 54

1 Find six grammatical mistakes in the text and correct them.

Yes, sir, this is slightly different as the Mark V. It looks same, but this one is black and white. The black and white sets are not as popular colour these days. If you've ever watched television in colour, you'll know that it isn't the same thing at all. Of course, it's not expensive as the colour set. However, it's certainly as reliable the Mark V, and you'll see that the style is similar the colour set.

2 Rewrite the sentences using the prompts so that they have the same meaning.

1 *Whizzo* is better than any other washing powder.
No other washing powder *is as good as Whizzo* _____.
2 *Whizzo* is different from other washing powders.
Whizzo isn't _____.
3 *Whizzo* washes whiter than all other washing powders.
Other washing powders don't _____.
4 *Whizzo* is the most popular washing powder.
Other washing powders aren't_____.
5 *Whizzo* is cheaper than other washing powders.
Whizzo isn't _____.

3 Work in pairs. Choose one product from the list and write four slogans similar to the ones in exercise 2.

- 'Life' mineral water
- 'Jump' training shoes
- 'Snap' digital cameras

VOCABULARY: adjectives (negative prefixes)

1 Look at audioscript 1.34 on page 138 and find seven adjectives that begin with negative prefixes. Add them to the table below.

un-	in-	im-	dis-
unlucky	incorrect	impatient	disloyal

Decide which negative prefix goes with these adjectives and put them in the table. Use a dictionary to help you.

accurate   honest   polite
prepared   probable   successful

2 Complete the sentences with a negative adjective from the table in exercise 1.

Top Tips for Telesales Staff

1 Never be _____ about why you are calling.

2 Never give your customer _____ information.

3 Never be _____ – do some research into your clients before you call.

4 Don't be _____ to make a sale – you may need to call the same person three or four times.

5 Even when customers are _____, make sure you stay calm and friendly.

6 Accept the fact that you are going to be _____ some of the time.

7 Offer to call your client back if the time is _____.

PRONUNCIATION: /s/, /z/ & /ʃ/

1 🔊 1.35 Listen to the underlined sounds in the sentence.

/z/   /ʃ/   /s/
Whizzo is the most popular wa**sh**ing powder in **S**cotland!

2 Look at the underlined letters and put the words in the box into three groups /s/, /z/ & /ʃ/.

~~amazing~~   ~~bus~~   ~~cash~~   certain   class
course   easy   efficient   mention   person
raise   send   shop   sure   thousand
times   using   wash

/s/ *bus*
/z/ *amazing*
/ʃ/ *cash*

🔊 1.36 Listen to the recording to check your answers.

3 Look at the words in the box. Which two sounds from exercise 2 do they each contain?

business   citizen   commercials   delicious
insufficient   salesman   surprise   stylish

🔊 1.37 Listen to the recording to check your answers.

SPEAKING

1 Work in pairs. You are going to do a market research survey. Prepare a list of 6–8 questions to ask people about their spending habits.

How much do you spend on clothes?
Where do you usually shop for food? Why?

2 Do your survey with as many students in the class as you can.

3 Give a short report to the rest of the class on the results of your survey.

Useful language

One or two people (spend more than …) …
Most of the class (prefer to …) …
Almost everyone (likes …) …

5c | The office

VOCABULARY: office activities

1 Match the verbs in column A to the phrases in column B in as many ways as possible.

	A	B
1	do	an email
2	make	a phone call
3	receive	a report
4	send	a photocopy
5	write	some photocopying
		the filing
		the coffee

2 Work in pairs. Discuss these questions.

- How many of the activities in exercise 1 do you do every day?
- Which activity do you think is the most difficult to do in a foreign language?
- Do you ever have to do any of them in English?

READING

1 Read the article below about different types of people who work in offices. Match the types of people a–d to the descriptions 1–4.

- a The trainee   c The workaholic
- b The office flirt   d The boss

2 Match the types a–d in exercise 1 to the activities 1–8.

Which office type …
1 has a habit of making terrible jokes?
2 does the most work and spends the most time in the office?
3 spends the least time at their desk?
4 is always very enthusiastic?
5 is friendly one minute and angry the next?
6 takes fewer days' holidays than anyone else?
7 usually makes the coffee for everyone else?
8 thinks that chatting is more interesting than working?

3 Here are three more common office types. What do you think their main characteristics are?

- The office joker • The lazy worker • The gossip

Office Stereotypes

Whether you love them or hate them, work just wouldn't be the same without them. Here is a description of some of the most common office types. Is there one in your office?

1 This person is always very keen to appear to be your 'friend'. They often ask you about your weekend or your family. But the next minute they're asking you whether you've written that urgent report. They often have the annoying habit of making jokes – very bad jokes – which you have to laugh at. But the worst thing is that their moods change so quickly. When there's a crisis in the office, the happy, joking 'friend' disappears and is replaced by a bossy bully.

2 For most people, the office is a place where you work from nine to five. But for this person, the office is their home. In fact they spend much less time at home than they do at their desk. If they have to take a holiday, they always make sure they have their cell phone and laptop with them so they can send and receive emails. And they make more business calls than when they're at work.

3 He or she is usually the youngest person in the office, but is also the person with the most energy and enthusiasm. They've probably just finished school and are getting some work experience before they start university. No task is too boring for them and no job is too repetitive. They just love making coffee and really don't mind doing all that last-minute photocopying.

4 This person spends more time chatting with their colleagues than working. They find work boring and they are always trying to make life in the office a little more interesting. They've always got a smile and a compliment for visitors – especially if they're young and good-looking. They spend very little time at their desks and are usually to be found by the photocopier or the coffee machine, trying to get a date for the next office party.

GRAMMAR: comparing nouns

Use *more* + noun + *than* to compare two things or people.

> He spends **more time** at work **than** with his family.

Use *less/fewer* + noun + *than* to make negative comparisons. Use *less* with uncountable nouns and *fewer* with countable nouns.

> He spends **less time** with his family **than** he does with his boss.

> He takes **fewer holidays than** anyone else in the office.

Use *the* + *most* + noun to compare more than two things or people.

> People who do things too quickly often make **the most mistakes**.

Use *the least/fewest* + noun to make negative comparisons.

> The workaholic always takes **the fewest days' holiday**.

> ❯ SEE LANGUAGE REFERENCE PAGE 54

1 Choose the correct words to complete the text. Then say which office type from Reading exercise 3 is being described.

They receive the (1) *more / most* emails of anyone in the office – usually funny messages from friends. They then share these jokes with everyone else, so they spend (2) *more / most* time walking round the office than at their desks. They do the (3) *less / least* work of anyone and think that their mission is to make sure that there are (4) *less / fewer* sad faces on a Monday morning.

2 Complete the sentences with words from the box so that they are true for you.

more	fewer	less
the most	the fewest	the least

1 I know _____ jokes than most of my friends.
2 I make _____ phone calls in the morning.
3 I do _____ work possible on Friday afternoons.
4 I have _____ free time than my friends.
5 I have _____ energy at the end of the week.
6 I do _____ work in the morning than in the afternoon.

3 Compare your sentences with a partner.

SPEAKING

1 Work in groups of four, A–D. Imagine that you work in an office. The company wants you to organize a party for the office staff.

A: Turn to page 127.   C: Turn to page 130.
B: Turn to page 134.   D: Turn to page 132.

Read the information on your role card and think about your answers to the questions below.

- What kind of party would you like: a meal in a restaurant, a disco, a buffet? Where would you like the party to be?
- What day of the week would you prefer to have the party? What time should it start and finish?
- Who should be invited to the party: only company staff, staff and their partners, staff and as many friends as they like?
- Who should pay for the party: the company, the staff, both the company and the staff?

2 Now work with your group. The boss has called a meeting to discuss the party. Share your opinions and decide what sort of party you are going to have.

Real life

5D | Paperwork

VOCABULARY: office supplies

1 Look at the photo above and tick the objects in the box you can see. What other objects can you see?

> biros   calculator   drawing pins   elastic bands
> highlighter   in tray   ink cartridge   mouse pad
> notepad   paperclips   pencil sharpener   phone
> Post-its®   rubber   scissors   Sellotape®
> stapler   Tipp-Ex®

2 Work in pairs. Discuss these questions.

- What can you tell about the person who works at this desk?
- Do you work at a desk every day? If not, where do you work/study?
- What does the place where you work/study look like?
- What do you think it says about you?

LISTENING

1 🔘 1.38 Listen to a telephone dialogue. Someone is ordering some office supplies from the stationery department. What does he want to order? Can he get it all?

2 🔘 1.38 Listen again and complete the order form below.

> Office supplies request form
>
> Department _____
> Requested by (full name required)
>
> _____
>
> Authorisation code _____
>
> | item | quantity |
> |------|----------|
> | | |
> | | |
> | | |
>
> Order taken by: _Pippa_____

3 Complete the sentences below with an appropriate verb. Then look at audioscript 1.38 on page 138 to check your answers.

1 I'd like to _____ an order, please.
2 I'm _____ from the IT department.
3 That's what it _____ on the form.
4 I'll _____ if I can find it.
5 Can you _____ on a sec?

FUNCTIONAL LANGUAGE: on the phone

1 How many phone expressions can you make from the words in the boxes below?

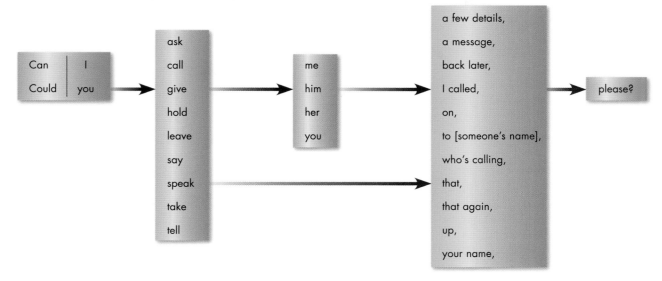

| Can | I |
| Could | you |

| ask |
| call |
| give |
| hold |
| leave |
| say |
| speak |
| take |
| tell |

| me |
| him |
| her |
| you |

| a few details, |
| a message, |
| back later, |
| I called, |
| on, |
| to [someone's name], |
| who's calling, |
| that, |
| that again, |
| up, |
| your name, |

| please? |

Can I leave her a message, please?
Could you say that again, please?

2 What questions from exercise 1 could you ask to get these replies?

1 Yes, the name's Bond. James Bond.
2 Yes, of course. I'll just get a pen and some paper.
3 Yes, I'll tell him as soon as he gets back.
4 Yes, but I don't think she'll be in the office until tomorrow morning.
5 Yes, OK. In about half an hour. Is that OK?
6 Yes, I'm sorry. It's a bad line, I think.

3 🔘 **1.39** Listen to the recording to check your answers.

4 Work in pairs, A and B. You are going to act out a telephone dialogue with an office supplies company.

A: Phone the office supplies company and place an order for some stationery.
B: You work for the office supplies company. Answer the phone and use the order form in Listening exercise 2 to take the order.

Then exchange roles.

DID YOU KNOW?

1 Work in pairs. Read about offices in London and answer the questions.

The most expensive offices in the world are in London's Mayfair and Park Lane districts – and these are also the most expensive properties in the game of Monopoly. Prices are almost twice as high as in the most popular parts of New York and Hong Kong. Besides having the most expensive offices and hotels, this part of London is close to the main shopping streets and some of the city's most fashionable squares.

- Where are most of the offices in your town/city? What is that part of your town/city like?
- Which is the best part of your town/city to work in?

Self-assessment (✓)

☐ I can answer the phone in a formal context.
☐ I can understand someone placing an order on the phone.
☐ I can place an order on the phone.
☐ I can describe an office.

GRAMMAR
Comparisions

We use comparatives to compare two things or people. We use *than* to join the two things we are comparing.

> *The supermarkets are cheaper **than** my local shops.*
> *Famous brand names are often more expensive **than** other brands.*

We can make negative comparisons with *less* + adjective + *than*.

> *Orange juice is **less popular than** fizzy drinks.*

We can make the difference between two things bigger or smaller with a modifier before the comparative adjective. With big differences we use *much, a lot, far* and with small differences we use *a little, slightly, a bit.*

> *Digital cameras are **much** more powerful these days.*
> *The shop now has a **slightly** wider range of goods.*

We use superlatives to compare more than two things or people. We put *the* before the superlative adjective.

> *She buys **the** cheapest clothes she can find.*
> *It's **the** most fashionable brand at the moment.*

We can make negative superlatives with *the least* + adjective.

> *Which shop is **the least friendly**?*

With short adjectives, we usually add *-er/-est*.

| fresh | fresher | the freshest |
| cheap | cheaper | the cheapest |

When an adjective ends in *-e*, we add *-r/-st*.

| wide | wider | the widest |
| late | later | the latest |

When an adjective ends in *-y* after a consonant, we change the *-y* to *-ier/-iest*.

| easy | easier | the easiest |
| busy | busier | the busiest |

When an adjective with one syllable ends with a consonant after a vowel, we double the consonant.

| big | bigger | the biggest |
| hot | hotter | the hottest |

With longer adjectives, we add *more/the most*.

| important | more important | the most important |
| reliable | more reliable | the most reliable |

Some adjectives have irregular comparative and superlative forms.

good	better	the best
bad	worse	the worst
far	further	the furthest

If we want to say that two things are the same, or almost the same, we can use the following structures:

1 *the same as*
> *Her trainers are **the same as** mine.*

2 *as* + adjective + *as*
> *Her trainers are **as old-fashioned as** mine.*

3 *similar to*
> *Her trainers are **similar to** mine.*

If we want to talk about the differences between two things or people, we can use the following structures:

1 *different from*
> *Her trainers are **different from** mine.*

2 *not as* + adjective + *as*
> *Her trainers are **not as nice as** mine.*
> (= My trainers are nicer.)

Comparing nouns

We can use comparative and superlative forms with nouns as well as adjectives.

We use *more* + noun + *than* to compare two things or people.

> *In the US, there are **more classroom advertisements than** in Europe.*

We use *less/fewer* + noun to make negative comparisons. We use *less* with uncountable nouns and *fewer* with plural (countable) nouns.

> *He does **less work** than his boss.*
> *The company wants everybody to take **fewer days** off.*

We use *the most/the least/the fewest* + noun to compare more than two things or people. We use *the least* with uncountable nouns and *the fewest* with plural (countable) nouns.

> *Who has **the most experience**?*
> *Of all the people in the office, she spends **the least time** behind her desk.*
> *Her department gets **the fewest complaints**.*

Functional language
On the phone

Can/Could I …
  ask who's calling?
  ask your name?
  call (you) back later?
  give him/her a message?
  leave a message?
  speak to (name)?
  take a few details?
  take a message?
  take your name?

Can/Could you …
  call (me) back later?
  give him/her a message?
  give me a few details?
  give me your name?
  hold on?
  say that again?
  speak up?
  take a message?
  tell him/her who's calling?
  tell him/her I called?

Word list
Adjectives (advertising)

comfortable ***	/ˈkʌmftəb(ə)l/
crowded *	/ˈkraʊdɪd/
delicious *	/dɪˈlɪʃəs/
efficient ***	/ɪˈfɪʃ(ə)nt/
fashionable **	/ˈfæʃ(ə)nəb(ə)l/
healthy ***	/ˈhelθi/
popular ***	/ˈpɒpjʊlə(r)/
reliable **	/rɪˈlaɪəb(ə)l/
strong ***	/strɒŋ/
stylish *	/ˈstaɪlɪʃ/

Adjectives (negative prefixes)

dishonest *	/dɪsˈɒnɪst/
disloyal	/dɪsˈlɔɪəl/
dissatisfied *	/dɪsˈsætɪsfaɪd/
impatient *	/ɪmˈpeɪʃ(ə)nt/
impolite *	/ˌɪmpəˈlaɪt/
impossible ***	/ɪmˈpɒsəb(ə)l/
improbable	/ɪmˈprɒbəb(ə)l/
inaccurate	/ɪnˈækjʊrət/
inconvenient	/ˌɪnkənˈviːniənt/
incorrect *	/ˌɪnkəˈrekt/
insufficient **	/ˌɪnsəˈfɪʃ(ə)nt/
unbelievable	/ˌʌnbɪˈliːvəb(ə)l/
unlucky	/ʌnˈlʌki/
unprepared	/ˌʌnprɪˈpeə(r)d/
unsuccessful *	/ˌʌnsəkˈsesf(ə)l/

Office activities

do a report	/duː ə rɪˈpɔː(r)t/
some photocopying	/duː sʌm ˈfəʊtəˌkɒpiɪŋ/
the filing	/duː ðə faɪlɪŋ/
make a phone call	/meɪk ə ˈfəʊn kɔːl/
a report	/meɪk ə rɪˈpɔː(r)t/
a photocopy	/meɪk ə ˈfəʊtəˌkɒpi/
the coffee	/meɪk ðə ˈkɒfi/
receive an email	/rɪˌsiːv ən ˈiːmeɪl/
a phone call	/rɪˌsiːv ə ˈfəʊn kɔːl/
send an email	/send ən ˈiːmeɪl/
a report	/send ə rɪˈpɔː(r)t/
write an email	/raɪt ən ˈiːmeɪl/
a report	/raɪt ə rɪˈpɔː(r)t/

Office supplies

biro *n C*	/ˈbaɪrəʊ/
calculator *n C* *	/ˈkælkjʊˌleɪtə(r)/
drawing pin *n C*	/ˈdrɔːɪŋ ˌpɪn/
elastic band *n C*	/ɪˌlæstɪk ˈbænd/
highlighter (pen) *n C*	/ˈhaɪˌlaɪtə(r) (pen)/
in-tray *n C*	/ˈɪntreɪ/
ink cartridge *n C*	/ˈɪŋk ˌkɑː(r)trɪdʒ/
mouse mat *n C*	/ˈmaʊs ˌmæt/
note pad *n C*	/ˈnəʊt ˌpæd/
paper clip *n C*	/ˈpeɪpə(r)ˌklɪp/
pencil sharpener *n C*	/ˈpens(ə)l ʃɑː(r)p(ə)nə(r)/
Post-its® *n pl*	/ˈpəʊstɪts/
rubber *n C*	/ˈrʌbə(r)/
scissors *n pl* *	/ˈsɪzə(r)z/
stapler *n C*	/ˈsteɪplə(r)/
Tipp-Ex® *n U*	/ˈtɪpeks/

Other words & phrases

advertiser *n C*	/ˈædvə(r)ˌtaɪzə(r)/
aggressive *adj* **	/əˈgresɪv/
annoying *adj* **	/əˈnɔɪɪŋ/
appeal *v* ***	/əˈpiːl/
appreciate *v* **	/əˈpriːʃiˌeɪt/
approval *n U* ***	/əˈpruːv(ə)l/
big business *n C*	/ˌbɪg ˈbɪznəs/
blank *adj* **	/blæŋk/
bossy *adj*	/ˈbɒsi/
brand *n C* **	/brænd/
buffet *n C*	/ˈbʊfeɪ/
bully *n C* *	/ˈbʊli/
catch (sb's) attention	/ˌkætʃ əˈtenʃ(ə)n/
cereal *n C/U* *	/ˈsɪəriəl/
client *n C* ***	/ˈklaɪənt/
code *n C* ***	/kəʊd/
commercial *n C* *	/kəˈmɜː(r)ʃ(ə)l/
compete *v* ***	/kəmˈpiːt/
compliment *n C* *	/ˈkɒmplɪmənt/
consumer *n C* ***	/kənˈsjuːmə(r)/
corridor *n C* **	/ˈkɒrɪdɔː(r)/
cover *n C* ***	/ˈkʌvə(r)/
credit limit *n C*	/ˈkredɪt ˌlɪmɪt/
crisis *n C* ***	/ˈkraɪsɪs/
cutback *n C*	/ˈkʌtˌbæk/
digital *adj* **	/ˈdɪdʒɪt(ə)l/
district *n C* ***	/ˈdɪstrɪkt/
double *v/adj* ***	/ˈdʌb(ə)l/
educational *adj* ***	/ˌedjʊˈkeɪʃ(ə)nəl/
educationalist *n C*	/ˌedjʊˈkeɪʃ(ə)n(ə)lɪst/
energy *n U* ***	/ˈenə(r)dʒi/
enthusiastic *adj* **	/ɪnˌθjuːziˈæstɪk/
existing *adj* ***	/ɪgˈzɪstɪŋ/
fizzy *adj*	/ˈfɪzi/
flirt *n C/v*	/flɜː(r)t/
fundraising *n U*	/ˈfʌndreɪzɪŋ/
gossip *v/n C/U*	/ˈgɒsɪp/
influence *v* ***	/ˈɪnfluəns/
interest rate *n C*	/ˈɪntrəst ˌreɪt/
joker *n C*	/ˈdʒəʊkə(r)/
laser *n C* **	/ˈleɪzə(r)/
loyalty *n U* **	/ˈlɔɪəlti/
market research *n U*	/ˌmɑː(r)kɪt rɪˈsɜː(r)tʃ/
mood *n C* ***	/muːd/
ordinary *adj* ***	/ˈɔː(r)d(ə)n(ə)ri/
percentage *n C* **	/pə(r)ˈsentɪdʒ/
persuade *v* ***	/pə(r)ˈsweɪd/
platinum *n U*	/ˈplætɪnəm/
procedure *n C* ***	/prəˈsiːdʒə(r)/
process *v* **	/ˈprəʊses/
property *n C/U* ***	/ˈprɒpə(r)ti/
repetitive *adj*	/rɪˈpetətɪv/
reward *v/n C* **	/rɪˈwɔː(r)d/
sale *n C* ***	/seɪl/
seal *n C* **	/siːl/
slogan *n C* *	/ˈsləʊgən/
snack *n C* *	/snæk/
staff *n U* ***	/stɑːf/
stationery *n U*	/ˈsteɪʃ(ə)n(ə)ri/
survey *n C* ***	/ˈsɜː(r)veɪ/
sweet *n C* *	/swiːt/
taxpayer *n C* **	/ˈtæksˌpeɪə(r)/
terrible *adj* ***	/ˈterəb(ə)l/
trainee *n C*	/ˌtreɪˈniː/
urgent *adj* **	/ˈɜː(r)dʒ(ə)nt/
voucher *n C*	/ˈvaʊtʃə(r)/
washing powder *n U*	/ˈwɒʃɪŋ ˌpaʊdə(r)/
workaholic *n C*	/ˌwɜː(r)kəˈhɒlɪk/

6A | Summer holiday

VOCABULARY: holidays 1

1 Choose the correct word or phrase to complete the collocations.

1 arrive *at the resort / a flight*
2 book *a flight / your way around*
3 check out of *the hotel / some holiday brochures*
4 choose *a destination / the packing*
5 do *the packing / the resort*
6 find *a deposit / your way around*
7 pay *a destination / a deposit*
8 pick up *the hotel / some holiday brochures*

2 What is the most logical order to do the things in exercise 1?

3 Work in pairs. Tell your partner about your last holiday. Use as many expressions as you can from exercise 1.

We chose our destination from a travel brochure. Then we …

READING

1 Read the questionnaire and answer each question for yourself.

2 Work in pairs and compare your answers. Do you have similar attitudes to travelling? Read your results on page 127 and see if you agree.

3 Find words or phrases in the questionnaire which match the definitions 1–8.

1 reading something to find specific information
2 happen unexpectedly or without planning it
3 a cheap holiday because you're booking late
4 do something after you've intended to do it for a long time
5 not take a lot of luggage
6 not prepare a long time ahead
7 made yourself comfortable
8 someone who looks after you when you're on holiday

4 Have you already decided what you're doing for your next holiday? Tell your partner about your plans.

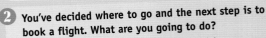

Travel questionnaire
What kind of holiday person are you?

1 It's the end of February and lots of people are already planning their summer holidays. What about you?

a) I've already decided that I'm going back to the same place as last year and the year before.

b) I've bookmarked some useful websites and I'm going to spend the weekend looking through them and deciding where I want to go.

c) I really don't know yet. I fancy somewhere different, but I don't really care where. I know something will turn up, maybe a last-minute bargain or an invitation from a friend.

2 You've decided where to go and the next step is to book a flight. What are you going to do?

a) I've already printed my tickets and itinerary.

b) I'm planning to have a look for some cheap flights on the internet tonight.

c) It's too early to decide yet, I'll probably get round to it in a week or two.

3 When do you usually do your packing?

a) I've already started doing some shopping. I always like to get everything ready at least a day or two before I leave.

b) I'm going to do it all the night before. I know what I need to take already and I'm going shopping tomorrow to buy sunscreen and some film for my camera.

c) I'll probably do it the morning before I leave. It usually only takes about half an hour. I always travel light.

4 When do you plan to get to the airport?

a) A taxi's picking me up first thing in the morning. I want to check in at least two and a half hours before my flight leaves.

b) I've already checked in online, but I'd still like to be at the airport about an hour to an hour and a half before my flight leaves.

c) I'll probably get there just in time – I always leave things till the last minute.

5 You've just settled into your hotel. What are you going to do first?

a) I'm meeting the travel rep and the other new arrivals for a welcome cocktail in the bar.

b) I'm going to find the tourist information centre and ask about where I can hire a car.

c) I don't know yet. I'll just wait and see what there is on offer.

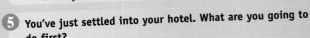

GRAMMAR: future 1 (future plans)

1 Look at question 5 of the questionnaire again and underline the future verb forms. Which verb form ...

a) describes an intention?
b) suggests that no definite plans have been made yet?
c) suggests that a firm arrangement has already been made?

2 Choose the best verb forms to complete the dialogue.

A: Hello, we were on the same flight, I think.
B: Yes, we were sitting just behind you. How long (1) *will you stay / are you staying*?
A: We're here for two weeks. And you?
B: We're not too sure. (2) *We're going to stay / We'll stay* for a couple of days and then (3) *we're deciding / we'll decide* if we want to move on. Have you made any plans for tomorrow?
A: Yes, we've hired a car, (4) *we're picking / we'll pick* it up in the morning and (5) *we'll drive / we're going to drive* around the island. We want to find the best beaches. What about you?
B: We haven't made any plans yet. We'll probably wait to see what the weather's like tomorrow and then (6) *we're making up / we'll make up* our minds!
A: Well, there's plenty of room in our car if you fancy coming along. (7) *We'll leave / We're leaving* at 9.30, straight after breakfast.
B: OK, thanks. That sounds like a good idea. We'll let you know tomorrow.

3 Work in pairs. Write the three options for the last two questions in the quiz.

> **6** You know you should send some postcards. When are you going to write them?

> **7** It's your last day. Your plane leaves at 7.30 this evening. What are you going to do?

4 Find out if any of your classmates are doing anything special this evening/tomorrow/at the weekend.

Use *be going to* + infinitive to talk about intentions: things you definitely want to do, but you haven't made firm arrangements for yet.
We're going to book some tickets on the internet this evening.
(= This is what we intend to do, but we haven't done it yet.)

Use the present continuous to talk about things you've already decided to do and made some arrangements for.
We're meeting at the pizza house at 8.30.
(= We've already spoken to our friends and arranged a time and a place to meet.)

Use *will* + infinitive ...
• to talk about the future when you haven't made any plans or arrangements.
• with *probably, possibly* or *perhaps.*
We haven't made any plans yet, we'll probably decide what to do when the others arrive tomorrow.

> ❯ SEE LANGUAGE REFERENCE PAGE 64

SPEAKING

1 Work in groups of three, A–C. It's your first morning in a hotel and you are sharing a breakfast table with some other guests. Find out what their plans are for the day.

A: Turn to page 127.
B: Turn to page 129.
C: Turn to page 134.

6B | Getting away

VOCABULARY: holidays 2

1 Read the information. Match the resorts to the photos A and B.

⚑ Negril

With eleven kilometres of beautiful white beaches, Negril is a very cosmopolitan resort, but manages to keep a laid-back atmosphere. It is ideal for a range of watersports and in the evenings you can dance to reggae in the lively clubs or join one of the crowded beach parties. Exotic, fun and completely unforgettable!

⚑ Port Antonio

Off the beaten track and away from the more well-known resorts, Port Antonio has some of the most exclusive and upmarket hotels on the island. With its romantic, secluded beaches and the picturesque scenery of the Blue Mountains, this is an area that you will never want to leave.

2 Read the information again and say if the sentences are true (T) or false (F). Correct the false sentences. Then underline the adjectives in the texts that helped you find each answer.

1 There are people from many different countries in Negril.
2 Negril has a very relaxed atmosphere.
3 The clubs in Negril are quiet and boring.
4 You will find Negril very similar to your home town.
5 Port Antonio is far from the places that people usually visit.
6 Port Antonio has cheap hotels.
7 The beaches in Port Antonio are all very crowded.
8 The Blue Mountains are very pretty.

3 Work in pairs. Discuss these questions.

● Would you prefer to go to Negril or Port Antonio? Why?
● What sort of holiday destination do you like? Use the adjectives in the texts about Negril and Port Antonio to describe it.

Buenos Aires is ideal for a range of cultural and fun activities. You can dance tango in La Boca or visit exclusive restaurants in Recoleta.

LISTENING

1 A radio reporter at Heathrow Airport asked six tourists the question: What are you most looking forward to on your holiday? Here are some of the things they mentioned. Which ones do you think were mentioned by men (M) and which by women (W)?

● the football
● the weather
● watersports
● romantic walks along the beach
● the shopping
● the beautiful women

2 🔊 1.40–1.45 Listen to the interviews to check your answers to exercise 1. Answer the questions below.

1 Where are they going?
2 How long are they staying?
3 What are they going to do?

3 🔊 1.40–1.45 Listen again. Complete the sentences with the correct number 1–6.

a Speaker _____ is travelling with his mother.
b Speaker _____ has some good news.
c Speaker _____ is going to spend a lot of money.
d Speaker _____ is going to be very tired by the time she gets home.
e Speaker _____ is interested in people-watching.
f Speaker _____ has just got married.

4 Look at the extracts below. What do the words in bold refer to?

Speaker 1: **That's** what everybody goes for, isn't it?
Speaker 2: We're planning to visit **every one**.
Speaker 3: What better place to see **them** than in the capital?
Speaker 4: That's definitely going to be **the highlight** of the four days.
Speaker 5: We're going to spend all of **it**.
Speaker 6: It looks like it's going to be wet and cold **here**.

🔊 1.40–1.45 Listen again to check your answers.

5 What do you most look forward to when you go on holiday?

GRAMMAR: future 2 (predictions)

> Use both *will* and *be going to* + infinitive to make predictions about the future.
> *That'll* definitely be the highlight of the trip.
> *That's* definitely **going to be** the highlight of the trip.
>
> Use *be going to* when you have present evidence for the prediction.
> *It's going to be* hot today. (= The skies are blue and it's already 25°C at nine o'clock in the morning.)
> *You're going to be late.* (= The class is about to start and you're still at home.)
>
> Note that often the two forms have a very similar meaning.

⊙ SEE LANGUAGE REFERENCE PAGE 64

1 Look at the pictures. Make two different predictions about what's going to happen next in each one.

2 🔊 1.46–1.47 Listen to the two dialogues. Were any of the predictions you made in exercise 1 correct?

3 Work in pairs. Look at the ideas in the box and predict five things for your partner.

| career | personal life | ten years from now |
| money | tomorrow | friends | exams | travel |

4 Tell your partner what your predictions are. Does he/she think they are possible?

SPEAKING

1 Work in groups of three, A–C. Read the information below.

> You work for a travel agency that specializes in 'made-to-measure' holidays for small groups. You have been asked to arrange a two-week summer holiday for a family group who are celebrating the grandparents' golden wedding anniversary.

2 Decide on the things below.

- destination
- accommodation
- possible activities and excursions
- facilities for the golden wedding party

  You will find more information about the special needs and interests of different people in the group at the back of the book.

  A: Turn to page 127.
  B: Turn to page 128.
  C: Turn to page 132.

3 Tell the rest of the class about the holiday you have planned.

> ### Useful language
>
> *We've decided to … because …*
> *We're going to arrange some …*
> *They won't want to …*
> *They'll probably be interested in …*
> *They'd like to … so we're going to …*

4 Now discuss the holidays with your group.

- Which holiday is …
  a) the most expensive?
  b) the most relaxing?
  c) the most fun?
- Which holiday do you think the family will choose?
- Which holiday would you enjoy most?

6c | Perfect day

SPEAKING

1 Work in pairs. Discuss these questions.

- Do you often go out for the day? Where do you usually go?
- Where's the best place to go for a day out in your area?

2 With your partner make a list of the five most important things for a good day out.

good weather, a nice restaurant ...

READING

1 Read the article and match the headings 1–4 to the excursions A–D.

1 Time travel   3 Bird's-eye view
2 Sports day   4 Song and dance

Emerald Tours

Discover the best of Ireland in a day.
We've put together an unbeatable selection of
one-day excursions from Dublin.

Call now to make your reservation!

C Ireland's west coast is one of the most beautiful and dramatic places on earth, and the ideal way to see it is from the air. In our brand new six-seater helicopter, you will first see the incredible lakes, mountains and rivers of Connemara. After you've had lunch in the pretty fishing village of Clifden, you'll be back in the air for breathtaking views of the wild Aran Islands. Don't forget to bring a camera with a zoom lens for once-in-a-lifetime shots of the seal colony.

A Those of you who've had enough of sightseeing will love this action-packed day. In the morning, you can experience the thrills of rock climbing under the guidance of an experienced instructor. After lunch, there's sea-kayaking in Dublin Bay. To round the day off, there's a visit to the National Aquatic Centre, Europe's largest indoor waterworld. Or if you've had enough of water sports, our guide will take you for a pony ride along the sandy beaches of the Bay.

D For those of you who like to lie in in the morning, the excursion to Dalkey leaves at the very respectable time of 11.30. Only a short drive from Dublin, the historic town of Dalkey has two castles and a little harbour, but it is also home to some of Ireland's best musicians (Bono, Van Morrison, Enya). Your day begins with a tour of three of the town's finest pubs, all with live music. Once you feel in the mood, our next stop will be a traditional Irish dancing club. Here you will learn the basic steps, in time for an evening of music and dance. The bus returns to Dublin at midnight, but you'll probably want to stay!

B For a taste of Ireland's ancient past, this excursion takes you to the magical area north of Dublin. As the sun sets, the highlight of the day will be a guided tour of the World Heritage Site of Newgrange, surrounded by its giant standing stones that are nearly 5,000 years old. Before we take you back into the depths of time, we will see the Hill of Tara, home of the ancient kings of Ireland, before the arrival of Christianity. This memorable day will begin with a visit to Slane Abbey where Saint Patrick brought the message of the Bible in the early 5th century.

2 Read the article again and match the comments 1–8 to the excursions A–D.

1 Great fun, but I fell in twice and the sea was freezing!
2 I was very nervous at first, but the pilot was very kind and he took us to some amazing places.
3 In one place, there was a brilliant harp player. I bought the CD.
4 Ireland's history is so fascinating. We learnt so much.
5 It was my first time on a horse, but it certainly won't be my last!
6 The guide made it really interesting with his funny stories about Irish heroes.

7 The scenery was absolutely fantastic and we'll never forget the sight of the seal cubs.

8 We loved it so much that we decided to stay until the very end. We had to get a taxi back to our hotel.

3 Which excursion A–D should these people choose to go on? Explain your reasons.

1 a young couple on their honeymoon
2 a businessman who wants to impress a customer
3 a group of four retired holidaymakers from Florida
4 two students from a Dublin language school who want to celebrate their last weekend in Ireland
5 a family with two teenage children
6 a delegation of European politicians on a cultural visit

4 Work in pairs. Discuss these questions.

• Which day trip would you choose to go on?
• What do you think the people in exercise 3 would like to see and do in your area?

GRAMMAR: present tenses in future time clauses

1 Look at the highlighted sentences in the article and answer the questions below.

1 Do the sentences refer to the present or the future?
2 Which two verb forms are used after the words *if, after, before* and *once*?
3 Which verb form is used in the other part of the sentence?

2 Complete the text. Put the verbs in brackets into the correct form.

> ### KING'S PARK HOLIDAY VILLAGE
>
> Thank you for booking your weekend away at King's Park. When we (1) _____ (*receive*) your payment, we (2) _____ (*send*) you a brochure with details of all our fantastic offers. If you (3) _____ (*want*) to hire a bicycle during your stay, please let us know and we (4) _____ (*make*) sure it's waiting for you on your arrival. Once you (5) _____ (*settle*) into your cabin, one of our guides (6) _____ (*come*) over to see that everything is to your liking. And as soon as you (7) _____ (*have*) a chance to have a look around, our reception staff (8) _____ (*be*) more than happy to take your bookings for dinner and your choice of evening entertainment. If there (9) _____ (*be*) anything else you need during your stay (*morning newspapers, extra bedding, food or drink in your cabin*), just let the staff know and they (10) _____ (*help*) you out as soon as they can.

3 Complete the sentences so that they are true for you.

1 I _____ as soon as I get some free time.
2 When I've done this exercise, I _____.
3 I _____ before I go to bed tonight.
4 Once I've _____, I _____.
5 I _____ as soon as I _____.

4 Compare your sentences with a partner.

> Use a present tense to talk about future time after conjunctions like *if, when, after, before, as soon as* and *once*. You often use *will* in the main clause of the sentence.
> *He'll get in touch with you as soon as he arrives.*
>
> Use the present perfect if you want to emphasize that the future action will have finished.
> ***Once I've** finished this, **I'll give** you a call.*

> ◆ SEE LANGUAGE REFERENCE PAGE 64

DID YOU KNOW?

1 Work in pairs. Read about Cork and discuss the questions.

In 2005, the city of Cork became the second Irish town (after Dublin) to become a European Capital of Culture. Visitors in search of culture can see the sculptures in the Crawford Gallery, go to a concert at the Opera House, take part in the Jazz and Blues festival, or simply find a bar in one of the historic streets and listen to some traditional Irish music. The most famous tourist attraction, however, is the Blarney Stone (just outside Cork). According to tradition, people who kiss the stone will become talkative and eloquent.

• What are the 'cultural capitals' of your country?
• What can you do in these cities?
• Which of these cities have you visited and what did you do there?

6D | Travel plans

SPEAKING

1 Work in pairs. Describe the photos.

2 Draw up a list of advantages and disadvantages of:
   a) Making travel arrangements online
   b) Booking through a travel agent's.

   Think about the topics in the box.

> time   money   connections and routes
> special offers   unexpected problems   choice
> advice   group discounts

3 Work in a group. Which do you think would be better in the situations below: making travel arrangements online or booking through a travel agent's?

- an activity holiday for a large group of friends
- a package holiday for a family
- a long-distance flight to visit family
- a train to another town

4 When was the last time you booked a trip? Did you book it online or did you go to a travel agent's? Why?

LISTENING

1 🔘 1.48 Listen to a short dialogue. Match it to one of the situations in Speaking exercise 3. What kind of trip is being organized? Who is going where and when?

2 🔘 1.48 Listen again and complete the form.

Flight enquiry ✈

Customer:	Avril Goodman
Destination:	
Option 1: airline	
cost	
Option 2: airline	
cost	

3 Work in pairs. Are the sentences below true (T) or false (F)? Correct the false sentences.

1 Avril knows the travel agent quite well.
2 She wants to book a flight for her boss.
3 Her boss knows the dates when he wants to fly.
4 The cost is more important than the flight time.
5 There isn't a big difference in cost between direct and indirect flights.
6 Avril gets all the information she wants.

4 🔊 **1.48** Listen again to check your answers.

FUNCTIONAL LANGUAGE: indirect questions

Use indirect questions when you are making polite enquiries. Direct questions can sometimes sound impolite.

Begin indirect questions with introduction + *if* or question word + indirect question.
  ***Do you know** if he wants to go direct?*

Here are some more common introductions to indirect questions:
I wonder …
I'd like to know …
Could you tell me …?
Do you think you could tell me …?

Note that the word order in an indirect question is the normal affirmative sentence word order (subject + verb).
  Can you tell me how long that takes?
  Not … *how long does that take?*

⊙ SEE LANGUAGE REFERENCE PAGE 64

1 Look at audioscript 1.48 on pages 139–140 and find seven examples of indirect questions.

2 Change the questions below into indirect questions. Use different introductions.

1 Where can I buy an American or English newspaper?
2 How many cinemas are there in the town?
3 What time do banks open in the morning?
4 Is there an internet café in the city centre?
5 Which restaurant is the best in town?
6 Are there any non-smoking restaurants near here?

3 Work in pairs. Look at the questions you made in exercise 2. Decide what you would say if a tourist asked you these questions about your city.

VOCABULARY: collocations with *sound*
PRONUNCIATION: word stress

1 🔊 **1.49** Listen to three short extracts from Avril's dialogue with the travel agent and tick the endings you hear.

1 That doesn't sound   a) much fun.
                        b) too bad.
                        c) very interesting.
2 Does that sound   a) all right?
                        b) like a good idea?
                        c) OK?
3 That sounds   a) fun.
                        b) great.
                        c) lovely.

2 Mark the adjectives positive (P) or negative (N).

1 amazing   5 fantastic
2 awful   6 horrible
3 dreadful   7 superb
4 excellent   8 terrible

3 Put the adjectives from exercise 2 under the correct stress pattern in the table.

• ●	● •	•●•	●••
		amazing	

4 🔊 **1.50** Listen to the exchanges and make a note of the intonation on the adjectives. Does it go up or down on the stressed syllable?

5 Tell your partner about three things that you have done today/that you did last week/that you are going to do at the weekend.

Your partner must respond using an expression with *sound*. Use an expression from the exercises above or choose a word from the box.

boring   different   enjoyable   exciting
fascinating   nice   painful   wonderful

A: Last week I had toothache so I went to the dentist's and he took out the tooth.
B: That sounds painful!

Self-assessment (✓)

☐ I can understand telephone travel enquiries.
☐ I can respond to personal news with appropriate phrases and intonation.
☐ I can use indirect questions to make polite enquiries.

Grammar
Future 1 (future plans)

We use *going to* + infinitive to talk about future plans and intentions. These are things that we definitely want to do, but we haven't made firm arrangements yet.

We're going to get some brochures tomorrow.

affirmative & negative
They're going to hire a car.
He's going to visit his parents.
question
What is she going to do next?

We use the present continuous to talk about things we have already decided to do and made arrangements for.

We're getting the two o'clock flight from Heathrow.
(= We've already bought the tickets.)

We tend not to use *going to* + infinitive with the verbs *go* and *come*. We prefer to use the present continuous.

They're going to Corfu next summer.
What time are you coming?

We use *will* + infinitive to talk about the future when we haven't made any plans or arrangements. This is often used with *probably, possibly* or *perhaps*.

We haven't made any plans yet, we'll probably decide what to do when the others arrive tomorrow.

Future 2 (predictions)

We can use both *will* and *going to* + infinitive to make predictions about the future.

You'll really enjoy the trip.
You're really going to enjoy the trip.

We use *going to* + infinitive when we have present evidence for the prediction.

It's going to rain later this morning.
(There are black clouds in the sky.)
I'm not going to finish this today.
(I still have a lot of work and it's already late.)

In many situations, it is possible to use both *will* and *going to*.

Present tenses in future time clauses

We use a present tense to talk about future time after conjunctions like *if, when, after, before, as soon as* and *once*. We often use *will* in the main clause of the sentence.

As soon as everybody gets here, the coach will leave.
We will have lunch after we get to Dalkey.

Sentences which include *if*, a present tense to talk about future and *will* in the main clause are often described as *first conditional* sentences.

We use the present perfect if we want to emphasize completion of a future action.

Once we have seen the castle, we'll visit some of the pubs.

Functional language
Indirect questions

We use indirect questions when we want to make polite enquiries. Indirect questions usually sound more polite than direct questions.

I'd like to know if I can buy a return ticket.
Could you tell me if this is the right train for Dublin?
Do you know what time the next train leaves?
Can you tell me where the station is, please?

Indirect questions begin with an introduction.

Do you know …?
Can you tell me …?
Could you tell me …?
Do you think you could tell me …?
I wonder …
I'd like to know …

For *yes/no* questions, we use *if* (or *whether*) after the introduction.

In the second part of an indirect question (after the introduction), we use normal affirmative sentence word order (subject + verb).

Can you tell me what time it arrives?
Not *Can you tell me what time does it arrive?*

WORD LIST

Holidays

action-packed *adj*	/ˌækʃ(ə)n ˈpækt/
airline *n C* **	/ˈeə(r)ˌlaɪn/
beach *n C* ***	/biːtʃ/
bedding *n U*	/ˈbedɪŋ/
brochure *n C* *	/ˈbrəʊʃə(r)/
capital *n C* ***	/ˈkæpɪt(ə)l/
check in *v*	/ˌtʃek ˈɪn/
check out of *v*	/ˌtʃek ˈaʊt əv/
cosmopolitan *adj*	/ˌkɒzməˈpɒlɪt(ə)n/
deposit *n C* **	/dɪˈpɒzɪt/
destination *n C* **	/ˌdestɪˈneɪʃ(ə)n/
exclusive *adj* **	/ɪkˈskluːsɪv/
excursion *n C*	/ɪkˈskɜː(r)ʃ(ə)n/
exotic *adj* *	/ɪgˈzɒtɪk/
find your way around	/faɪnd jə(r) ˌweɪ əˈraʊnd/
flight *n C* ***	/flaɪt/
fun *adj* **	/fʌn/
guided tour *n*	/ˌgaɪdɪd ˈtʊə(r)/
itinerary *n C*	/aɪˈtɪnərəri/
laid-back *adj*	/ˌleɪdˈbæk/
off the beaten track	/ˌɒf ðə ˌbiːt(ə)n ˈtræk/
packing *n U* *	/ˈpækɪŋ/
postcard *n C* *	/ˈpəʊs(t)ˌkɑː(r)d/
picturesque *adj* *	/ˌpɪktʃəˈresk/
resort *n C* *	/rɪˈzɔː(r)t/
romantic *adj* **	/rəʊˈmæntɪk/
sandy *adj* *	/ˈsændi/
secluded *adj*	/sɪˈkluːdɪd/
sightseeing *n U*	/ˈsaɪtˌsiːɪŋ/
souvenir *n C* *	/ˌsuːvəˈnɪə(r)/
stop off *n C/v*	/ˈstɒp əv/ /ˌstɒp ˈɒv/
suitcase *n C* *	/ˈsuːtˌkeɪs/
sunscreen *n U*	/ˈsʌnˌskriːn/
tourist attraction *n C*	/ˈtʊərɪst əˌtrækʃ(ə)n/
travel agent *n C*	/ˈtræv(ə)l ˌeɪdʒ(ə)nt/
travel rep *n C*	/ˈtræv(ə)l ˌrep/
upmarket *adj*	/ʌpˈmɑː(r)kɪt/

Other words & phrases

abbey *n C*	/ˈæbi/
ahead *adv* ***	/əˈhed/
amazing *adj* **	/əˈmeɪzɪŋ/
ancient *adj* ***	/ˈeɪnʃ(ə)nt/
awful adj **	/ˈɔːf(ə)l/
babysitter *n C* *	/ˈbeɪbiˌsɪtə(r)/
bargain *n C* **	/ˈbɑː(r)gɪn/
battery *n C* **	/ˈbæt(ə)ri/
bay *n C* **	/beɪ/
bird's-eye view *n C*	/ˌbɜːdzaɪ ˈvjuː/
bookmark *v*	/ˈbʊkˌmɑː(r)k/
boring *adj* **	/ˈbɔːrɪŋ/
brand-new *adj* *	/ˌbrændˈnjuː/
breathtaking *adj* *	/ˈbreθˌteɪkɪŋ/
cabin *n C* **	/ˈkæbɪn/
catch up on *v*	/ˌkætʃ ˈʌp ˌɒn/
cocktail *n C*	/ˈkɒkˌteɪl/
colony *n C* **	/ˈkɒləni/
congratulations *n pl*	/kənˌgrætʃʊˈleɪʃ(ə)nz/
delegation *n C* **	/ˌdeləˈgeɪʃ(ə)n/
depth *n C* ***	/depθ/
dramatic *adj* ***	/drəˈmætɪk/
dreadful *adj* **	/ˈdredf(ə)l/
eloquent *adj*	/ˈeləkwənt/
enjoyable *adj* *	/ɪnˈdʒɔɪəb(ə)l/
exhausted *adj* *	/ɪgˈzɔːstɪd/
fan *n C* **	/fæn/
fantastic *adj* **	/fænˈtæstɪk/
fascinating *adj* **	/ˈfæsɪneɪtɪŋ/
fate *n U* **	/feɪt/
firm *adj* ***	/fɜː(r)m/
flexibility *n U* **	/ˌfleksəˈbɪləti/
get round to (sth)	/get ˈraʊnd tə/
giant *adj/n C* *	/ˈdʒaɪənt/
goalkeeper *n C* *	/ˈgəʊlˌkiːpə(r)/
gorgeous *adj* *	/ˈgɔː(r)dʒəs/
guidance *n U* **	/ˈgaɪd(ə)ns/
harbour *n C* **	/ˈhɑː(r)bə(r)/
harp *n C*	/hɑː(r)p/
hero *n C* **	/ˈhɪərəʊ/
heritage *n U* **	/ˈherɪtɪdʒ/
highlight *n C* *	/ˈhaɪˌlaɪt/
hill *n C* ***	/hɪl/
honeymoon *n C* *	/ˈhʌniˌmuːn/

horrible *adj* **	/ˈhɒrəb(ə)l/
hyper-organized *adj*	/ˌhaɪpə(r)ˈɔː(r)gənaɪzd/
in particular	/ˌɪn pə(r)ˈtɪkjʊlə(r)/
in person	/ˌɪn ˈpɜː(r)s(ə)n/
indoor *adj* *	/ˈɪndɔː(r)/
instructor *n C*	/ɪnˈstrʌktə(r)/
kayak *n C*	/ˈkaɪæk/
knockout *n C*	/ˈnɒkaʊt/
last-minute *adj* *	/ˌlɑːst ˈmɪnɪt/
lens *n C* *	/lenz/
lie in *v*	/ˈlaɪ ˌɪn/
logical *adj* **	/ˈlɒdʒɪk(ə)l/
make up your mind	/ˌmeɪk ʌp jə(r) ˈmaɪnd/
memorable *adj*	/ˈmem(ə)rəb(ə)l/
option *n C* ***	/ˈɒpʃ(ə)n/
penny *n C*	/ˈpeni/
pilot *n C* ***	/ˈpaɪlət/
pony *n C*	/ˈpəʊni/
precise *adj* **	/prɪˈsaɪs/
range *n C* ***	/reɪndʒ/
reckon *v* ***	/ˈrekən/
respectable *adj* *	/rɪˈspektəb(ə)l/
rock climbing *n U*	/ˌrɒk ˈklaɪmɪŋ/
round (sth) off *v*	/ˌraʊnd ˈɒf/
saint *n C*	/seɪnt/
sculpture *n C* **	/ˈskʌlptʃə(r)/
seal *n C* **	/siːl/
settle into *v*	/ˌset(ə)l ˈɪntuː/
shot *n C* ***	/ʃɒt/
site *n C* **	/saɪt/
step *n C* ***	/step/
stunning *adj* *	/ˈstʌnɪŋ/
superb *adj* **	/sʊˈpɜː(r)b/
talkative *adj*	/ˈtɔːkətɪv/
terrible *adj* ***	/ˈterəb(ə)l/
thrill *n C/v*	/θrɪl/
unbeatable *adj*	/ʌnˈbiːtəb(ə)l/
unexpectedly *adv*	/ˌʌnɪkˈspektɪdli/
via *prep* ***	/ˈvaɪə/ /ˈviːə/
wild *adj* ***	/waɪld/
windsurfing *n U*	/ˈwɪn(d)ˌsɜː(r)fɪŋ/
zoom *v*	/zuːm/

7A | Moving

VOCABULARY: phrasal verbs with *live*

1 Complete the sentences with words from the box.

for	off	on	out of	through	up to

1 I love travelling and I'm quite happy living _____ a suitcase.
2 I don't need much money to live _____ – just enough for food and basics.
3 I can't understand people who live _____ their work – there are more important things in life.
4 You haven't really lived if you haven't lived _____ difficult times.
5 I want to live my own life. I'm not interested in living _____ my parents' expectations.
6 There's no point working if you can live _____ social security.

🔊 **2.1** Listen to check your answers.

2 Work in pairs. Do you agree or disagree with the sentences in exercise 1?

READING

1 Read the article below about a woman who has moved from the city to the country. Answer these questions.

1 What was Zoe doing before she moved?
2 Why did she move?
3 Is she happy with her decision? Why or why not?

2 Read the article again and put the phrases a–g in the gaps 1–7.

a and I just didn't feel like looking for another job
b and a busy social life of expensive restaurants and late-night clubs
c and she blushed with embarrassment
d and I knew I wanted to stay
e and one of Kathy's wonderful dinners
f and says she has no regrets
g and she has learnt to drive a tractor

3 Work in pairs. Discuss these questions.

- Zoe says that she has no regrets. Do you think that she will have any regrets later?
- Are you happy with your lifestyle? Why or why not?
- Would you like to make a radical change to your lifestyle? What kind of change?

Redundancy was the best thing that ever happened to me

Like many of her colleagues, Zoe Chambers lived for her work. She was a successful PR consultant and life was going well – she had a 5 great job, a beautiful flat on London's fashionable King's Road (1) _____. Then, the unthinkable happened. One evening in June last year, she received a text message telling her 10 she was out of work.

Suddenly, as she put it, life was 'hell'. 'The first two weeks were the most difficult to live through,' she said. 'After everything I'd done for the 15 company, they fired me by text! I was so angry (2) _____. I hated everything about the city and my life.'

Then, Zoe received an invitation from 20 an old schoolfriend, Kathy, to come and stay. Kathy and her husband,

Huw, had just bought a farm in north-west Wales. Zoe jumped at the 25 chance to spend a weekend away from London, and now, ten months later, she is still on the farm.

'The moment I arrived at Kathy's farm, I loved it (3) _____,' said 30 Zoe. 'Everything about my past life suddenly seemed superficial. When I asked Kathy if I could work for her, she refused to take me seriously at first. She told me how much farm hands get paid (4) _____.'

35 Zoe has been working on the farm since October of last year (5) _____. 'It's a hard life, physically very tiring,' she says. 'In London I was stressed and often 40 mentally exhausted. But this is a good, healthy tiredness. Here, all I need to put me in a good mood is a hot bath (6) _____.'

After ten months on the farm, Zoe 45 says she has never felt bored. Every day brings a new experience. Kathy has been teaching her how to ride a horse (7) _____. Since Christmas, she has been helping with the 50 lambing – watching a lamb being born is incredible, she says. 'It's one of the most moving experiences I've ever had. I could never go back to city life 55 now. Redundancy is the best thing that has ever happened to me!'

Glossary
superficial *adj* not deep, serious or important

GRAMMAR: present perfect continuous 1

Use the present perfect continuous …
- to talk about actions which started in the past and are still in progress now.
  I've been living here for six months. (=I still live here.)
- often with time expressions and *for* or *since*. Use *for* + time expression to talk about the length of time the action has been taking place. Use *since* + time expression to talk about the starting point of the action.
  for ten years, for a long time, for the last six months, …
  since I left London, since last September, since last Saturday …
- in questions with *How long …?*
  How long have you been waiting?

Make the present perfect continuous with *have/has + been + verb + -ing.*
  I've been working here for over six months.
  He's been working here since he was a boy.

Use the present perfect simple (not the continuous) with stative verbs.
  I've been here since last autumn. Not *I've been being here.*

> FOR MORE INFORMATION ABOUT STATIVE VERBS AND CONTINUOUS VERB FORMS, SEE PAGE 14
> SEE LANGUAGE REFERENCE PAGE 74

1 Complete the text. Put the verbs in brackets into the present perfect continuous.

Dave is a violinist. He (1) _____ (*study*) music for the last ten years and last year he moved to London to look for work. Dave (2) _____ (*live*) in London for five months now and while he is looking for a job with one of the London orchestras, he (3) _____ (*work*) as a waiter in an Italian restaurant. One of his colleagues in the restaurant (4) _____ (*also / look*) for a job as a violinist and for the past two months they (5) _____ (*play*) their violins for the customers in the restaurant. Their concerts (6) _____ (*get*) a lot of attention in the local press and they (7) _____ (*receive*) requests to perform in restaurants all over the city. Could this be the beginning of a new career?

2 Look at the time expressions in the box. Which ones can we use with *for* and which ones with *since*? Mark the expressions *for* (F) or *since* (S).

a long time	I left school
last summer	about three hours
I started work	the last two weeks
1996	ages
	as long as I can remember

3 Find four mistakes in the sentences and correct them. Explain why the verbs are incorrect.

1 I haven't been understanding any of your explanation.
2 How long have you been studying English?
3 How long have you been knowing your best friend?
4 How long have you been being in the classroom?
5 How long have you been doing this lesson?
6 How long have you been having your mobile phone?

4 Work in pairs. Answer questions 2–6 in exercise 3 using expressions with *for* and *since*.

5 Choose five of the expressions in exercise 2 and write sentences that are true for you, or a member of your family, using the present perfect continuous.

My dad's been collecting jazz CDs for as long as I can remember.

7B Life changes

VOCABULARY: metaphor

1 🔊 **2.2** Listen to a poem from *The Lord of the Rings* by JRR Tolkien. What is it about?

> The Road goes ever on and on
> Down from the door where it began.
> Now far ahead the Road has gone,
> And I must follow, if I can,
> Pursuing¹ it with eager² feet,
> Until it joins some larger way
> Where many paths and errands³ meet.

1 following   2 with enthusiasm   3 things you must do

2 The sentences below contain metaphors of life as a journey. Translate them into your own language.

1 His life **took an unexpected turn**.
2 His life was **at a crossroads**.
3 He and his partner went **their separate ways**.
4 He **embarked on a new stage of his life.**
5 He felt that it was time to **move on**.
6 He realized that there was **no turning back**.
7 He wanted to take **a new direction**.
8 Suddenly, his life **took off**.

3 Complete the text with the phrases in bold in exercise 2.

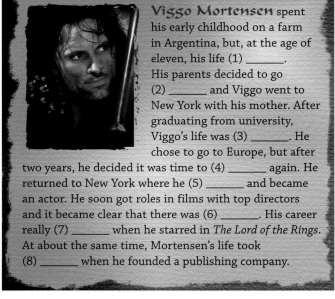

Viggo Mortensen spent his early childhood on a farm in Argentina, but, at the age of eleven, his life (1) _____. His parents decided to go (2) _____ and Viggo went to New York with his mother. After graduating from university, Viggo's life was (3) _____. He chose to go to Europe, but after two years, he decided it was time to (4) _____ again. He returned to New York where he (5) _____ and became an actor. He soon got roles in films with top directors and it became clear that there was (6) _____. His career really (7) _____ when he starred in *The Lord of the Rings*. At about the same time, Mortensen's life took (8) _____ when he founded a publishing company.

4 🔊 **2.3** Listen to the recording to check your answers.

5 Work in pairs. Discuss these questions.

• Do you know anyone whose life has taken an unexpected turn?
• Have you ever made a decision and felt that there was no turning back?
• Have you ever felt that you were at a crossroads in your life?
• Have you ever wanted to take a new direction in life? What did you do?

LISTENING

1 🔊 **2.4** Listen to an interview with a man whose life has taken a new direction. Answer the questions.

1 How has his life changed?
2 How has this changed his day-to-day life?

2 🔊 **2.4** Listen again and answer the questions.

1 Why did he decide to leave his job?
2 Why didn't his wife leave her job?
3 Why did he feel guilty about going to work?
4 How long has he been looking after Ben?
5 Does he enjoy his new lifestyle? Why or why not?
6 Is it an easy lifestyle? Why or why not?
7 Would he like to go back to work one day? Why or why not?

3 Find these expressions in audioscript 2.4 on pages 140–141. Explain what the words in italics refer to.

1 *It* didn't make much sense.
2 We were missing out on *it* all.
3 Neither of us was there to see *it*.
4 *It* all turns into a game.
5 *That's* great.

4 Would you be happy as a 'stay at home' parent? Why or why not?

SPEAKING

1 Work in pairs. Look at the list of life-changing events below and discuss these questions.

- Which are the three most important changes?
- Which is the most difficult decision to make?
- Which is the easiest change to deal with? Which is the most stressful?
- Have you had to make any of these changes in your life? If yes, what difficulties (if any) did you face?

2 Imagine that you have just made a big life change. Use your imagination or choose one of the ideas on page 127. Write your answers to these questions in note form.

- What change have you just made?
- Why did you decide to make this change?
- How long have you been doing what you are now doing?
- What difficulties did you face at the beginning?
- Are you happy with the change?
- Are there any aspects you particularly enjoy? Are there any that you really don't like?
- How long do you think you'll continue with this new lifestyle?

3 Work in pairs. Interview your partner about their life change. Find out as much as you can about their new lifestyle.

Useful language

I think the most difficult thing was …
I really didn't know what to expect …
At first I was excited/nervous/unsure …
It took me some time to …
From the start I really enjoyed/loved/hated …
It's the best thing I've ever done!
I'd recommend it to anyone!

DID YOU KNOW?

1 Work in pairs. Read about legal ages and discuss the questions.

From a legal point of view, life in England and Wales begins at the age of ten. The law says that children from ten upwards can understand the consequences of their actions. The next big birthday is at sixteen, when you can leave school, get a job and pay tax. You can also leave home and get married (if your parents agree). At seventeen, you can drive or ride a small motorbike. At eighteen, you can get married without your parents' permission and you can finally vote. You can also buy alcohol, smoke, play the National Lottery and get a tattoo.

- Are these ages the same or different in your country?
- What do you think the various minimum legal ages should be?

7c | Happy birthday

SPEAKING & VOCABULARY: life stages

1 Match the sentences 1–7 to the pictures A–G.

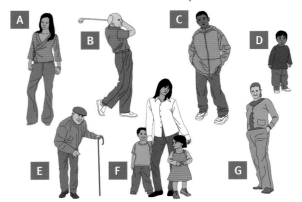

1 He retired many years ago and lives in a home for the **elderly**.
2 He's a **pensioner** now, but he's still very active.
3 He's a **toddler**.
4 He's a typical **adolescent**.
5 She's **middle-aged**, probably in her late forties or early fifties.
6 She's still a **teenager**, but she's very adult in some ways.
7 She's **thirty something** and she's got two young children.

2 Use the words in bold in exercise 1 to make sentences about people you know. Talk about these people with a partner.

3 Work in pairs. Discuss these questions.

- Which stage of life do you associate with the following adjectives: wise, rebellious, overworked, lively, irresponsible, happy, bored?
- Which stage are you in at the moment? What are the advantages and disadvantages of being your age?
- Which stage are you most looking forward to? Why?

READING

1 You are going to read an article about a woman who is celebrating her 113th birthday. Answer the questions.

1 How do you think she's going to celebrate her birthday?
2 In what way has the world changed since she was a young girl? What do you think are the changes that have shocked her most?

2 Read the article and compare your ideas to the information in the article. Has Florrie led a happy life?

Florrie prepares to celebrate her 113th birthday

Florence Baldwin says that eating a fried egg sandwich every morning has helped her live so long. That and the occasional glass of sherry.

5 England's oldest woman, who has lived in three centuries, is today celebrating her 113th birthday surrounded by four generations of her family. She is fit and healthy and does not need any regular medication. Her
10 short-term memory is fading, but her long-term memory is still going strong. She still remembers seeing Queen Victoria when she was four, and being amazed when she first saw a car.

Her family put her long life down to hard work and a
15 strong character. She started working at the age of sixteen and didn't retire until she was 75. For most of her working life she walked up and down a long steep hill twice a day and her doctor is sure that this is part of the secret of her health and long life.

20 'It's wonderful to be the oldest lady in Britain,' she said, 'but to be honest I don't remember how old I am most of the time.'

Her friends and family have been preparing a special celebration for her in the nursing home where she lives.
25 The nursing home staff have been working hard to prepare for the special day. The chef has baked a special cake with 113 iced flowers. All four generations of the family will be there, including her daughter, Maisie, who is a youthful 88.

Florrie was born in Leeds, one of a family of eight.
30 In 1919 she married painter and decorator Clifford Baldwin. They had one daughter and lived happily together until he died at the age of 73. She continued to live in their three-bedroom house until the age of 105, fiercely independent, cooking and cleaning for herself until she
35 finally moved to a nursing home eight years ago. She was born before telephones, televisions and washing machines were invented and has seen 27 prime ministers, four kings, two queens and two world wars.

Florrie has one daughter, two grandsons, six great
40 grandchildren and five great-great grandchildren. All the family have been helping with the preparations for the party and everybody is looking forward to toasting her incredible life with a glass of buck's fizz,
45 and helping Florrie blow out her 113 candles.

Glossary
sherry *n* a kind of strong wine
fade *v* slowly become less clear
buck's fizz *n* a drink of
    champagne and orange juice

3 Read the article again and put the topics in the correct order.

☐ Florrie's childhood
☐ her husband
☐ Florrie's secret for a long life
☐ Florrie's health
☐ the changes that Florrie has seen
☐ preparations for her birthday party

4 Work in pairs, A and B. Test your partner's memory.

A: Turn to page 128. Ask your partner the questions.
B: Turn to page 131. Ask your partner the questions.

5 Would you like to live to be 113 years old? Why or why not?

GRAMMAR: present perfect continuous 2

Use the present perfect continuous …
• to talk about an action that has been in progress recently. The action may or may not still be in progress.
They've been planning the party for weeks.
They've been decorating the living room.

• to emphasize an action, or the duration of an action.
They've been writing invitations all day.

Use the present perfect simple (not the continuous) …
• to talk about the result of an action.
They've written more than a hundred invitations.

• to talk about single, completed actions.
The chef has baked a special cake.

❯ FOR MORE INFORMATION ABOUT THE PRESENT PERFECT SIMPLE, SEE PAGE 24
❯ SEE LANGUAGE REFERENCE PAGE 74

1 Complete the text. Put the verbs in brackets into the present perfect simple or continuous.

It's my mum and dad's golden wedding anniversary next weekend. We (1) _____ (*arrange*) a surprise party for them for the last three months. We (2) _____ (*book*) a room in a local hotel and we (3) _____ (*order*) an enormous cake with a photo of their wedding on top. We (4) _____ (*work*) hard trying to get in touch with friends and family from all over the world and so far we (5) _____ (*receive*) more than 50 replies to our invitations. Mum and Dad suspect that we (6) _____ (*plan*) something special, but they don't really know what. I know that Mum (7) _____ (*think*) very carefully about their outfits. She (8) _____ (*buy*) a new dress and she (9) _____ (*persuade*) my dad that he needs a new suit.

2 Work in pairs. Look at the picture. Write as many sentences as possible to say what the people have been doing recently.

They've been preparing food for the party.

SPEAKING

1 Work in two groups, A and B. You are going to talk about the changes that have taken place in your lifetime.

Group A: Look at the questions on page 128.
Group B: Look at the questions on page 131.

2 Use your notes and the Useful language to help you report back to the class on your discussion.

Useful language

Our group has been discussing …
We spent a lot of time talking about …
We think that the biggest changes have been …
We agreed that the …
We thought it was particularly interesting that …

7D | Dilemmas

SPEAKING

1 Read the three situations. Who has the most difficult decision to make?

At a Crossroads

Lynn is engaged to be married. At work, she is offered promotion, but the new job will involve a lot of travelling – sometimes she will need to be away for two weeks at a time. Her future husband, Tony, has a good job, and they do not need the extra money. He has old-fashioned values and Lynn is afraid that he will not be happy about the possibility of her travelling so much.

Eighteen-year-old Steve receives two letters. In the first, there is an offer of a place at a top university. He has won a scholarship and all his fees will be paid. In the second letter, he receives an offer of a professional contract with a top London football club. He can't do both.

Gabita (Mexican) and Sandy (British) live in Mexico. Gabita has a good job in an international company, but Sandy is unhappy. He cannot speak very good Spanish, he can't find a good job and he wants to return to Britain, where he hopes to return to his career as a journalist. Gabita wants her husband to be happy, but she doesn't want to leave her family, friends and career in Mexico.

2 Work in pairs. Discuss these questions.

* What advice would you give the three people in exercise 1?
* Have you ever had an important or difficult decision to make? What was it?

LISTENING & FUNCTIONAL LANGUAGE: giving advice

1 🔊 **2.5** Listen to a dialogue between Lynn (from Speaking exercise 1) and Carl, a close friend. Answer the questions.

1 What is Lynn's main worry?
2 What does Carl suggest?
3 What does she think about his suggestions?

2 🔊 **2.5** Listen to the dialogue between Lynn and Carl again. Complete the sentences in column A with a phrase from column B.

A
1 I think you should
2 Why don't you
3 What you need to do is
4 Have you thought about
5 If I were you, I'd
6 There's no harm in
7 Why not

B
a call them right now.
b change the date of the wedding?
c explain to him how important this is to you.
d go and see him in the morning?
e speaking to his parents first?
f take it.
g telling him.

3 Find the highlighted responses in audioscript 2.5 on page 141. Match the responses to the advice 1–7 in exercise 2.

4 Rearrange the words to make six pieces of advice.

1 her   dinner   take   why   out   to   you   don't ?
2 wants   she   harm   asking   no   what   there's   her   in .
3 flowers   were   I'd   her   get   you   if   some   I .
4 weekend   to   away   need   what   do   take   her   you   is   for   the .
5 should   theatre   her   the   some   get   I   tickets   think   you   for .
6 gift   thought   voucher   giving   have   her   you   about   a ?

5 Read the advice in exercise 4 again. What do you think has happened? Why is the person giving this advice?

6 Work in pairs, A and B. Perform the roleplay.

A: You want some advice about a problem. Turn to page 128.
B: You want to help your friend with a problem. Turn to page 133.

7 Now exchange roles.

A: Turn to page 130.   B: Turn to page 132.

VOCABULARY: exclamations with *what*

1 Match the comments 1–8 to an appropriate response a–h.

1 I thought it was something serious, but the doctor said it was nothing really.
2 … and then he said that Slovakia was the capital of the Czech Republic!
3 You'll never guess what! For the first time in my life, he bought me some flowers!
4 Mum! Look, I've got tomato ketchup all over my T-shirt. And on my trousers, too.
5 I thought we were going to win, but the other team scored a goal in the last minute.
6 So, she's lost her job, her husband's left her and now she's broken her leg!
7 There was no hot water this morning, so I couldn't have a shower.
8 I can't remember his address. Oh, I know, I'll see if it's in the phone book.

a	What a good idea!	e	What a relief!
b	What a mess!	f	What a shame!
c	What a nightmare!	g	What a surprise!
d	What a nuisance!	h	What an idiot!

2 Work in pairs. Think of four situations in which somebody would say these things.

- What a day!
- What a night!
- What a waste of time!
- What bad luck!

PRONUNCIATION: intonation (feelings)

1 2.6 Listen to this extract from Lynn and Carl's dialogue. Choose the best explanation of the word *what* in the extract.

1 I didn't hear you very well.
2 I'm really angry with you.
3 I'm really surprised.

2 2.7 Now listen to these three words. Match each word to a feeling from the box.

1 hello   2 right   3 yes

| anger   surprise   happiness |
| boredom   interest |

3 Practise saying the words in exercise 2 with as many different feelings as you can.

Self-assessment (✓)

☐ I can understand a discussion about personal problems.
☐ I can talk about personal problems.
☐ I can give advice.

GRAMMAR
Present perfect continuous

We can use the present perfect continuous to talk about actions which started in the past and are still in progress now.

I've been studying geography for two years.
(= I'm still studying geography.)

To describe the period of time between the start of the action and now, we can use *for* and *since*. We use *for* + an expression that describes the length of time.

for five years/a long time/the last two years/three weeks

We use *since* + an expression that refers to the time when the action started.

since two o'clock/last year/2002/I met you

We use *how long …* in questions to ask about the length of time.

How long have you been living here?

We also use the present perfect continuous to talk about an action that has been in progress recently. The action may or may not still be in progress.

She's been getting ready for the party.
They've been swimming in the river.

We use the present perfect continuous to emphasize the action itself, or the duration of the action. However, we use the present perfect simple (not the continuous) to talk about the result of the action.

She's been writing letters.
(Here the speaker is interested in the action of writing.)
She's written 50 letters.
(Here the speaker is interested in the result of the action – the number of letters that have been completed.)

We also use the present perfect simple (not the continuous) to talk about single, completed actions.

She's chosen a new outfit.
They've booked a holiday.

affirmative & negative		
I/You/We/They	*'ve/haven't*	*been working.*
He/She	*'s/hasn't*	

question			
What	*have*	*I/you/we/they*	*been doing?*
	has	*he/she*	

We use the present perfect simple (not the continuous) with stative verbs.

I've been here since last autumn.
Not *I've been being here.*

For more information about stative verbs and continuous verb forms, see unit 1 (Language reference page 14).

For more information about the present perfect simple, see unit 2 (Language reference page 24).

FUNCTIONAL LANGUAGE
Giving advice

Have you thought about + -ing form?
Have you tried + -ing form?
I think you should + infinitive
If I were you, I'd + infinitive
There's no harm in + -ing form
What you need to do is + infinitive
Why don't you + infinitive?

WORD LIST

Phrasal verbs with *live*

live for (sth)	/ˈlɪv fə(r)/
live off (sth/sb)	/ˈlɪv ɒf/
live on (sth)	/ˈlɪv ɒn/
live out of (sth)	/ˈlɪv aʊt əv/
live through (sth)	/ˈlɪv θruː/
live up to (sth)	/lɪv ˈʌp tə/

Metaphor

at a crossroads	/ˌæt ə ˈkrɒsrəʊdz/
embark on a new stage of life	/ɪmˌbɑː(r)k ɒn ə ˌnjuː ˌsteɪdʒ əv ˈlaɪf/
go their separate ways	/ˌgəʊ ðeə(r) sep(ə)rət ˈweɪz/
his life took off	/hɪz ˌlaɪf tʊk ˈɒf/
move on	/ˌmuːv ˈɒn/
no turning back	/ˌnəʊ tɜː(r)nɪŋ ˈbæk/
take a new direction	/ˌteɪk ə ˌnjuː dɪˈrekʃ(ə)n/
take an unexpected turn	/ˌteɪk ən ˌʌnɪkspektɪd ˈtɜː(r)n/

Life stages

adolescent *adj/n C*	/ˌædəˈles(ə)nt/
adult *n C/adj* ***	/ˈædʌlt; əˈdʌlt/
elderly *adj* ***	/ˈeldə(r)li/
in your early /late forties	/ˌɪn jɔː(r) ˌɜː(r)li /ˌleɪt ˈfɔː(r)tiz/
middle-aged *adj* *	/ˌmɪd(ə)lˈeɪdʒd/
pensioner *n C* **	/ˈpenʃ(ə)nə(r)/
retired *adj* *	/rɪˈtaɪə(r)d/
teenager *n C* **	/ˈtiːnˌeɪdʒə(r)/
toddler *n C* *	/ˈtɒdlə(r)/

Exclamations with *what*

What a good idea!	/ˌwɒt ə ˌgʊd aɪˈdɪə/
What a day!	/ˌwɒt ə ˈdeɪ/
What a mess!	/ˌwɒt ə ˈmes/
What a night!	/ˌwɒt ə ˈnaɪt/
What a nightmare!	/ˌwɒt ə ˈnaɪtˌmeə(r)/
What a nuisance!	/ˌwɒt ə ˈnjuːs(ə)ns/
What a relief!	/ˌwɒt ə rɪˈliːf/
What a shame!	/ˌwɒt ə ˈʃeɪm/
What a surprise!	/ˌwɒt ə sə(r)ˈpraɪz/
What a waste of time!	/ˌwɒt ə ˌweɪst əv ˈtaɪm/
What bad luck!	/ˌwɒt ˌbæd ˈlʌk/
What an idiot!	/ˌwɒt ən ˈɪdɪət/

Other words & phrases

anniversary *n C* **	/ˌænɪˈvɜː(r)s(ə)ri/
bake *v* *	/beɪk/
ballistic *adj*	/bəˈlɪstɪk/
basically *adv* **	/ˈbeɪsɪkli/
blow out *v*	/ˌbləʊ ˈaʊt/
blush *v* *	/blʌʃ/
boss *n C* ***	/bɒs/
candle *n C* **	/ˈkænd(ə)l/
childcare *n U*	/ˈtʃaɪldˌkeə(r)/
consequence *n C* ***	/ˈkɒnsɪkwəns/
consultant *n C* **	/kənˈsʌltənt/
contract *n C* ***	/ˈkɒntrækt/
decorator *n C*	/ˈdekəˌreɪtə(r)/
embarrassment *n U* *	/ɪmˈbærəsmənt/
expectation *n C* ***	/ˌekspekˈteɪʃ(ə)n/
fade *v* **	/feɪd/
farm hand *n C*	/ˈfɑː(r)mˌhænd/
fee *n C* ***	/fiː/
fiercely *adv*	/ˈfɪə(r)sli/
fire *v* ***	/ˈfaɪə(r)/
found *v* ***	/faʊnd/
generation *n C* ***	/ˌdʒenəˈreɪʃ(ə)n/
get in touch with (sb)	/ˌget ɪn ˈtʌtʃ wɪð/
graduate *n C/v* **	/ˈgrædʒuət; ˈgrædʒueɪt/
guilty *adj* ***	/ˈgɪlti/
hell *n U* ***	/hel/
hill *n C* ***	/hɪl/
iced *adj*	/aɪst/
invitation *n C* **	/ˌɪnvɪˈteɪʃ(ə)n/
irresponsible *adj*	/ˌɪrɪˈspɒnsəb(ə)l/
lamb *n C* **	/læm/
make sense	/ˌmeɪk ˈsens/
medication *n U*	/ˌmedɪˈkeɪʃ(ə)n/
mentally *adv*	/ˈment(ə)li/
miss out on (sth) *v*	/ˌmɪsˈaʊt ɒn/
moving *adj* **	/ˈmuːvɪŋ/
nappy *n C*	/ˈnæpi/
nursery *n C* **	/ˈnɜː(r)s(ə)ri/
orchestra *n C* **	/ˈɔː(r)kɪstrə/
outfit *n C* *	/ˈaʊtfɪt/
overworked *adj*	/ˌəʊvə(r)ˈwɜː(r)kt/
playgroup *n C*	/ˈpleɪˌgruːp/
PR (public relations)	/ˌpiː ˈɑː(r)/
promotion *n C/U* ***	/prəˈməʊʃ(ə)n/
put two and two together	/ˌpʊt ˌtuː ən ˌtuː təˈgeðə(r)/
radical *adj* **	/ˈrædɪk(ə)l/
rebellious *adj*	/rɪˈbeljəs/
redundancy *n C* **	/rɪˈdʌndənsi/
regret *v/n C* **	/rɪˈgret/
scholarship *n C* *	/ˈskɒlə(r)ʃɪp/
sherry *n U*	/ˈʃeri/
social security *n U* *	/ˌsəʊʃ(ə)l sɪˈkjʊərəti/
steep *adj* **	/stiːp/
stressful *adj*	/ˈstresf(ə)l/
superficial *adj* *	/ˌsuːpə(r)ˈfɪʃ(ə)l/
suspect *v* ***	/səˈspekt/
take (sth/sb) seriously	/ˌteɪk ˈsɪərɪəsli/
tattoo *n C*	/tæˈtuː/
toast *v*	/təʊst/
tractor *n C*	/ˈtræktə(r)/
travel expenses *n pl*	/ˈtræv(ə)l ɪkˌspensəz/
unsure *adj* *	/ʌnˈʃʊə(r)/
unthinkable *adj*	/ʌnˈθɪŋkəb(ə)l/
violinist *n C*	/ˌvaɪəˈlɪnɪst/
wise *adj* **	/waɪz/
youthful *adj*	/ˈjuːθf(ə)l/

8A | Breaking news

VOCABULARY: newspapers

1 Complete the text with words from the box.

> articles   circulation   daily   features   right-wing   headline
> journalists   news coverage   quality newspapers

The best-selling (1) _____ newspaper in the UK is *The Sun*, with a (2) _____ of many millions. Its front page has a large (3) _____ and photo, but there is not much news. Inside, you find (4) _____ about pop stars and other celebrities, details of TV programmes, sports news, games, crosswords and competitions.

Readers who want to know what is happening in the world choose one of the (5) _____ and *The Daily Telegraph* is the most popular. It has (6) _____ all over the world and, as well as its (7) _____, it contains special (8) _____ on subjects such as gardening, motoring and travel. It is widely accepted that it is a (9) _____ newspaper and it supports the Conservative party.

2 Work in pairs. Discuss these questions.

- What are the most popular quality newspapers in your country?
- Which paper do you think has the best international news coverage? What about local news?
- Are there any daily newspapers like *The Sun*?
- Which newspapers are considered right-wing or left-wing?
- Which newspaper do you read? How often?
- What kind of articles do you find most interesting?

LISTENING

1 🔘 **2.8** Listen to an interview with a journalist, Colin Ashley. Tick the four topics that are discussed.

- ☐ his advice to other journalists
- ☐ his attitude towards America
- ☐ his education and qualifications
- ☐ his new book
- ☐ his private life
- ☐ his work for television

2 🔘 **2.8** Choose the best answer, a or b, to the questions. Then listen again to check your answers.

1 What is Colin Ashley's new book about?
   a) the developing world
   b) the World Bank
2 Where do the ideas in his book come from?
   a) Joseph E. Stiglitz
   b) his own research
3 Where does Colin come from?
   a) America
   b) Australia
4 What was his last book about?
   a) oil companies
   b) the Pentagon
5 Where does Colin have a lot of friends?
   a) Wall Street
   b) West Africa
6 Who does he not want to work for?
   a) some TV companies
   b) Wall Street
7 What does he think a journalist needs?
   a) experience
   b) patience

3 Find these sentences in audioscript 2.8 on pages 141–142. Explain what the words in italics refer to.

1 Most of the time, *it* does the complete opposite.
2 I'm not the first person to say *it*.
3 I wouldn't say *that*.
4 The one before *that*.
5 I don't think of *them* as enemies.
6 I'd love to do *more*.

GRAMMAR: *would*

> Use *would* + infinitive …
> * to give an opinion about hypothetical future situations.
>   *I'd never **work** for CNN.*
>   *It **would be** great to have more money.*
>
> * to ask for and offer advice or suggestions.
>   *What **would** you **say** to someone who wants to become a journalist?*
>
> * with *like, love, prefer*, etc. to express preferences.
>   *I'd **love** to do more TV work.*

> ❯ SEE LANGUAGE REFERENCE PAGE 84

1 Replace *'d* in the sentences with *would* or *had*.

1 I'd already read two of his books.
2 I'd hate to do that.
3 I'd never forgive myself.
4 I'd never speak to you again.
5 You'd never heard of him?
6 You'd regret it.

2 Complete the dialogue with verbs from the box.

> be (x2)   hate   like   love (x2)   mind   prefer

A: Would you (1) _____ to be a journalist?
B: I wouldn't (2) _____, but I'd (3) _____ to be a photographer.
A: What? A news photographer?
B: Yes, I'd (4) _____ that.
A: You mean working for one of the big newspapers?
B: Yes, that would (5) _____ really nice.
A: Personally, I'd (6) _____ it! Being away from home all the time, travelling to countries at war, …
B: Oh, I'd (7) _____ to. It would (8) _____ really interesting.

3 🔊 2.9 Listen to the recording to check your answers.

4 Work in pairs. Discuss these questions.

* As a journalist, which country would you like to work in?
* Who would you like to interview?
* What questions would you ask?
* Would you prefer to work for a newspaper or for TV?
* Is there anywhere in the world where you would never work?

SPEAKING

1 Work in two groups, A and B.

You work for the editorial team of a popular newspaper. You must choose one main story and one secondary story for the front page of the newspaper.

* Choose stories that will make people buy your newspaper and explain the reasons for your choice.
* Decide what kind of photo you want to use on the front page.
* Write headlines for the stories that you choose.

Group A: Turn to page 128 for a list of possible stories.
Group B: Turn to page 130 for a list of possible stories.

2 Work in new groups that contain students from Group A and Group B. Compare the ideas from exercise 1 and decide together which stories you will use.

DID YOU KNOW?

1 Work in pairs. Read about newspapers and discuss the questions.

> Most Australian daily newspapers are owned by News Corporation, a company that was founded by Rupert Murdoch and is still controlled by his family. In Britain, the company controls about a third of the national newspapers, including *The Sun* and *The Times*, and also owns a big part of Sky TV, a cable TV company. In the US, News Corporation controls the Fox cable TV networks, 20th Century Fox studios, many local TV stations and *The New York Post*. In Asia, the company owns Star TV. It is the world's third biggest media company. Like other large media groups, News Corporation sometimes makes news (such as a phone-hacking scandal in 2011) as well as reporting it.

* Who owns the newspapers and TV stations in your country?
* Which TV station do you think gives the best news coverage in your country?

8B | Protests

READING

1 Work in pairs. Discuss these questions.

- When was the last big demonstration in your town? What was it about?
- Have you ever been on a demonstration? What was it about?
- For what reasons would you go on a demonstration?

2 Match the headlines a–g to the newspaper articles 1–5. There are two headlines you do not need.

a Dads stop cars
b Health workers refuse to go back to work
c Jail protest continues
d Pie man strikes again
e Police stop anti-war demonstration
f Prison officers demand pay rise
g Strip protest

3 The last sentence of each article is missing. Match the sentences a–e to the articles 1–5.

a His favourite targets are self-important people without a sense of humour.
b He said that the protest was the result of overcrowding.
c The men failed to deliver their heart-shaped message, but said they were happy with the protest.
d Leaders of UNISON, the nurses' union, are meeting employers again later today.
e The protest ended with hot protesters cooling off in the Cibeles fountain.

4 Find words in the articles which match the definitions 1–7.

1 used to describe someone who thinks he/she is very important
2 people who suffer from the actions of other people
3 not wearing any clothes
4 a protest where people stop working
5 places where legal decisions are taken
6 discussions where people try to agree something
7 a man who speaks for other people

5 Which of the protests in the newspaper articles do you sympathize with most? Which is the best form of protest?

1 **Bill Gates**, the president of Microsoft, has been hit in the face with a cream pie during a visit to Brussels. The attack was the work of Noel Godin. For the last 30 years, Godin says he 'has been sending the suits of our most pompous public figures to the dry cleaner's.' Godin chooses his victims carefully.

2 60 cyclists rode naked through the centre of Madrid today to protest against the lack of facilities for cyclists in the Spanish capital. They decided to take their clothes off as a symbol of their vulnerability in the dangerous Madrid traffic.

3 Over 5,000 Scottish nurses have entered the second week of a strike.
The nurses are demanding better pay. Maggie Hunter, a nurse with eighteen years' experience told our reporter: 'My annual salary is £17,000 and the starting salary is £15,650. How would you feel if you were living on that kind of money?'

4 Traffic in London came to a stop earlier today as a group of Elvis Presley look-alikes danced to the London family courts – or 'Heartbreak Hotel', as they call it. The men, all divorced fathers, were protesting at being refused access to their children. In a statement to the press, one of the men said: 'If we had courts that were fair to men, we would be able to see our children. But they only think about the mothers.'

5 After a day of negotiations, four of the prisoners in the rooftop protest at Wealstun prison have come down. But a group of twenty prisoners are still refusing to move. A spokesman for the prisoners said: 'If we had decent living conditions, this wouldn't be necessary.' Colin Moses, of the Prison Officers' Association agreed that there was a problem at the jail.

GRAMMAR: unreal conditions (type 2)

> Use a conditional clause beginning with *if* to imagine impossible or improbable situations in the present or in the future.
>
> Note that you use a past tense in the conditional clause.
> *If we **had** decent living conditions, this wouldn't be necessary.*
> (= but we don't have decent living conditions)
> *If we **had** courts that were fair to men, we would be able to see our children.*
> (= but we don't have courts that are fair to men)
>
> Use *would ('d)* + infinitive to talk about the consequence or the result of the imagined situation.
> *How **would** you **feel** if you were living on that kind of money?*
>
> ● SEE LANGUAGE REFERENCE PAGE 84

1 Put *if* in the correct place in the sentences.

1 Conditions would be better there were fewer prisoners.
2 Godin wouldn't throw cream pies at these people they were less pompous.
3 He had the chance he would attack the British prime minister.
4 Courts were fairer to men it wouldn't happen.
5 Maggie didn't like her job she wouldn't do it.
6 She would be happier she earned more money.

2 Complete the questions. Put the verbs in brackets into the correct form.

1 What _____ (you / do) if someone _____ (throw) a cream pie in your face?
2 _____ (you / go) on strike if you _____ (be) unhappy about something at work?
3 How _____ (you / feel) if you _____ (not / paid) a reasonable salary?
4 If you _____ (meet) the leader of your country, what _____ (you / say)?
5 If you _____ (be) able to change three things in the world, what _____ (you / do)?

3 Work in pairs. Ask and answer the questions in exercise 2.

PRONUNCIATION: /ʊ/ & /uː/

1 Mark the words in the box short /ʊ/ (S) or long /uː/ (L).

book *S*	choose *L*	few	food	foot	good
group	moved	pull	put	stood	suit
took	true	two	whose	would	

2 ● 2.10 Listen to the recording to check your answers.

3 Complete the poem with words from the box.

clue	could	do	good	Hood

A man who was called Robin _____
Went on demos* whenever he _____.
He hadn't a _____
What he wanted to _____,
But he felt it was doing him _____.

* demos = demonstrations

4 ● 2.11 Listen to the recording to check your answers. Then practise saying the poem.

SPEAKING

1 Look at the three newspaper headlines and say what you think the stories are about.

LOCAL RESIDENTS PROMISE TO FIGHT NEW ROAD

New road endangers wildlife says report

New road will cut journey times by 12 minutes

2 Work in groups of three. Read the stories and share the information with the other students in your group.

A: Turn to page 128.
B: Turn to page 131.
C: Turn to page 134.

3 Discuss these questions with your group.

- What would you do if you lived in one of the houses that will be destroyed?
- What would be the best form of protest?
- How would you encourage other people to join your protest?

4 Compare your ideas with the ideas of other groups. Decide whose ideas are best.

8c | Bank robbers

SPEAKING

1 Work in pairs. Discuss these questions.

- How many different films can you think of in which a robbery takes place?
- What are the titles of these films in your language?
  Ocean's Thirteen   The Italian Job   The Pink Panther
- What can you remember about these films?

One of the most famous gangster movies of all time, *Bonnie and Clyde*, won two Oscars®. The film, starring Warren Beatty and Faye Dunaway, tells the story of two young gangsters in 1920s America.

2 Work in pairs, A and B. Read the information about Bonnie and Clyde above. Then practise reading a dialogue from the Bonnie and Clyde story.

A: Turn to page 129. B: Turn to page 132.

3 What do you think happens next? Continue the dialogue with your partner.

VOCABULARY: law & order

1 Complete the article with words from the box.

guilty   judge   police
prison   stolen   thieves

The robbery happened at ten o'clock and more than £10,000 was (1) _____. There were many **witnesses** who saw it happen – both customers and bank staff. The (2) _____ also had other **evidence** – a bag that the (3) _____ had left behind. It did not take them long to **arrest** the criminals. The **trial** began two months later in the High **Court**. The **jury** found the men (4) _____ and the (5) _____ **sentenced** the men to ten years in (6) _____.

2 Match the words in bold in exercise 1 to the definitions 1–7.

1 a place where legal decisions are taken
2 to catch (a thief)
3 information that helps to show who is responsible for a crime
4 a group of ordinary members of the public who decide if a person is guilty or innocent
5 people who see a crime
6 gave a punishment
7 the process of deciding if a person is guilty

READING

1 Read the newspaper article on the next page and think of a headline for it.

2 Read the article again and answer the questions.

1 Why did the judge have to speak to the jury?
2 Why did the judge say that the robbery was not a joke?
3 Why did the robbers go into a toy shop?
4 Why did they go into a launderette?
5 Why did Michael fall over?
6 Why did no one reply to Laurence's demands?
7 When did the police arrest the brothers?

3 Do you agree with the judge's sentence? Why or why not?

Earlier today, a judge at the Central Criminal Court sentenced two men to twelve years in prison for attempting to rob a branch of the Chelmsford Savings Bank.
5 During the trial, the judge repeatedly had to ask members of the jury to stop laughing as they listened to the evidence. In his summing-up, the judge said that the robbery was not funny, but he described the men as pathetic. He continued, 'If everything had
10 gone according to plan, this would have been no joke.' He told the jury to find the men guilty.

In January of this year, the two men, brothers Michael (42) and Laurence Parsons (39), took the bus into Chelmsford town centre. They got off just
15 outside the bank, but left their bag, containing an old Webley revolver, on the bus. Not wanting to abandon their plans, the men went into a toy shop opposite the bank and bought two water pistols.

The tights they were wearing over their heads
20 were too small and the men had difficulty seeing where they were going. Wearing their masks, they crossed the road, ran into the launderette next to the bank and shouted, 'This is a stick-up!' Surprised customers laughed and suggested that they try
25 next door.

At the second attempt, the men found the bank. Witnesses described how Michael slipped and fell on the polished floor as the two men ran into the bank. Meanwhile, his brother went up to a counter,
30 not realizing that it was unattended, pointed his gun and demanded £5,000. Surprised customers laughed as Laurence repeated his demand. Getting no reply, he decided to give up the attempt, but tripped and fell over his brother who was still on the floor.
35 Later in the day, the men received treatment in hospital for their injuries. They explained what had happened to the doctors, who then called the police. At first, the police refused to believe the men's story, but arrested them the following day when the
40 missing bag was found.

Glossary
summing-up *n* conclusion
launderette *n* place to wash clothes
trip *v* hit your foot on something and fall

GRAMMAR: unreal conditions (type 3)

Use a conditional clause beginning with *if* to imagine situations in the past which are the opposite of what actually happened. Note that you use *had* + past participle in the conditional clause.
> If everything **had gone** according to plan, …
> (= but things didn't go according to plan)
> If they **hadn't left** their bag on the bus, …
> (= but they left their bag on the bus)

Use *would* ('*d*) + *have* + past participle to talk about the consequence or the result of the imagined situation.
> If they had had their own masks, they **would have seen** what they were doing.

> ❯ SEE LANGUAGE REFERENCE PAGE 84

1 Complete these sentences which all refer to the past. Put the verbs in brackets into the correct form.

1 The sentence _____ (*be*) longer if they _____ (*steal*) any money.
2 If the toy shop _____ (*be*) closed, they _____ (*go*) home.
3 If he _____ (*not / run*) into the bank, he _____ (*not / fall*) over.
4 The customers _____ (*be*) frightened if they _____ (*think*) it was a real robbery.
5 The police _____ (*not / believe*) them if they _____ (*not / find*) the missing bag.

2 Read the story. Write five sentences about the story with *if* and the past perfect.

One evening, a thief broke into a house in the village of Lachelle. The owners were not there because they had gone to visit some friends. The thief had not eaten all day and was extremely hungry. He found a packet of biscuits in the kitchen and ate them. He then felt thirsty and, finding a bottle of champagne in the fridge, drank that. He now felt sleepy and he decided to have a little rest before robbing the house. Unfortunately, he didn't wake up and the owners of the house found him on their bed when they returned. He was still asleep when the police arrived.

If the owners had been at home, the thief wouldn't have broken into the house.

3 Think of five important events in your life. Imagine what would have happened if these events hadn't taken place. Tell a partner.

If I hadn't got married, I wouldn't have had any children.

8D | Driving

SPEAKING & VOCABULARY: compound nouns (driving)

1 Who are better drivers – men or women? Why?

2 Complete the compound nouns in the phrases 1–8 with a word from the box.

belt	licence	lights	limit
phone	street	way	zone

1 driving a car 20 kph over the speed _____
2 driving a car while you are using a mobile _____
3 driving a car without a driving _____
4 driving a car without a seat _____
5 driving the wrong way down a one-way _____
6 driving very slowly in the fast lane of a motor _____
7 not stopping at the traffic _____ when they are red
8 parking your car in a no-parking _____

3 Work in pairs. Choose the three most serious actions from exercise 2. What should the punishment for these actions be?

4 What annoys you most about other drivers? What kind of driver are you?

LISTENING

1 Look at the photos. What do you think is happening in each photo? Have you ever been in a similar situation?

2 🔘 2.12–2.13 Read the summaries of two dialogues. Then listen to the dialogues and correct the two mistakes in each of the summaries.

Dialogue 1
A woman's car has broken down. She thinks it is a problem with the oil. She asks someone to help her. He says that the oil level is low and that she should go to a garage immediately.

Dialogue 2
A driver is trying to find the centre of a town. She asks two police officers for help. She finds it difficult to understand the first policeman, but the second tells her to turn left at the end of the street and look for a sign.

3 🔘 2.12–2.13 Choose the correct verb to complete the conversational expressions. Then listen again to check your answers.

1 I'll *give / pass* you a hand. (= I'll help you.)
2 You never *know / tell*. (= It's possible, but not probable.)
3 Nothing to *lose / waste* sleep over. (= Don't worry about it.)
4 I didn't quite *follow / take* you. (= I didn't understand everything.)
5 You can't *lose / miss* it. (= It's easy to see.)
6 You've *got / had* it. (= You understand.)

FUNCTIONAL LANGUAGE: offers

1 Complete the offers from the dialogues in Listening exercise 1 with a verb from the box.

| can 'll let like shall want |

1 _____ I check it for you?
2 I _____ come with you, if you like.
3 _____ me explain, all right?
4 Do you _____ me to have a look?
5 Would you _____ me to repeat it?
6 _____ I do anything for you?

2 Look at audioscripts 2.12–2.13 on page 142. Match the responses a–f to the offers 1–6 in exercise 1.

a OK, thanks.
b That's very kind of you.
c If you wouldn't mind.
d No, that's OK, thank you.
e Yes, that would be great.
f No, I'll manage, thanks.

3 How many different ways can you offer to help in the situations below? Tell the rest of the class your ideas.

1 A friend's car has broken down. It will probably take a week to repair.
2 A friend has broken a leg. He will not be able to walk for a long time.
3 A friend has lost a bag on the metro. It contained money, credit cards, ID card and mobile phone.
4 A friend is going away for two weeks and will not be able to attend English classes.
5 A friend is organizing a huge party for 100 people.
6 A friend is moving house and is feeling very stressed.
7 A friend is going to have a baby next week.

4 Work in pairs. Choose three situations from exercise 3. Act out a dialogue for each situation.

SPEAKING

1 Work in pairs. Imagine a world without cars and make a list of the advantages and disadvantages.

advantages	disadvantages
less pollution	*many things would take a lot longer*

2 Discuss these questions with your partner.

• Do you think that governments should do more to discourage people from driving? Why or why not?
• What could governments do to encourage people to drive less?

Self-assessment (✓)

☐ I can talk about cars and driving.
☐ I can make and respond to offers.
☐ I can discuss the advantages and disadvantages of a hypothetical situation.

GRAMMAR
Would

We use *would* + infinitive to give an opinion about hypothetical present and future situations.

> It **would be** nice to have a pay rise.
> They**'d** probably **say** no.
> I **wouldn't go** there for a holiday.

We use *would* + infinitive to ask for and offer advice or suggestions.

> What **would** you **do** in my situation?
> I**'d** probably **tell** her the truth.

We use *would* with *like*, *love*, *prefer* and *hate* to express preferences.

> **Would** you **prefer** to have coffee or tea?
> I**'d love** to be a journalist.

Unreal conditions

We can talk about impossible or improbable (hypothetical) situations in a conditional clause that begins with *if*. When we want to refer to a hypothetical situation in present or future time, we use a past tense in the conditional clause.

> If she **had** a car, …
> (= but she doesn't/won't have a car)
> If I **were*** the president of the US, …
> (= but I'm not/won't be the president of the US)

* With the verb *be*, we can use *were* for *I/she/he/it* in a conditional clause.

We use *would* + infinitive in the main clause of the sentence to talk about the consequence or result of the hypothetical situation.

> If she had a car, she **would drive** to work.
> She **would drive** to work if she had a car.
> If I were the president of the US, I**'d do** things very differently.

These sentences are sometimes called second conditional sentences.

Compare the following pair of sentences:

> If you listened, you **would understand**.
> (The condition here is hypothetical. The speaker is saying that you don't or you won't listen.)
> If you listen, you**'ll understand**.
> (The condition here is real. The speaker is saying that it is possible that you will listen.)

Unreal conditions in the past

When we want to refer to a hypothetical situation in the past, we use the past perfect (*had* + past participle) in the conditional clause. These clauses express the opposite of what actually happened.

> If you **had listened** to me, …
> (= but you didn't listen to me)
> If he **hadn't missed** the train, …
> (= but he missed the train)

We use *would* + *have* + past participle in the main clause of the sentence to talk about the consequence or result of the hypothetical situation.

> If you had listened to me, you **would've understood**.
> You **would've understood** if you'd listened to me.
> If he hadn't missed the train, he **would have been** on time.

These sentences are sometimes called third conditional sentences.

FUNCTIONAL LANGUAGE
Making offers

Can I + infinitive … *for you?*
Do you want me to + infinitive …?
I'll + infinitive …, *if you like.*
Let me + infinitive …
Shall I + infinitive …?
Would you like me to + infinitive …?

Responding to offers

Thank you.
Thanks.
That's (really) kind of you.
That would be nice/lovely.

No, I'll manage, thanks.
No, it's/that's OK, thank you.
No, that's all right, thanks.

WORD LIST

Newspapers

article *n C* ***	/ˈɑː(r)tɪk(ə)l/
circulation *n U* **	/ˌsɜː(r)kjʊˈleɪʃ(ə)n/
daily *adj/n C* ***	/ˈdeɪli/
feature *n C/v* ***	/ˈfiːtʃə(r)/
headline *n C* **	/ˈhedˌlaɪn/
journalist *n C* **	/ˈdʒɜː(r)nəlɪst/
left-wing *adj*	/ˈleft ˌwɪŋ/
news coverage *n U*	/ˈnjuːz ˌkʌv(ə)rɪdʒ/
press *n U* ***	/pres/
quality	/ˈkwɒləti
newspaper *n C* ***	ˈnjuːzpeɪpə(r)/
right-wing *adj*	/ˈraɪt ˌwɪŋ/

Compound nouns (driving)

credit card *n C* **	/ˈkredɪt ˌkɑː(r)d/
driving licence *n C*	/ˈdraɪvɪŋ ˌlaɪs(ə)ns/
ID card *n C*	/aɪˈdiː ˌkɑː(r)d/
mobile phone *n C* **	/ˌməʊbaɪl ˈfəʊn/
motorway *n C* **	/ˈməʊtə(r)ˌweɪ/
no-parking zone *n C*	/nəʊˈpɑː(r)kɪŋ ˌzəʊn/
one-way street *n C*	/ˌwʌnweɪ ˈstriːt/
police station *n C* *	/pəˈliːs ˌsteɪʃ(ə)n/
seat belt *n C*	/ˈsiːtbelt/
speed limit *n C*	/ˈspiːd ˌlɪmɪt/
traffic lights *n C*	/ˈtræfɪk ˌlaɪts/

Law and order

arrest *v* **	/əˈrest/
clue *n C* **	/kluː/
court *n C* ***	/kɔː(r)t/
crime *n C/U* ***	/kraɪm/
criminal *n C* *	/ˈkrɪmɪn(ə)l/
evidence *n U* ***	/ˈevɪd(ə)ns/
gangster *n C*	/ˈgæŋstə(r)/
guilty *adj* ***	/ˈgɪlti/
hold-up *n C*	/ˈhəʊldʌp/
innocent *adj* *	/ˈɪnəs(ə)nt/
jail *n C* *	/dʒeɪl/
judge *n C* ***	/dʒʌdʒ/
jury *n C* **	/ˈdʒʊəri/
mask *n C* **	/mɑːsk/
punishment *n C* **	/ˈpʌnɪʃmənt/
revolver *n C*	/rɪˈvɒlvə(r)/
rob *v* **	/rɒb/
robber *n C* *	/ˈrɒbə(r)/
robbery *n C* *	/ˈrɒbəri/
sentence *v* **	/ˈsentəns/
solicitor *n C*	/səˈlɪsɪtə(r)/
stick-up *n C*	/ˈstɪkʌp/

thief *n C* **	/θiːf/
trial *n C* ***	/ˈtraɪəl/
victim *n C* ***	/ˈvɪktɪm/
violent *adj* **	/ˈvaɪələnt/
witness *n C* **	/ˈwɪtnəs/

Other words & phrases

abandon *v* **	/əˈbændən/
access *n U* ***	/ˈækses/
annual *adj* ***	/ˈænjuəl/
attitude *n C* ***	/ˈætɪˌtjuːd/
best-selling *adj*	/ˌbestˈselɪŋ/
biscuit *n C* **	/ˈbɪskɪt/
cable *n C* **	/ˈkeɪb(ə)l/
cool off *v*	/ˈkuːlˌɒf/
cream *n U* **	/kriːm/
crossword *n C* *	/ˈkrɒsˌwɜː(r)d/
cyclist *n C* *	/ˈsaɪklɪst/
demand *v* ***	/dɪˈmɑːnd/
demonstration *n C* **	/ˌdemənˈstreɪʃ(ə)n/
developing world *n*	/dɪˌveləpɪŋ ˈwɜː(r)ld/
divorced *adj* **	/dɪˈvɔː(r)st/
employer *n C* ***	/ɪmˈplɔɪə(r)/
endanger *v*	/ɪnˈdeɪndʒə(r)/
engineering *n U* ***	/ˌendʒɪˈnɪərɪŋ/
exaggerated *adj*	/ɪgˈzædʒəˌreɪtɪd/
facilities *n pl*	/fəˈsɪlətiz/
flash *v* **	/flæʃ/
fountain *n C* *	/ˈfaʊntɪn/
globalization *n U*	/ˌgləʊbəlaɪˈzeɪʃ(ə)n/
hypothetical *adj* *	/ˌhaɪpəˈθetɪk(ə)l/
investigative *adj*	/ɪnˈvestɪgətɪv/
launderette *n C*	/ˌlɔːndəˈret; ˌlɒndˈret/
living conditions *n pl*	/ˈlɪvɪŋ kənˌdɪʃənz/
look-alike *n C*	/ˈlʊkəˌlaɪk/
media *n*	/ˈmiːdiə/
movie *n C* *	/ˈmuːvi/
naked *adj* **	/ˈneɪkɪd/
negotiation *n C* **	/nɪˌgəʊʃiˈeɪʃ(ə)n/
network *n C* ***	/ˈnetˌwɜː(r)k/
nude *adj*	/njuːd/
overcrowding *n U*	/ˌəʊvə(r)ˈkraʊdɪŋ/
pathetic *adj* *	/pəˈθetɪk/
patience *n U* *	/ˈpeɪʃ(ə)ns/
pie *n C/U* *	/paɪ/
pompous *adj*	/ˈpɒmpəs/
protest *n C/v* **	/ˈprəʊtest, prəˈtest/
protester *n C* *	/prəˈtestə(r)/
public figure *n C*	/ˌpʌblɪk ˈfɪgə(r)/
publish *v* ***	/ˈpʌblɪʃ/
reasonable *adj* ***	/ˈriːz(ə)nəb(ə)l/
roof *n C* **	/ruːf/
salary *n C* **	/ˈsæləri/
slip *v* ***	/slɪp/
species *n C* ***	/ˈspiːʃiːz/

statement *n C* ***	/ˈsteɪtmənt/
strike *n C/v* ***	/straɪk/
strip *v* **	/strɪp/
studio *n C* ***	/ˈstjuːdiəʊ/
summing-up *n C*	/ˌsʌmɪŋ ˈʌp/
support *v* ***	/səˈpɔː(r)t/
symbol *n C* **	/ˈsɪmb(ə)l/
sympathize *v*	/ˈsɪmpəθaɪz/
target *n C* ***	/ˈtɑː(r)gɪt/
thriller *n C* *	/ˈθrɪlə(r)/
toy *n C* **	/tɔɪ/
traffic *n U* ***	/ˈtræfɪk/
treatment *n U/C* ***	/ˈtriːtmənt/
trip *v* **	/trɪp/
union *n C* ***	/ˈjuːnjən/
valley *n C* ***	/ˈvæli/
valuable *adj* ***	/ˈvæljʊb(ə)l/
value *n C* ***	/ˈvæljuː/
vulnerability *n C*	/ˌvʌln(ə)rəˈbɪləti/
widely *adv* ***	/ˈwaɪdli/

9A | The shopping basket

VOCABULARY: containers

1 Look at the photo of the shopping basket on page 87 and complete the phrases 1–8 with a word or phrase from the box.

> cat food   jam   lemonade   margarine
> milk   mineral water   nappies   tissues

1 a bottle of _____   5 a jar of _____
2 a box of _____   6 a packet of _____
3 a can of _____   7 a tin of _____
4 a carton of _____   8 a tub of _____

2 Think of two more items that can go in each of the containers in exercise 1.

3 What can you tell about this family from the items in their shopping basket?

They've got a baby because there are nappies in the basket.

4 Work in pairs. Discuss these questions.

- How many of the things in the shopping basket do you (or your family) buy regularly?
- Which five items are always in your shopping basket?

PRONUNCIATION: *of*

1 🔘 2.14 Listen to a phone dialogue. Complete the phrases with the name of the container.

1 some _____ of beer
2 a _____ of carrot soup
3 a _____ of cranberry juice
4 a _____ of jam
5 a couple of _____ of peanuts
6 a _____ of tuna

2 🔘 2.14 Listen again. What do you notice about the pronunciation of *of*?

3 🔘 2.15 Listen to the complete shopping list and repeat. Then close your book and repeat the list from memory.

4 Turn to page 134. You have one minute to remember all the objects on the page.

5 Work in pairs. Take it in turns to remember and say as many of the objects from page 134 as you can.

READING

1 Read the article and answer the questions.

1 What is the 'nation's shopping basket'?
2 What is its purpose?
3 How often do the contents change?
4 How have British people's holidays changed the things they buy?
5 What are the two main ways that the contents have changed?

2 Read the article again. Circle the products that are in the nation's shopping basket at present. Underline the products that are no longer in the basket.

3 Work in pairs. Discuss these questions.

- What are the differences between the typical British shopping basket and a typical basket in your country?
- Have eating habits in your country changed in the last 20 years?
- What do you think will be in a typical shopping basket in 20 years' time?

GRAMMAR: articles & determiners

1 Choose the correct words to complete the text.

(1) *A / The* nation's shopping basket not only contains items of (2) *the / –* food. It also includes (3) *any / –* electronic and household goods. Here are (4) *some / –* new items that have appeared recently: DVD players, digital cameras, CDs bought over (5) *the /an* internet. Have you bought (6) *any / –* of these items recently? I'm sure you have. And what about (7) *the / any* products that are falling out of favour? When was the last time you bought (8) *the / an* exercise bike or (9) *the / a* typewriter? (10) *Some / A* quick look at anyone's birthday wish list shows their lack of (11) *the / –* popularity.

2 Correct the six grammatical mistakes in the dialogue.

A: Do you ever buy the traditional British food items?
B: No, I don't think I know some traditional British foods.
A: Oh, come on! The packet of English tea bags? Any jar of marmalade? Some crackers?
B: Crackers?
A: Yes, a biscuits that we eat with cheese. Or some Cadbury's chocolate?
B: Sorry, I've never bought any of these things.
A: You should. Any British food is really nice.

Checking out the
check out

The 18ᵗʰ century French writer, Brillat-Savarin, wrote that we are what we eat. But in the consumer world of the 21ˢᵗ century, it is perhaps truer to say that we are what we buy.

Every year, in order to find out more about who we are, the
5 National Office of Statistics draws up a list of the typical contents of the nation's shopping basket. The list is designed to analyze the nation's buying habits as accurately as possible. Every year they remove any items that are becoming less popular and replace them with new products.

10 In this year's basket they have included: a carton of low-fat milk, a bottle of mineral water, a tub of olive-oil-based margarine, a bag of pre-washed salad leaves, a cereal bar, a loaf of garlic bread and some free-range chicken. The basket no longer contains a box of matches (apparently we prefer lighters), a carton of fruit drink (it
15 seems that we now like our fruit drinks in plastic bottles), lipstick (lip gloss is more popular) or a packet of cheese slices (Parmesan cheese is now more popular).

Changes in the basket show that traditional British foods, like bread and butter or bacon and eggs and a cup of tea, which used

20 to be so popular, are being replaced by a more Mediterranean diet. Twenty years ago very few households included olive oil or fresh pasta on their shopping lists. Now they are among the top ten most likely items on the Great British shopping list.

Ten years ago very few families bought bottled mineral water to
25 drink at home – they thought it was a luxury item. But, influenced by holidays in other European countries, we're now buying so much that it has taken over from more traditional drinks, such as lemonade. And it would seem that the typical British consumer is also spending more money on organic fruit and vegetables,
30 vegetarian burgers and decaffeinated coffee. At the same time, less healthy food items have been crossed off the list.

So it seems that Britain as a nation is looking more to its European neighbours and thinking more about its health. The next time you're in the supermarket, take a quick look at the contents of
40 your trolley and see if you're a part of modern Britain.

3 🔊 **2.16** Listen to the recording to check your answers.

Use *the* …
- to refer to something because you have already mentioned it or it is defined by the context of the sentence.
  The *basket will include* …
  (= the basket I was talking about earlier)
- to refer to something when it's the only one in the context.
  The *nation's shopping basket* …
  (= we know which nation we're talking about)

Use zero article to talk about things in general.
  Very few households bought fresh pasta.

Use *a/an* …
- to talk about things in general.
  a *more Mediterranean diet*
- to introduce new information or to refer to something for the first time.
  The Office of National Statistics draws up **a** *list.*
- to refer to one of a group of things.
  It seems that Britain as **a** *nation* …

Use *some* and *any* to describe an unspecified number or quantity. Note that *some* is common in positive sentences, and *any* in negative sentences and questions.
  a bag of salad leaves and **some** *chicken*
  There isn't **any** *butter in the shopping basket.*

Use *any* in positive sentences to show that the quantity is not important.
  They remove **any** *items that are becoming less popular.*

➤ SEE LANGUAGE REFERENCE PAGE 94

9B | Shoppers

VOCABULARY: shopping

1 Match the words in the box to the categories 1–3.

> shop assistant   shopping centre/mall   window-shopping
> shoplifter   corner shop   discount shop   online shopping
> high street shopping   shopaholic

1 people   2 types of shopping   3 places to go shopping

2 Complete the quiz with a word or phrase from exercise 1.

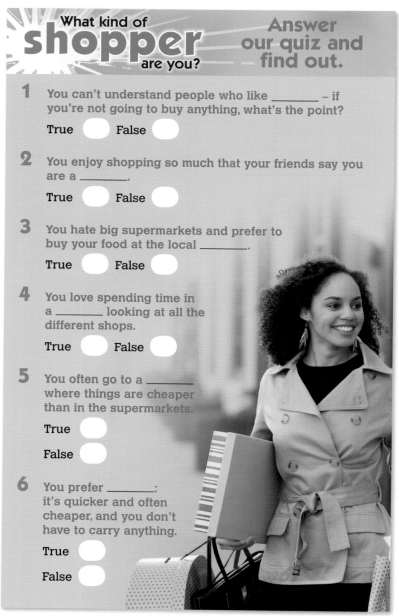

What kind of shopper are you? Answer our quiz and find out.

1 You can't understand people who like _____ – if you're not going to buy anything, what's the point?
True ☐   False ☐

2 You enjoy shopping so much that your friends say you are a _____.
True ☐   False ☐

3 You hate big supermarkets and prefer to buy your food at the local _____.
True ☐   False ☐

4 You love spending time in a _____ looking at all the different shops.
True ☐   False ☐

5 You often go to a _____ where things are cheaper than in the supermarkets.
True ☐
False ☐

6 You prefer _____: it's quicker and often cheaper, and you don't have to carry anything.
True ☐
False ☐

3 Which of the sentences in exercise 2 are true for you? Compare your answers with a partner.

LISTENING

1 🔘 **2.17** Listen to an interview with Katy, a shopaholic. Which of the questions does the interviewer not ask?

1 Are you really an addict?
2 When do you usually go shopping?
3 Is there an ideal time to go shopping?
4 Where do you most like shopping?
5 Do you travel a lot?
6 How much do you usually spend a week?
7 What's your favourite country for shopping?
8 What do you most enjoy shopping for?
9 When did you last go shopping?
10 What did you buy?

2 🔘 **2.17** Listen again and make notes on Katy's answers.

3 Work in pairs, A and B. Make up a short dialogue between Katy and one of her friends who wants to give her some advice about her shopping addiction.

A: You are Katy.
B: You are one of Katy's friends.

GRAMMAR: quantifiers 1

1 Add one word to each sentence.

          his
1 My brother spends most of ⋏ money on presents for his new girlfriend.

2 All friends prefer shopping to doing sport.

3 None them actually enjoys going shopping.

4 My mum spends most her free time on the internet finding new shopping sites.

5 Last week I spent all money on a really expensive bottle of champagne for my boss.

6 My boyfriend never likes any of clothes I buy for him.

7 Some the best shops in town are down the little side streets.

2 🔘 **2.18** Listen to the recording to check your answers.

3 Complete the sentences so that they are true for your town. Use *some, many, most, all, any, none* or *no* with or without *of* as appropriate.

1   <u>Most of</u> the big shopping centres are on the outskirts of town.
2   _____ people prefer to drive to the big supermarkets to do their shopping.
3   _____ the shops in the town centre sell tourist souvenirs.
4   _____ shops in the centre have private parking facilities.
5   _____ smaller shops have had to close because they can't compete with the big malls.
6   _____ the people you meet can tell you that the town centre has changed a lot in the last ten years.
7   And _____ them will say that they are happy with the changes.

Use *some, any, many, most* and *all* with or without *of*.

some any many most all	of	the + noun my/his, etc. + noun them/us, etc.

Most *of the time I go out of my way …*
Many *of my good friends think I'm an addict.*
All *of them seem to agree.*

some any many most	+ noun
all	+ the/my/his, etc. + noun

Some *people complain that they're boring.*
Most *countries are good for something.*
All *the shops look alike.*

Always use *of* when *none* is followed by a noun or a pronoun.

none of	the + noun my/his/her, etc. + noun us/them, etc.

None of the shops *in the centre …*
Not ~~*None shops in the centre*~~ *…*

Use *no* followed by a noun without an article or a possessive determiner.
No country *I know is better than Italy.*

⟩ SEE LANGUAGE REFERENCE PAGE 94

SPEAKING

1 Work in three groups, A–C. Read the information.

> The local council is planning to develop a new shopping area in your town. They want the area to include cinemas, cafés, an arts centre and a sports centre.

2 Prepare a proposal for the new shopping area. Your proposal must cover the points below.

- exact location and reasons for choosing this location
- parking and transport arrangements
- parks and green areas
- leisure facilities (sports, cinema, concerts, exhibitions, etc.)

Group A: Turn to page 131.
Group B: Turn to page 132.
Group C: Turn to page 134.

3 Work in new groups of three or more. Each group must include at least one student from groups A, B and C in exercise 1. Explain your proposal to your partners and decide together on a joint proposal for the shopping centre.

4 Present your proposal to the class.

> *Useful language*
>
> *First of all, we'll talk about …*
> *Then, we'll move on to consider …*
> *We have decided to …*
> *We propose to …*
> *We believe that it is important that …*
> *In conclusion we'd like to say that …*

9c | E-shopping

READING

1 Read the situations a–e and look at the website. Decide which link you would click on for each.

a This is your first visit to the site. You don't want anything now, but you want to find out what's on offer.

b A friend has told you this site has very cheap DVDs and you want to find out how much it costs to get the *Lord of the Rings* trilogy.

c You have ordered a shirt and a pair of jeans from the site, but they haven't arrived.

d You've just ordered some CDs for a friend's birthday. You want to send them to your friend's address with a special birthday greeting.

e You're a music fan who is looking for cheap CDs and music downloads.

2 Turn to page 133. Read the descriptions and match them to stores in the mall.

3 Read the descriptions again (both the one on this page and the three on page 133). Answer the questions.

1 Which stores offer discount prices on selected items?

2 Which store is running a special prize competition?

3 Which store specializes in presents, both traditional and unconventional?

4 Which store offers a special advice service?

5 Which stores claim to cater for all age groups?

6 Which store regularly features products associated with a famous person?

File Edit View Favourites Tools Help Links »

Eezeemall.com

Our stores

- Toyland
- Sports time
- Fashion parade
- House and home
- Gardeners' corner
- The food hall
- Movie world
- **The music centre**

Everything you're looking for on the music scene. Loads of <u>new releases</u> for the music connoisseurs, lots of <u>chart successes</u> for our younger customers and plenty of <u>classics</u> for those of you who are a little older. There are hundreds of bargains, too.
Take a look at our <u>bargain basement</u> for more information.

Welcome to Eezeemall – a new concept in e-shopping.

Click on the store you want to visit and come inside to look around. <u>Click here</u> to find out more.

<u>Or take a guided tour around the mall.</u>

Take a little time to get to know us. It's worth it! There are a lot of things to see, loads of stores to visit, and nothing else for you to do but sit back and enjoy the ride!

Our services

- ✳ guided tour
- ✳ gift wrapping
- ✳ special deliveries
- ✳ your account
- ✳ wish list
- ✳ special dates
- ✳ contact us

Sending a present to someone special? Take advantage of our free gift-wrapping and delivery service. Guaranteed to arrive in style and always in plenty of time for that important day.

VOCABULARY: collocations with *take*

1 Complete the texts with a word or phrase from the box.

> our word   your breath   a look
> a little time   our advice   advantage

1 Take _____ at our summer sales. You're sure to find something to wear on that special occasion!
2 Looking for something to read on the beach? Take _____ for it – you've come to the right place.
3 Take _____ of our special offer – running this week only. 50% off all frozen products.
4 Can't find that special present? Take _____, buy a gift voucher! Let your friends choose from our huge range of new releases and all-time classics, films and video games!
5 Enjoy the atmosphere of our historic towns, relax on our spectacular beaches and let the beauty of the landscape take _____ away.
6 Take _____ out of your busy day to look after yourself. Work out at the gym, take it easy in the Jacuzzi, or play a friendly game of tennis. We've got exactly what you need.

2 What products are the texts trying to sell?

3 Write a short advert for another popular product. Include at least one phrase with *take*. Your classmates must guess what the product is.

GRAMMAR: quantifiers 2

1 Work in pairs. Decide whether the sentences in each pair have the same (S) or different (D) meaning.

1 a A few sites offer free gift wrapping.
  b A couple of sites offer free gift wrapping.
2 a The government is doing little to protect e-shoppers against credit card fraud.
  b The government is doing enough to protect e-shoppers against credit card fraud.
3 a People spend too much money on clothes.
  b People spend plenty of money on clothes.
4 a Not many websites offer such a wide range of goods.
  b Few websites offer such a wide range of goods.
5 a Most internet users spend a little time window-shopping online.
  b Most internet users don't spend a lot of time window-shopping online.

2 Put these quantifiers in the table: *few, too many, lots of, loads of, little, much, plenty of, enough, too much*. Then choose the correct words to complete the rules.

countable	uncountable	both
not many	*not much*	*a lot of*

Use *few* and *little* without *a* with a *negative / positive* meaning. (*few* = not many; *little* = not much)
> *The government is doing **little** to protect e-shoppers.*

Use *enough* when you mean that the quantity is *sufficient / more than sufficient* for the purpose.
> *We've got **enough** for two, but not for three.*

Use *plenty* when you mean that the quantity is *sufficient / more than sufficient* for the purpose.
> *We've got **plenty** of time to get to the station. There's no need to hurry.*

Use *too much* and *too many* (of something) when you mean that this is a *good / bad* thing.
> *Ugh! There's **too much** salt in this soup!*

> SEE LANGUAGE REFERENCE PAGE 94

3 Complete the sentences so that they are true for you. Choose a positive or negative verb and add a quantifier.

1 I *spend / don't spend* _____ money on clothes.
2 I *know / don't know* _____ people who hate shopping.
3 I *buy / don't buy* _____ books every year.
4 I *have / don't have* _____ time to shop online.
5 There *are / aren't* _____ online shops for young people.

4 Work in pairs. Compare your sentences. How similar are your shopping habits?

SPEAKING

1 Work in groups. You are going to prepare a quiz to find out if your classmates are cybernauts or technophobes. Use the prompts below to help you prepare questions for the quiz.

- Do you know what ...?
- How often do you ...?
- When did you first ...?
- Have you ever used ...?
- Would you like to ...?
- How important is ...?

2 Work in pairs. Interview a student from another group. After the quiz, give them a score out of 10 (1 = total technophobe ➜ 10 = absolute cybernaut).

Does your partner agree with your score?

9D | Phone calls

SPEAKING

1 Work in small groups. Discuss these questions.

- What kind of phone do you have? What kind of phone would you like?
- What do you mostly use your phone for (calling, text messages, internet, music, camera, …)?
- Which phone company do you use? How happy are you with them?
- What sort of problems have you had with your phone?

2 Work in pairs. Talk about the last three phone dialogues you have had or the last three text messages you have sent.

LISTENING & FUNCTIONAL LANGUAGE: complaints

1 🔘 **2.19–2.20** Listen to two dialogues and answer the questions.

1 What are the people unhappy about in each dialogue?
2 Are the people satisfied at the end of each dialogue? Why or why not?

A little video for everyone. iPod nano

2 🔘 **2.19–2.20** Listen to the dialogues again and complete the extracts.

Dialogue 1
1 I've got a _____ with my phone.
2 I think there's something _____ with the battery.
3 I can't do that because the phone doesn't _____.
4 I'm sorry, but this is _____ unacceptable.
5 Could I _____ to the manager, please?
6 I want a refund, I want my _____ back.

Dialogue 2
7 I'm having _____ understanding it.
8 I'm not sure I can _____ you, I'm afraid.
9 I'm not sure what to _____.
10 Could you get someone else to have a _____?
11 I'm afraid that's not _____ enough.
12 I'll _____ to it this afternoon.

3 Match the sentences in exercise 2 to the four groups a–d.

a Explaining the problem (4 sentences)
b Saying what you want (3 sentences)
c Expressing dissatisfaction (2 sentences)
d Responding to a complaint (3 sentences)

4 Work in pairs. You are going to act out a dialogue where someone makes a complaint. Choose one of the situations below. Prepare and perform the roleplay.

1 You have recently opened an account with an internet service provider (ISP). Every time you log on to the net, your computer crashes. Telephone the ISP to complain.
2 You ordered some DVDs from a website. After four weeks, they still have not arrived. You have received no replies to your emails. Telephone the company to complain.
3 You bought an expensive digital camera from a local shop to take on holiday with you. It didn't work. You couldn't even switch it on. You return from your holiday and go back to the shop to complain.

VOCABULARY: prepositional phrases

1 Complete the sentences with an appropriate preposition.

1 Have you ever telephoned the wrong number _____ mistake?
2 Do you switch off your telephone _____ class?
3 How many telephone numbers do you know _____ heart?
4 Have you ever been _____ trouble for using your phone?
5 How much do you spend _____ average per month on your phone?
6 Do you write words _____ full when you text?
7 How many people do you regularly keep _____ touch with by phone?
8 Do you look at your telephone bill _____ detail?

🔘 **2.21** Listen to the recording to check your answers.

2 Work in pairs. Choose five questions to ask your partner.

DID YOU KNOW?

1 Work in pairs. Read about phone boxes in the UK and discuss the questions.

The red phone box was a traditional symbol of Britain for over 80 years. Until the 1990s, there were over 100,000 of them in the country. But, as a result of the popularity of mobile phones, they have now mostly disappeared. Some of the older ones are protected as historical monuments. Others were sold to people who wanted to use them as a shower in their bathrooms; a few have been turned into works of art.

There have been other changes to British telephones in recent years. As in other countries, there are now many companies that offer telephone services (such as Vodafone™ and T-Mobile). Mobile phones are now much more popular than fixed landlines, and for international phone calls Skype™ and other online options are becoming increasingly popular.

● How many phone companies are there in your country?
● Which is the most popular?
● What advice would you give to someone who wants to have a mobile phone account in your country?

Self-assessment (✓)

☐ I can make and respond to complaints.
☐ I can discuss my own use of the telephone.
☐ I can discuss phone services in my country.

GRAMMAR
Articles, determiners & quantifiers

We use the definite article, *the* ...
* to refer to something or someone because we have already mentioned it, or it is defined by the context of the sentence.
  *The Office of Statistics draws up a list of goods. **The** list is designed to reflect the nation's buying habits.*
* to refer to something or someone when it's the only one in the context.
  *In **the** consumer world of **the** 21st century ...*

We use the zero article with uncountable or plural nouns to talk about things in general.

  They replace them with Ø new products.
  We prefer Ø lighters.

We use the indefinite article, *a* or *an* ...
* to talk about things in general (with singular nouns).
  *The basket does not contain **a** box of matches.*
* to introduce new information or to refer to something for the first time (with singular countable nouns).
  *The Office of Statistics draws up **a** list of goods.*
* to refer to one of a group of things.
  *... to see if you're **a** part of modern Britain.*

We use the determiners *some* and *any* to describe an unspecified number or quantity (with uncountable and plural nouns).

  *We should get **some** mineral water.*
  ***Some** families are spending more on organic food.*

Some is common in positive sentences. In negative sentences and questions, *any* is more common.

  *It does not contain **any** luxury goods like caviar.*
  *Have you bought **any** coffee recently?*

We can also use *any* in positive sentences to show that the quantity is not important.

  *If you see **any** special offers at the shops, let me know.*
  (= it doesn't matter how many/which special offers)

We can use the quantifiers *some, any, many, most* and *all* in two different ways: with or without *of*.

with *of*		
some		
any		*the* + noun
many	*of*	*my/his/her*, etc. + noun
most		*them/us/you*
all		

  ***Some of** the shops are very expensive.*
  *I don't know **any of** your friends.*

without *of*	
some	
any	
many	+ noun
most	
all	

  ***Some people** hate shopping.*
  *Are there **any shops** that sell souvenirs?*

We use *none* to talk about no amount or quantity of something. When *none* is followed by a noun or pronoun, we always use *of*.

none of	*the* + noun
	my/his/her, etc. + noun
	them/us/you

  ***None of the shops** are open.*
  Not ~~none shops are open~~ ...
  ***None of my friends** smoke.*
  ***None of them** has time to help you.*

When *none* is the subject of a sentence, it is used with an affirmative verb. The verb can be singular or plural.

We use *no* followed by a noun without an article or a possessive determiner.

  *There were **no** parking facilities.*
  ***No** website is better for cheap flights.*

Quantifiers that can be used with both plural countable nouns and uncountable nouns:

  a lot of, lots of, enough, not enough, plenty of

Enough means the quantity is sufficient for the purpose.

  *Do we have **enough** money to go out for a meal?*
  *I think you've probably had **enough** time.*

Plenty of means the quantity is more than sufficient for the purpose.

  *You've got **plenty of** time to catch the train.*
  *There's **plenty of** room for everybody.*

quantifiers with plural countable nouns	quantifiers with uncountable nouns
many	—
not many	*not much*
too many	*too much*
a few	*a little*
few	*little*

We do not usually use *much* in affirmative sentences in modern English. We use *a lot of/lots of* instead.

  *They gave us **a lot of** advice.*
  Not ~~They gave us much advice.~~

We use *too many/too much* when we want to be critical of something.

> *There were **too many** people.*
> (= I was not happy about this.)

A few and *a little* mean a small amount or quantity. *Few* and *little* without the indefinite article mean *not many* or *not much*. Compare:

> ***A few** beaches are really nice.*
> (= a small number of beaches)
> ***Few** beaches are really nice.*
> (= not many)

Few and *little* (without *a*) are usually used with an affirmative verb.

FUNCTIONAL LANGUAGE
Complaints

I'm having problems + -ing form …
I think there's a problem with …
I think there's something wrong with …
I've got a problem with …
… doesn't work.

What seems to be the problem?
I'll see to it/look into it.
I'll get back to you.

Could you ask/get someone to + infinitive …?
Could I speak to …?

I'm afraid that's not good enough.
It's totally unacceptable.
I'd like a refund.
I want to have my money back.

WORD LIST

Shopping

corner shop *n C*	/ˌkɔː(r)nə(r) ˈʃɒp/
discount shop *n C*	/ˈdɪskaʊnt ˌʃɒp/
high street shopping *n U*	/ˌhaɪ ˌstriːt ˈʃɒpɪŋ/
online shopping *n U*	/ˌɒnlaɪn ˈʃɒpɪŋ/
shop assistant *n C*	/ˈʃɒp əˌsɪst(ə)nt/
shopaholic *n C*	/ˌʃɒpəˈhɒlɪk/
shoplifter *n C*	/ˈʃɒpˌlɪftə(r)/
shopping centre *n C*	/ˈʃɒpɪŋ ˌsentə(r)/
shopping mall *n C*	/ˈʃɒpɪŋ ˌmɔːl/
window-shopping *n U*	/ˈwɪndəʊ ˌʃɒpɪŋ/

Containers

bottle *n C* ***	/ˈbɒt(ə)l/
box *n C* ***	/bɒks/
can *n C* **	/kæn/
carton *n C*	/ˈkɑː(r)t(ə)n/
jar *n C* *	/dʒɑː(r)/
packet *n C* **	/ˈpækɪt/
tin *n C* **	/tɪn/
tub *n C*	/tʌb/

Collocations with *take*

take a look at (sth)	/ˈteɪk ə ˈlʊk ət/
take advantage of (sth)	/ˌteɪk ədˈvɑːntɪdʒ əv/
take (sb's) advice	/ˌteɪk ədˈvaɪs/
take (sb's) breath away	/ˌteɪk ˈbreθ əˌweɪ/
take (sb's) word for (sth)	/ˌteɪk ˈwɜː(r)d fə(r)/
take time	/ˌteɪk ˈtaɪm/

Prepositional phrases

by heart	/baɪ ˈhɑː(r)t/
by mistake	/baɪ mɪˈsteɪk/
in class	/ɪn ˈklɑːs/
in detail	/ɪn ˈdiːteɪl/
in full	/ɪn ˈfʊl/
in touch	/ɪn ˈtʌtʃ/
in trouble	/ɪn ˈtrʌb(ə)l/
on average	/ɒn ˈæv(ə)rɪdʒ/

Other words & phrases

accessible *adj*	/əkˈsesəb(ə)l/
accurately *adv*	/ˈækjʊrətli/
analyze *v*	/ˈænəlaɪz/
appeal *v* ***	/əˈpiːl/
association *n C* ***	/əˌsəʊsiˈeɪʃ(ə)n/
basement *n C* *	/ˈbeɪsmənt/
basket *n C* **	/ˈbɑːskɪt/
buff *n C*	/bʌf/
burger *n C* *	/ˈbɜː(r)gə(r)/
cater *v* **	/ˈkeɪtə(r)/
chart *n C* **	/tʃɑː(r)t/
classic *n C/adj* **	/ˈklæsɪk/
complaint *n C* ***	/kəmˈpleɪnt/
council *n C* ***	/ˈkaʊns(ə)l/
cracker *n C*	/ˈkrækə(r)/
cranberry *n C*	/ˈkrænb(ə)ri/
cross off *v*	/ˌkrɒs ˈɒf/
cybernaut *n C*	/ˈsaɪbə(r)ˌnɔːt/
decaffeinated *adj*	/diːˈkæfɪˌneɪtɪd/
delivery *n C* ***	/dɪˈlɪv(ə)ri/

diet *n C* ***	/ˈdaɪət/
discount *n C* **	/ˈdɪsˌkaʊnt/
electronic *adj* ***	/ˌelekˈtrɒnɪk/
favour *n C* ***	/ˈfeɪvə(r)/
fraud *n U* **	/frɔːd/
free-range *adj*	/ˌfriːˈreɪndʒ/
frustrated *adj* *	/frʌˈstreɪtɪd/
gift *n C* ***	/gɪft/
greeting *n C* *	/ˈgriːtɪŋ/
guarantee *n C/v* **	/ˌgærənˈtiː/
hand-made *adj*	/ˌhæn(d)ˈmeɪd/
herb *n C* *	/hɜː(r)b/
hot-air balloon *n C*	/ˌhɒt ˌeə(r) bəˌluːn/
household *n C/adj* ***	/ˈhaʊsˌhəʊld/
landscape *n C* **	/ˈlæn(d)ˌskeɪp/
leaf *n C* ***	/liːf/
lemonade *n U*	/ˌleməˈneɪd/
lighter *n C*	/ˈlaɪtə(r)/
low-fat *adj*	/ˈləʊˌfæt/
luxury *n C* *	/ˈlʌkʃəri/
margarine *n U*	/ˌmɑː(r)dʒəˈriːn/
marmalade *n U*	/ˈmɑː(r)məleɪd/
memorabilia *n U*	/ˌmem(ə)rəˈbɪliə/
nation *n C* ***	/ˈneɪʃ(ə)n/
olive oil *n U*	/ˌɒlɪv ˈɔɪl/
organic *adj* *	/ɔː(r)ˈgænɪk/
out of favour	/ˌaʊt əv ˈfeɪvə(r)/
outskirts *n pl*	/ˈaʊtˌskɜː(r)ts/
parade *n C* *	/pəˈreɪd/
peanut *n C*	/ˈpiːˌnʌt/
precious *adj* **	/ˈpreʃəs/
product *n C* ***	/ˈprɒdʌkt/
proposal *n C* ***	/prəˈpəʊz(ə)l/
query *n C* *	/ˈkwɪəri/
release *n C/v* ***	/rɪˈliːs/
salad *n U/C* **	/ˈsæləd/
screenplay *n C*	/ˈskriːnˌpleɪ/
slice *n C* **	/slaɪs/
spice *n C* *	/spaɪs/
statistic *n C*	/stəˈtɪstɪk/
system *n C* ***	/ˈsɪstəm/
technophobe *n C*	/ˈteknəʊfəʊb/
tissue *n C* **	/ˈtɪʃuː/
trilogy *n C*	/ˈtrɪlədʒi/
trolley *n C* *	/ˈtrɒli/
tuna *n U/C*	/ˈtjuːnə/
unconventional *adj*	/ˌʌnkənˈvenʃ(ə)nəl/
vegetarian *adj/n C*	/ˌvedʒəˈteəriən/
wheelchair *n C*	/ˈwiːlˌtʃeə(r)/
wish list *n C*	/ˈwɪʃ ˌlɪst/
wrap *v* **	/ræp/

10A | Secrets

VOCABULARY: illusions

1 Read the text below and replace the words in italics with a word from the box.

audience   fake   performed   pretended
stage   vanished

I once saw a magician who (1) *did* an incredible trick. He took a long knife and put it into his mouth. He (2) *acted as if* it was really painful. I was sure that the knife was (3) *not real*, but then he took it out of his mouth and used it to cut an apple in half. Then he ate the apple.

He then asked a member of the (4) *public* to come to the (5) *front of the theatre* and he put the knife into her mouth. He closed her mouth and then opened it again. The knife had completely (6) *disappeared* and in its place were the two pieces of apple.

2 What are the best magic tricks you have seen? Do you have any idea how the tricks work?

READING

1 Read the magazine article and choose the best explanation for *the secret is really out of the bag*.

a   someone has given a secret away
b   someone has a new secret

2 Read the article again and say if the sentences are true (T) or false (F). Correct the false sentences.

1   Most people want to understand how magic tricks are done.
2   Videos on the internet explain how some tricks work.
3   You need special powers to do the most amazing tricks.
4   Only magicians can buy equipment for tricks.
5   Magicians who reveal their secrets are not popular with other magicians.
6   Some magicians have lost a lot of money.
7   Magic is not interesting when we understand the magicians' secrets.

3 Find the words 1–5 in the article and choose the best definition for each, a or b.

1   hidden   a) you can see it   b) you can't see it
2   reveal   a) give away   b) keep
3   traitors   a) people who   b) people who
                   keep secrets   don't keep secrets
4   spoiled   a) made better   b) made worse
5   routines   a) performances   b) secrets

The Tricks of the Trade

Everybody loves a secret and nobody loves a secret more than magicians. As we sit and watch the magician pulling a rabbit out of a hat, there is only one question on most people's minds:
5 how did he do that? Skilled magicians will take advantage of the fact we want to know how the tricks are done and will even pretend to make a mistake. Just when we think that we understand the trick, he does it another way and we know
10 that we must be wrong. But now the secret is really out of the bag and magicians around the world are furious.

In the last few years, it has become possible to go online and find out how to do some of the world's
15 most amazing tricks. Magicians like Derren Brown, Penn & Teller and Val Valentino explain the tricks of their trade on Youtube videos and other sites. There are no real surprises. Hidden assistants, fake boxes, locks and other special
20 equipment are the usual, simple explanations. If you have $500, you can even buy the equipment for the 'floating-on-a-chair' trick on the internet.

It is well-known that magicians share a code of secrecy and agree never to reveal their secrets.
25 Understandably, many of them feel that Derren Brown and the others are traitors.

Once we know the secret of a trick, the magic vanishes. Magicians who have spent thousands of dollars are less than happy to find their equipment
30 worthless and their shows spoiled. One man in Brazil has lost more than $500,000 as a result of the TV show and may have to close his magic store.

The revelations about magicians' secrets are
35 not, however, going to stop. A best-selling new book called *Sleights of Mind*, written by two neuroscientists (and helped by famous magicians like Teller and James Randi), explains even more secrets and looks at the psychology of magic.
40 Great magic is not about secrets, explain the authors. Great magicians are performers who spend hours and hours practising their routines. Even when we know their secrets, we are still amazed by what they have done.

GRAMMAR: modals of speculation 1 (present time)

Use a modal verb + infinitive to make guesses or speculate about the present or the future.

sure ↑ less sure ↓ sure	subject	*must* *might* (*not*) *may* (*not*) *could* *can't*	infinitive (*be, have,* etc.)

*We **must be** wrong.*
*They **may not be able to** repeat the trick a second time.*

❯ SEE LANGUAGE REFERENCE PAGE 104

1 Choose the correct verbs to complete the dialogue.

A: Look! Over there! It's David Copperfield, the magician!
B: No! It (1) *can't / must* be him. He's too old.
A: Are you sure? I think it (2) *might / might not* be him. He looks very similar.
B: No, it (3) *may / must* be someone else. David Copperfield has got brown eyes, not blue.
A: Oh, yes, you're right. But it (4) *could / must* be his cousin …
B: Why don't you ask him?
A: No, he (5) *must / might* get angry!

2 Look at the photo and write as many sentences as you can about it using modal verbs.

There must be something invisible that is holding her up.

3 Work in pairs. Compare your sentences in exercise 2. Explain why you chose your modal verbs.

PRONUNCIATION: sentence stress

1 🔊 2.22 Listen to a sentence said in two different ways. Underline the word that is stressed each time.

1 The show might be fun.
2 The show might be fun.

The position of the stress in the sentence changes its meaning.

	stressed modal	unstressed modal
may *might* *could*	less sure	more sure
must *can't*	more sure	less sure

2 🔊 2.23 Listen to the sentences below. Is the speaker more (M) or less (L) sure of what he is saying?

1 I might be able to help you.
2 They may be very busy later.
3 I'll answer the phone – it could be for me.
4 You must be very tired.
5 You can't be serious!

3 Work in pairs. Practise saying the sentences in exercise 2. Your partner must decide if you are more or less sure of what you are saying.

SPEAKING

1 Work in two groups, A and B. You are going to do a magic trick.

Group A: Turn to page 130.
Group B: Turn to page 133.

In your groups, read the instructions and practise the trick.

2 Work in pairs with one student from Group A and one student from Group B. Show your partner the trick. Can he /she guess how it's done?

10B Fact or fiction?

SPEAKING & VOCABULARY: word families

1 Complete the table with the correct words.

adjective	noun	negative adjective	negative noun	adverb
possible	(1) _____	(2) _____	(3) _____	(4) _____
(5) _____	(6) _____	(7) _____	(8) _____	probably
(9) _____	(10) _____	unlikely		
(11) _____	certainty	(12) _____	(13) _____	(14) _____
definite				(15) _____

2 Complete the sentences. Put the words in brackets into the correct form.

1 I _definitely_ agree with that. (*definite*)
2 That's very _____ to be true. I find it very hard to believe. (*likely*)
3 There's very little _____ of that being true. (*probable*)
4 That's _____ a lot of nonsense. (*certain*)
5 Nobody could believe that – it's an absolute _____. (*possible*)
6 I can't say with any _____ that that's correct. (*certain*)
7 That sounds a very _____ idea. I'd be very surprised. (*probable*)
8 That might just _____ be true, but I doubt it. (*possible*)

3 Work in pairs. Discuss these conspiracy theories. How true do you think the conspiracy theories are?

1 Some businesses control our minds through hidden messages in television pictures.
2 The HIV virus was developed as a biological weapon.
3 Oil companies have found an alternative source of cheap energy, but they are keeping it a secret.
4 Pharmaceutical companies could find cures for many diseases if they really wanted to.
5 The secret services can listen to everything we say.
6 American scientists have made contact with aliens.
7 A secret group of politicians and businessmen control most of the world.

4 Work with your partner. Make your own conspiracy theory by completing the text.

The world is controlled by (1) _____ with the help of (2) _____. They want to (3) _____ and they have been responsible for many important events, including (4) _____. In the next few years, they will probably (5) _____.

LISTENING

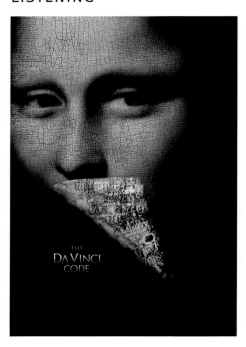

After being accused of a murder in the Louvre museum, a Harvard professor, Robert Langdon, discovers a secret organization that plans to take over the world.

1 Have you seen the film or read the book *The Da Vinci Code*? What can you remember about it? What did you think of it?

2 2.24 Listen to part of a radio programme about *The Da Vinci Code*. How many of the callers think there may be some truth to the story of the book?

3 2.24 Listen again. What information do the speakers use to justify their opinions?

1 The secret society in *The Da Vinci Code* is definitely a fact.
2 A secret organization controls the world's banks.
3 The secret organization in *The Da Vinci Code* is the CIA.
4 The secret in *The Da Vinci Code* is not a secret.
5 The Freemasons are very powerful.
6 You should not take *The Da Vinci Code* seriously.

4 Do you think it is likely that there are secret organizations that want to control the world?

GRAMMAR: modals of speculation 2 (present time)

Use a modal verb + *be* + verb + *-ing* to make guesses or speculations about actions in progress now.

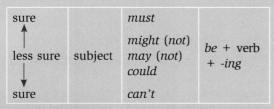

sure ↑ less sure ↓ sure	subject	*must* *might* (*not*) *may* (*not*) *could* *can't*	*be* + verb + *-ing*

*Someone **might be watching** you.*
*You **must be joking**.*
***Could** he **be telling** the truth?*

> SEE LANGUAGE REFERENCE PAGE 104

1 Find three examples of modal verbs followed by *be* + verb + *-ing* in audioscript 2.24 on pages 143–144.

2 🔘 2.25 Listen to the recording. You will hear seven different actions from the story of *The Da Vinci Code*. After each action, say what you think Robert Langdon is doing. Use a modal verb of speculation and the ideas below to help you.

He might be hiding his gun.

- escaping from the police in the Louvre
- hiding his gun
- looking for a key in a desk
- looking for information in a library
- looking for information on the internet
- reading about himself in a newspaper
- trying to open a locked door
- typing a letter to his girlfriend
- walking around an old church

3 Think of four people you know. What do you think they are doing now? Write two sentences with modals of deduction for each person.

My friend Pete could be presenting sales figures in a meeting.
He can't be sitting at home.

DID YOU KNOW?

1 Work in pairs. Read about Glastonbury and discuss the questions.

Glastonbury

Glastonbury, a town in the south-west of England, is a magical and mysterious place. There are many legends and myths about it. A large number of people believe that one of the followers of Jesus Christ, a man called Joseph of Arimathea, brought the Holy Grail (the cup that Christ used at the Last Supper) to England, and buried it at Glastonbury. They also say that he built the first church in England in Glastonbury. Archaeological research shows that there may have been an early Christian church in the town.

There is also a connection with King Arthur and his knights of the Round Table, who spent their lives looking for the Grail. In the 12th century, some monks announced that they had found King Arthur's grave at Glastonbury, along with a stone. On the stone there was some writing that said, 'Here lies Arthur, king.'

- Are there any magical or mysterious places in your country?
- What stories are associated with these places?

10c | Mysteries

READING

1 Every year around the world, thousands of people fake their own deaths. How many reasons can you think of for doing this? Look at the headlines.

Police say missing woman faked disappearance

SOLDIER STAGED HIS OWN DEATH

Missing politician was suffering from stress

2 Read the article about John Darwin and put the paragraphs in the correct order.

3 Read the article again. Tick the five facts below that are mentioned in the article and identify the corresponding section of the text. Then match the facts 1–8 to the paragraphs A–E.

1 The search for John Darwin was unsuccessful.
2 Before moving into his own home, John Darwin lived in a tent.
3 John and Anne Darwin lied to their children.
4 A newspaper revealed the Darwins' lie.
5 The Darwins' children had no sympathy for their parents.
6 The relationship between the Darwins broke down after they were arrested.
7 In the end, the Darwins did not get rich.
8 The Darwins left prison after serving half of the six-year sentence.

4 Work in pairs. What do you think was the Darwins' worst crime: faking the death or lying to their children?

6

☐ A But a few days later, the mystery deepened when *The Daily Mirror* published a photo of John and Anne Darwin in Panama. The photo was a year old and the couple seemed to be happy together. Could the Darwins have faked John's disappearance, asked the newspaper. The police began to investigate and, shortly afterwards, arrested the couple.

John Darwin

☐ B One cold March morning, John Darwin went paddling in his canoe off a beach in the north-west of England. Later that day, when he failed to turn up for work, the coastguards tried to find him. They managed to recover his paddle, and, the following day, parts of his canoe, but there was no sign of John Darwin himself. It was clear that he must have had an accident. One year later, the authorities issued his death certificate.

Anne Darwin

☐ C But the Darwin sons were angry with their parents and felt they deserved to go to prison. The judge agreed with them. He sentenced them both to six years and ordered them to repay all the money they had.

☐ D Darwin pretended to be dead for one simple reason: money. He and his wife collected £150,000 from a life insurance policy after receiving the death certificate. For two years, and completely unknown to the couple's two sons, Darwin lived in a secret hiding-place in the family home. Later, the couple moved to Panama. The reasons for Darwin's return to England are not entirely clear. It is known that he had visa problems, but he may have been unhappy about not seeing his sons for so long.

☐ E Five and a half years later, a man walked into a London police station and said he was John Darwin. He claimed to be unable to remember anything about the last five years of his life. By this time, his wife, Anne, was living in Panama. At first, she refused to believe that her husband had returned, but the police confirmed his identity. She said she was both shocked and happy.

The beach where Darwin disappeared

GRAMMAR: modals of speculation (past time)

> Use a modal verb + *have* + past participle to make guesses or to speculate about the past.

sure ↑ less sure ↓ sure	subject	*must* *might* (*not*) *may* (*not*) *could* *can't* *couldn't*	*have*	past participle (*had*, *known*, *seen*, *said*, etc.)

He **may have been** unhappy.
He **must have had** an accident.
Could they **have faked** his disappearance?

> ❯ SEE LANGUAGE REFERENCE PAGE 104

1 Match the sentences 1–6 to one of the newspaper headlines A–D.

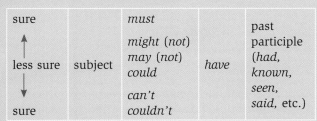

A Politician's clothes found on beach

B POLICE FIND BOX OF SNAKES ON HIGHWAY

C Alien attacks teacher

D SIX PEOPLE SEE MONSTER IN CHINESE MOUNTAINS

1 I'm sure they didn't come from a zoo.
2 Someone definitely left them there.
3 It's possible that they attacked someone.
4 Maybe they fell off the back of a lorry.
5 Perhaps they weren't dangerous.
6 There's a possibility that someone intended to pick them up later.

2 Rewrite the sentences in exercise 1 beginning with the words given below and a modal verb.

1 They can't have come from a zoo.

1 They ...	4 They ...	
2 Someone ...	5 They ...	
3 They ...	6 Someone ...	

3 Now make deductions about the other headlines.

It can't have been an alien!
It might have been someone dressed as an alien.

4 🔊 **2.26–2.29** Listen to the recordings to find out what really happened.

VOCABULARY: verbs followed by infinitive

1 These words are highlighted in the story about John Darwin. Underline the words and the two words that follow them in the story.

> began   claimed   deserved   managed
> pretended   refused   seemed   tried

2 Work in pairs. Complete the text with words from the box in exercise 1.

Before their wedding, Nicola's husband (1) _seemed_ to be normal in every way. But afterwards, he (2) _____ to act very strangely. He often came home late from work and he (3) _____ to say where he had been. Nicola (4) _____ not to mind, but she was very worried. She (5) _____ to speak to him, but he never explained why he was late. Then, one day at dinner, he suddenly (6) _____ to be an alien. He said that all humans were bad and (7) _____ to die. He was very excited, but Nicola (8) _____ to calm him down. But the next morning, her husband had gone and she never saw him again.

SPEAKING

1 Work in groups, A and B. You are going to work out the answer to a mystery.

Group A: Read the information below. Find out more information by asking the students in Group B questions. They can only answer *Yes, Sort of, No* or *Not exactly*.

> A woman went to the shops and bought a new pair of shoes. Later that day, she went to work and died. How did she die?

After every eight questions, discuss what you have learnt with your group.

Group B: Turn to page 132. Read the explanation of the situation and answer the questions the students in Group A ask you. You can only answer *Yes, Sort of, No* or *Not exactly*.

2 Now exchange roles.

Group B: Try to work out the answer to the mystery.

> A man was staying in a motel. He went outside to his car and hooted on the horn. He then returned to his room. Why did he hoot on the car horn?

Group A: Turn to page 128 and answer the questions the students in Group B ask you.

10D | Strictly confidential

SPEAKING

1 Work in pairs. Which of the following pieces of information about you are the most confidential?

• your age
• the way that you vote
• your emails and where you surf on the internet
• your financial situation
• your employment record
• your school record

2 Which pieces of information in exercise 1 do you think the following people have the right to know? Explain your reasons.

• parents about their children
• husbands or wives about their partners
• employers about their staff
• schools or universities about their students
• governments about the people

LISTENING

1 🔘 2.30 Listen to a management meeting in a company. Answer the questions.

1 What are they thinking of doing?
2 What do they finally decide?

2 🔘 2.30 Listen to the dialogue again. Put the points in the order that you hear them.

The new system …
☐ will stop people wasting time.
☐ will show the staff that it is important to improve efficiency.
☐ will stop people from visiting gambling websites.
☐ will help to avoid problems with computer viruses.
☐ will make people feel unhappy.
☐ will cost money in the long term.

3 Do you think it is a good idea for companies (or schools) to introduce systems like this?

FUNCTIONAL LANGUAGE: advantages & disadvantages

1 Choose the correct words and phrases to complete the sentences.

1 We should think a little more about the *drawbacks / pros* and cons.
2 The *benefits / troubles* of this are pretty obvious.
3 There may be one or two hidden *drawbacks / problems.*
4 The good *disadvantage / thing* about this system is that it stops time-wasting.
5 The *advantages / trouble* is that our computer system is open to viruses.
6 You were worried about some of the *disadvantages / thing* of doing this.
7 I can't see any *gained / point* in waiting.
8 The other *benefits / problem* with this is the whole question of confidentiality.
9 I think there's a lot to be *benefit / gained*.

2 Look at audioscript 2.30 on page 144 to check your answers.

3 Complete the dialogue with the words in italics from exercise 1. Sometimes more than one answer is possible.

A: We've designed a new system that scans customers' emails to look for particular words.
B: What's the (1) _____ in that?
A: Well, the great (2) _____ of it is that we can send advertisements that match the things that people talk about.
B: But isn't there a (3) _____ with people who don't want to receive advertisements?
A: Maybe, but there are so many other (4) _____ – special offers, low prices and so on – that they'll want to use our service.
B: And it's a good (5) _____ for the advertisers, of course.
A: Yes, there's a lot to be (6) _____ for them. One of the (7) _____ in the past was that they didn't know who to send the advertisements to.

SPEAKING

1 Read the magazine article about installing CCTV in schools.

Have your say:

Spying

on our kids?

As we know, the behaviour of school children is getting worse across the **UK. Vandalism, violence and bullying are all on the increase in our schools.** More and more schools are trying to help solve this problem by installing CCTV cameras in our schools so that the small minority who cause trouble can be caught.

In Crookton, our Mayor is thinking about spending some of his budget on such cameras. The cameras will be in classrooms, corridors, toilets and playgrounds.

A public debate on this issue will take place in the town hall this Friday. If you want to have your say, come along.

2 Work in four groups, A–D. You are going to prepare a list of five reasons for or against the introduction of CCTV cameras.

Group A: You represent the teachers in your town's schools. You are against the introduction of CCTV.

Group B: You represent the parents of school children in your town. You support the introduction of CCTV.

Group C: You represent school children in your town. You are against the introduction of CCTV.

Group D: You represent the local government in your town. You support the introduction of CCTV.

In your groups, prepare your reasons for or against the introduction of CCTV.

3 Now choose a representative from each group. Present your arguments for or against the introduction of CCTV.

VOCABULARY: idioms

1 Complete the idiomatic expressions with a word from the box.

bright	cracking	feet	high	point	safe

1 Do you like to get up _____ and early or do you prefer to stay in bed as long as possible?
2 Do you know anyone who goes on and on and never gets to the _____ when they are speaking?
3 In general, do you live dangerously or play it _____?
4 What was the _____ point of your day yesterday and what was the worst moment?
5 When there is something you have to do, do you prefer to get _____ immediately or do you prefer to wait a bit?
6 When was the last time you didn't want to do something and you dragged your _____?

2 Find and underline these idioms in audioscript 2.30 on page 144.

3 Work in pairs. Ask and answer the questions in exercise 1. Do you know any more English idioms? What are they?

Self-assessment (✓)

- ☐ I can talk about the advantages and disadvantages of a plan.
- ☐ I can explain the reasons behind my decisions.
- ☐ I can express my opinions about confidentiality.

GRAMMAR
Modals of speculation (present & past time)

We can use modal verbs to make guesses about the present, the past and the future.
The choice of modal verb shows how sure we are about our guess.

sure   less sure   sure

must   *might (not), may (not), could*   *can't, couldn't*

We use the modal verb + infinitive to make guesses about the present or the future.

> You **must be** very tired.
> I **might need** your help later.
> He **can't be** serious.

We use the modal verb + *be* + *-ing* form to make guesses about actions in progress now.

> She **must be having** problems at work.
> I'm not sure where he is. He **could be having** a bath.
> She **might be working** for the CIA.

We use the modal verb + *have* + past participle to make guesses about the past.

> They **must have arrived** by now.
> He **might not have known** her true identity.
> It **can't have been** a surprise.

FUNCTIONAL LANGUAGE
Advantages & disadvantages

The pros and cons of + noun/*-ing* form
The good/bad thing about + noun/*-ing* form *is* …
The advantage of + noun/*-ing* form
The benefit/benefits of + noun/*-ing* form
There's a lot to be gained from + *-ing* form
The disadvantage of + noun/*-ing* form
The drawback of + noun/*-ing* form
The trouble with + noun/*-ing* form
The problem with + noun/*-ing* form
There's no point in/There isn't any point in + *-ing* form
There's nothing to be gained from + *-ing* form

WORD LIST

Illusions

act *v* ***	/ækt/
audience *n C* ***	/'ɔːdiəns/
fake *adj/n C*	/feɪk/
magician *n C*	/mə'dʒɪʃ(ə)n/
perform *v* ***	/pə(r)'fɔː(r)m/
pretend *v* **	/prɪ'tend/
public *n* ***	/'pʌblɪk/
reveal *v* ***	/rɪ'viːl/
stage *n C/v* ***	/steɪdʒ/
trick *n C* **	/trɪk/
vanish *v* **	/'vænɪʃ/

Word families

certain *adj* ***	/'sɜː(r)t(ə)n/
certainly *adv* ***	/'sɜː(r)t(ə)nli/
certainty *n C* **	/'sɜː(r)t(ə)nti/
definite *adj* **	/'def(ə)nət/
definitely *adv* **	/'def(ə)nətli/
impossibility *n C*	/ɪm,pɒsə'bɪləti/
impossible *adj* ***	/ɪm'pɒsəb(ə)l/
improbability *n C*	/ɪm,prɒbə'bɪləti/
improbable *adj*	/ɪm'prɒbəb(ə)l/
likelihood *n U* *	/'laɪklihʊd/
likely *adj* ***	/'laɪkli/
possibility *n C* ***	/,pɒsə'bɪləti/
possible *adj* ***	/'pɒsəb(ə)l/
possibly *adv* ***	/'pɒsəbli/
probability *n C* **	/,prɒbə'bɪləti/
probable *adj* **	/'prɒbəb(ə)l/
probably *adv* ***	/'prɒbəbli/
uncertain *adj* **	/ʌn'sɜː(r)t(ə)n/
uncertainty *n C* **	/ʌn'sɜː(r)t(ə)nti/
unlikely *adj* ***	/ʌn'laɪkli/

Verbs followed by infinitive

begin ***	/bɪ'gɪn/
claim ***	/kleɪm/
deserve **	/dɪ'zɜː(r)v/
manage ***	/'mænɪdʒ/
pretend **	/prɪ'tend/
refuse ***	/rɪ'fjuːz/
seem ***	/siːm/
try ***	/traɪ/

Idioms

bright and early	/,braɪt ən 'ɜː(r)li/
drag your feet	/,dræg jə(r) 'fiːt/
get cracking	/,get 'krækɪŋ/
get to the point	/,get tə ðə 'pɔɪnt/
high point	/'haɪ ,pɔɪnt/
play it safe	/,pleɪ ɪt 'seɪf/

Other words & phrases

accuse *v* ***	/ə'kjuːz/
alien *n C* **	/'eɪliən/
ape *n C*	/eɪp/
archaeological *adj*	/,ɑː(r)kiə'lɒdʒɪk(ə)l/
biological *adj* **	/,baɪə'lɒdʒɪk(ə)l/
bullying *n U*	/'bʊliɪŋ/
bury *v* **	/'beri/
canoe *n C* *	/kə'nuː/
casino *n C*	/kə'siːnəʊ/
CCTV *n C*	/,siː siː tiː 'viː/
certificate *n C* **	/sə(r)'tɪfɪkət/
collar *n C* **	/'kɒlə(r)/
confidentiality *n U*	/,kɒnfɪdenʃi'æləti/
crazy *adj* **	/'kreɪzi/
cure *n C/v* **	/kjʊə(r)/
dating agency *n C*	/'deɪtɪŋ ,eɪdʒ(ə)nsi/
deaf *adj* **	/def/
deepen *v*	/'diːpən/
elbow *n C* **	/'elbəʊ/
equipment *n U* ***	/ɪ'kwɪpmənt/
float *v* **	/fləʊt/
furious *adj* **	/'fjʊəriəs/
grave *n C* **	/greɪv/
guardian *n C*	/'gɑː(r)diən/
gun *n C* ***	/gʌn/
hack into *v*	/'hæk ,ɪntuː/
hide *v* ***	/haɪd/
hoot *v*	/huːt/
in the long/short term	/ɪn ðə 'lɒŋ/'ʃɔː(r)t tɜː(r)m/
knight *n C*	/naɪt/
knot *n C* **	/nɒt/
legend *n C* **	/'ledʒ(ə)nd/
minority *n C* ***	/maɪ'nɒrəti/
monk *n C* *	/mʌŋk/
motel *n C*	/məʊ'tel/
murder *n C/v* ***	/'mɜː(r)də(r)/
murderer *n C* *	/'mɜː(r)dərə(r)/
mysterious *adj* **	/mɪ'stɪəriəs/
myth *n C* **	/mɪθ/
neuroscientist *n C*	/'njʊərəʊ,saɪəntɪst/
obvious *adj* ***	/'ɒbviəs/
paddle *n C/v*	/'pæd(ə)l/
pharmaceutical *adj*	/,fɑː(r)mə'sjuːtɪk(ə)l/

rabbit *n C* **	/'ræbɪt/
revelation *n C*	/,revə'leɪʃ(ə)n/
routine *n C* **	/ruː'tiːn/
rub *v* **	/rʌb/
scan *v* **	/skæn/
scare *v* *	/skeə(r)/
secrecy *n U*	/'siːkrəsi/
secret agent *n C*	/,siːkrət 'eɪdʒ(ə)nt/
snap *n C/v* **	/snæp/
software *n U* ***	/'sɒf(t),weə(r)/
spoil *v* **	/spɔɪl/
spy on *v*	/'spaɪ ,ɒn/
tent *n C* **	/tent/
tie *v* ***	/taɪ/
traitor *n C* *	/'treɪtə(r)/
understandably *adv*	/,ʌndə(r)'stændəbli/
vandalism *n U*	/'vændə,lɪz(ə)m/
virus *n C* ***	/'vaɪrəs/
weapon *n C* ***	/'wepən/
worthless *adj*	/'wɜː(r)θləs/

11A | Total sport

SPEAKING & VOCABULARY: sport

1 Work in pairs. Match at least one sport to each verb.

> catch   hit   jump   kick   pass   run
> serve   throw

> athletics   baseball   boxing   football
> gymnastics   rugby   volleyball   water polo

2 Can you think of one more sport for each verb?

3 🌐 2.31 Listen to someone describing how to play a sport. Which sport is the person talking about?

4 Now choose a different sport and describe it using the verbs in exercise 1.

5 Work in groups. Look at the sports in exercise 1 and discuss these questions.

- Which two sports are the most popular in your country?
- Which two sports is your country best at?
- Which two sports are the most enjoyable to do?
- Which two sports are the most interesting to watch?

READING

1 Who, in your opinion, is the world's greatest sportsman or sportswoman? Explain your reasons.

2 Read the article about a world champion sportswoman. Answer the question in the article's title and explain your reasons.

3 Read the article again. Which topic 1–6 is not mentioned in the article?

1 a description of triathlon
2 Chrissie's other interests
3 Chrissie's preparation for competitions
4 Chrissie's success as an athlete
5 the increasing popularity of triathlon
6 the relationship between sport and politics

4 Complete the sentences with words from the article.

1 Can you name two athletes who are h_____ names in your country?
2 In which sport would you like to c_____ in the Olympic Games®?
3 What was the last sporting e_____ that you went to?
4 Which companies are the best-known s_____ of sport in your country?

5 Work in pairs. Ask and answer the questions in exercise 4.

GRAMMAR: passive

1 Complete the table with examples from the article.

active	passive
present simple They **don't talk** about it.	1 It is _____.
present continuous They **are organizing** more events.	2 More events _____.
past simple They **recognized** her achievements.	3 Her achievements _____.
present perfect One or two **have beaten** her.	4 She _____.
future simple They **will not show** it on TV.	5 It _____.
modal verbs They **must complete** the triathlon.	6 The triathlon _____.

2 Choose the correct verb form to complete the sentences.

1 Where *did the first modern Olympics® hold / were the first modern Olympics® held* in 1896?
2 How many times *have the Olympics® cancelled / have the Olympics® been cancelled* because of war?
3 Approximately how many gold medals *are awarded / award* at the Olympics®?
4 Which country *has won / has been won* the most gold medals since the Olympics® started?
5 How many different sports *can watch / can be watched* at the Olympics®?
6 When *did the Olympics® see / were the Olympics® seen* on TV for the first time?
7 How many people *watch / are watched* the Olympics® on TV?
8 Which sport *introduced / was introduced* as an Olympic® event in 1996?
9 When *did the Olympic® flag use / was the Olympic® flag used* for the first time?

The world's greatest sportswoman?

It is not talked about like football or tennis. It will not be shown on prime-time TV and its stars are not household names. But the
5 sport of triathlon is as tough as it gets. There are many varieties of the sport, but in the toughest, which is known as the Ironman triathlon, competitors swim 3.8
10 kilometres, ride 180 kilometres on a bicycle and then run a marathon. The athletes do not get a break. Perhaps the biggest triathlon event each year is the Ironman World
15 Championships, which have been held in Hawaii since 1978. Under a hot sun, with strong winds and no wetsuit for protection in the water, the triathlon must be completed in under nine hours for an athlete to stand a chance of a medal.

20 The biggest name in triathlon, the winner of many Ironman championships and the world-record holder is Christine (Chrissie) Wellington. Although not as fast as the fastest men, in some races she has been beaten by only one or two of them. Her achievements were recognized when she was voted *The Sunday Times* 'Sportswoman of the Year' and given a medal by the British government.

25 Triathlon was introduced into the Olympic Games® in 2000 and it is quickly gaining in popularity. It has attracted international sponsors like Coca Cola®. Top athletes like Chrissie Wellington are professionals, but more and more events are being organized for amateurs. Chrissie is already in her thirties and knows that she cannot continue to compete in top events for ever. But she is hoping that the
30 new media attention to triathlon will help her to achieve her non-sporting goals.

Chrissie's two passions are sport and international development, and she believes that the two can be combined. Before becoming a professional, she worked for a development project in Nepal. Now she wants to use her sporting success to help the developing world. She believes that sport can change the world we live in. It
35 can help people to communicate and to understand each other.

3 Match the answers in the box to the questions in exercise 2. Check your answers on page 129. Now turn the answers into full sentences.

Athens	beach volleyball
the United States	three
28	300	1920	1960
4.7 billion

1 The first modern Olympics® were held in Athens in 1896.

4 Work in pairs. Write three similar quiz questions about sports in your country. Use passives where possible. Then test your classmates.

Use the passive …
• to talk about an action when the agent (the person or thing that does the action) is unknown or unimportant.
• to emphasize what happened rather than who did it.

If we want to name the agent, we use *by*.
*The modern Olympics® were started **by** Pierre de Coubertin.*
(We only name the agent when the information is important or unusual.)

Make the passive with the appropriate tense of the verb *to be* + past participle.
*How **are** Olympic® sports **chosen**?*
*The 2016 games **are being held** in Brazil.*
*Tickets **must be bought** a long time in advance.*

SEE LANGUAGE REFERENCE PAGE 114

11B | Olympic dreams

VOCABULARY: nouns & adjectives (describing people)

1 Match the adjectives in the box to the sentences.

> agile ambitious determined
> enthusiastic intelligent powerful
> ruthless talented

1 He will not let anything stop him from doing what he has decided to do.
2 He's always really interested in and excited by his sport.
3 I've never known anyone who wants so much to be successful.
4 She can really move very quickly and very easily.
5 She has so much natural ability.
6 She is very, very strong.
7 She thinks clearly and quickly.
8 The only thing that is important to him is success. He doesn't mind if other people suffer in the process.

2 Make nouns from the adjectives in exercise 1. Use a dictionary to help you.

agile   agility

3 Work in pairs. Discuss these questions.

• Think of a well-known sports personality. Which of the words in exercises 1 and 2 can you use to describe this person?
• What special qualities do you think children need to become very successful at sport?

LISTENING

1 Look at the photos. How old do you think the athletes are? Do you think it's good for children to compete at international level when they're so young? Why or why not?

2 🔊 2.32 Listen to a psychologist talking about child sports stars and answer these questions.

1 Which two sports do they talk about?
2 Does the psychologist think the child star phenomenon is a positive one? Why or why not?

3 🔊 2.32 Listen to the interview again and answer the questions.

1 How old should tennis players be when they win their first important competition?
2 How did the Williams sisters learn to play tennis?
3 What was special about Nadia Comaneci?
4 What do some young gymnasts suffer from?
5 What is 'one hundred times more difficult' for a child?
6 Why do these children not have a real choice?
7 How do some parents benefit from their children's success?

4 Think of famous Olympic® or professional sports stars from your country or region. How old are they? Do you know when they started to compete? Are young children in your country encouraged to start sports training at a young age? If yes, what sports do they usually do?

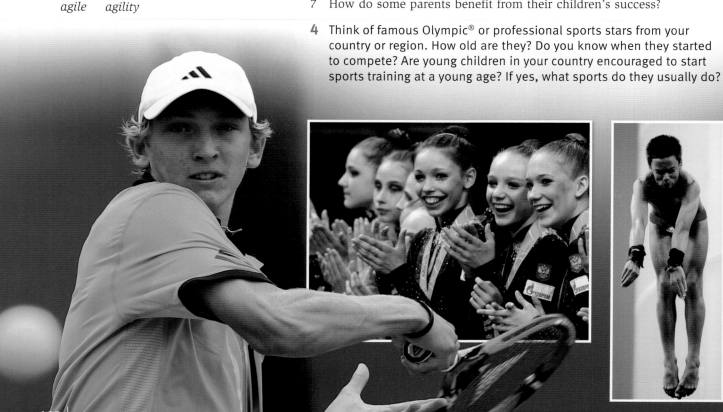

GRAMMAR: verbs with two objects

Some verbs can have two objects: an indirect object and a direct object.

	indirect object	direct object
His parents bought	*him*	*a tennis racquet.*
The judges gave	*Nadia*	*ten points.*

You can also put the direct object immediately after the verb. You need a preposition (*to* or *for*) before the indirect object.

*His parents bought a tennis racquet **for** him.*
*The judges gave ten points **to** Nadia.*

Note that in passive sentences both the direct and indirect objects can become the subject of the sentence.

Active:
Their parents taught them the basics of the game at a very young age.

Passive 1: indirect object as subject
They were taught the basics of the game at a very young age.

Passive 2: direct object as subject
The basics of the game were taught to them at a very young age.

> ➲ SEE LANGUAGE REFERENCE PAGE 114

---

1 Rewrite the sentences by putting the indirect object before the direct object.

1 They gave their daughter some skis for her second birthday.

1 They gave some skis to their daughter for her second birthday.
2 Every day, they showed films about skiing to her.
3 Before bed, they read stories about the mountains to her.
4 They also bought a house in the mountains for her.
5 They found the best ski instructor in the world for her.
6 They promised all sorts of rewards to her.

2 Rearrange the words to make sentences.

1 He was given a lot of support.

1 a   given   he   lot   of   support   was .
2 game   he   of   taught   the   the   was   rules .
3 father's   he   his   medals   shown   was .
4 bought   equipment   expensive   for   him   most   the   was .
5 drugs   given   he   special   was .
6 a   judges   lot   money   of   offered   the   to   was .

3 Work in pairs. Answer the questions for you. Give details about what and who.

When was the last time you …

- bought something for somebody?
- lent something to somebody?
- made something for somebody?
- were given a present?
- were shown some photos?

I bought an mp3 player for my boyfriend.

SPEAKING

1 Work in groups. Discuss these questions.

- Why do so many countries want to host the Olympic® Games?
- Has your country ever hosted the Olympic® Games?
- If yes, when? Which city was the host?

2 Work in groups. Choose a city in your country which you think could host the Olympic® Games. Then make a list of five reasons why it would be an ideal location.

3 Explain to the class which city you think it should be and why.

> **Useful language**
>
> *We believe … is ideally suited because of its …*
> *It would make the ideal host thanks to its …*
> *In addition, it has …*
> *What's more, it can offer …*
> *In conclusion, we are confident that …*

11c | Strange sports

READING

1 Look at the photos A–C and describe what you can see. Then read the emails 1–3 and match them to the photos.

2 Read the emails again and answer the questions.

Which sport, A, B or C, …
1 cannot be played in all countries?
2 has six people in each team?
3 is harder for men than for women?
4 was not fun to watch?
5 requires strength?
6 is accompanied by music?

3 Complete the three words from the emails that mean *strange*.

1 b _ _ _ _ _ _   2 o _ _   3 w _ _ _ _

4 Which of these sports would you like to try or watch? Why or why not?

1

:File Edit View Favourites Tools Help Links ➤

Well, we didn't win! Ryan dropped me when we were running through the water obstacle! It was my fault apparently – he said I was too heavy for him. Now he's insisting on having his neck massaged every few minutes. Any excuse! It was great fun, but some of the other competitors were taking it really seriously. One couple we met said it was their fifth Wife Carrying championships.

We almost didn't make it at all. Our van broke down on the way to Sonkajärvi, so we lost a day while we had it fixed. Anyway, we got here in the end and it's been a good laugh. I'll show you the photos when we get back.

2

:File Edit View Favourites Tools Help Links ➤

I saw a really weird thing this afternoon. I went to the pool for a swim, and there was a 'closed' sign on the door. I thought they were having the place cleaned or something, so I asked, but they told me it was closed for Octopush training. They said I could watch if I wanted. Twelve people in the water, under the water most of the time, with little sticks that they use to push a little round red thing along the bottom. Really bizarre, and not exactly a spectator sport!

3

:File Edit View Favourites Tools Help Links ➤

Hey, have you ever heard of Bossaball? I've just been learning how to play and it's a bit odd, but it's brilliant. It's a kind of volleyball, but you play it on an inflatable court, with a trampoline in the middle. You have to use your hands and feet and even your head, and it's exhausting because you're bouncing up and down all the time. You'd love it! And while you're playing, a DJ plays loud Brazilian samba. They don't have it in England, so it's another reason for coming out here to visit me, OK?

GRAMMAR: causative

Use *have* something *done* to talk about an action that you ask someone else to do for you.
> We **had** the car **fixed**.
> (= We asked or paid for someone to fix the car.)

Note that it is not necessary to say who does the action, as it is usually understood. If you want to say who does the action, use *by* + the person.
> We had the car fixed **by a local garage**.

form	object	past participle
has/have *is/are having* *had* *was/were having* *is/are going to* *have*	*hats,* *them,* etc.	*made,* *delivered,* etc.

> SEE LANGUAGE REFERENCE PAGE 114

1 Find the mistake in five of these sentences and correct them.

1 We had pizzas send to our room.
2 He's having repaired his bike.
3 He has his shorts ironing for him.
4 She's going to have her hair cut very short.
5 They were their house painted last week.
6 She's having her hair dyed.
7 You should have your eyes testing.
8 Why don't you have your shopping delivered?

2 Rewrite the sentences using the words given and the causative.

1 The newsagent delivers the sports press to his house every morning.
He has the _____ every morning.
2 An assistant shaves his head before every match.
He has his _____ before every match.
3 His sponsors make special boots for him.
He has _____ by his sponsors.
4 A top fashion designer designs his clothes.
He has his _____.
5 His accountant looks after his money.
He has _____.

3 Work in pairs. All the sentences in exercise 2 are about one of the people in the box. Who?

a singer   an actor   a football player
a tennis coach   a teacher   a foreign student

4 Choose another person from the box in exercise 3. Write three sentences about him/her using the causative. Ask the class to guess who you are talking about.

She has the board cleaned by a student.

SPEAKING & VOCABULARY: services

1 Complete the questions with the past participles of the verbs in the box.

bring   test   cook   cut
deliver   service   serve   iron

1 Where do you usually …
  a) have your hair _____?
  b) have your car _____?
2 How often do you …
  a) have your eyes _____?
  b) have your meals _____ for you?
  c) have your clothes _____ for you?
3 Would you like to …
  a) have champagne _____ to your bedroom?
  b) have breakfast _____ in bed?
  c) have flowers _____ to your home every day?

2 Work in pairs. Ask and answer the questions in exercise 1.

PRONUNCIATION: /ɪə/ & /eə/

1 2.33 Listen to the pronunciation of these words. Can you think of any other words that contain these sounds?

ear /ɪə/   air /eə/

2 Underline all the words in this text that contain /ɪə/. Circle all the words that contain /eə/.

If you have a moment to spare on Christmas morning, go down to the beach near Brighton town centre where you can see a British sporting tradition. Every year, a group of about 50 people go for a swim in the sea. With a water temperature that is rarely more than seven degrees and an air temperature that is close to zero, most people keep their swim very short. More experienced swimmers stay in the water for nearly 20 minutes. The idea began in 1860 and there are similar events in other parts of the country.

3 2.34 Listen to the recording to check your answers to exercise 2.

11D | Sport relief

SPEAKING

1 Work in small groups. Look at the ideas for ways to raise money for charity and answer the questions.

1 A tennis match between the Wimbledon champion and the president of your country. How much would you pay for a ticket to watch the match?
2 A friend of yours is going to run a marathon and wants people to sponsor her/him. How much money would you give him/her?
3 A lottery. The prize is an evening out with the sports personality of your choice. How much would you spend on tickets in this lottery?

2 Work in groups of three students, A–C. You have three minutes to read some information about a charity.

Then close your books and tell the other people in your group as much as you can remember about your charity.

A: Turn to page 129.
B: Turn to page 131.
C: Turn to page 132.

3 Now imagine that your group works for the national lottery. You have £100,000 that you can give to the sports charities in exercise 2. You can either give all of the money to one charity or divide it between several charities.

Decide as a group what you will do with the money.

4 Tell the rest of the class your decision and explain your reasons.

LISTENING

1 🔘 2.35–2.39 Listen to five short dialogues and say if the sentences are true (T) or false (F). Correct the false sentences.

1 Dan is going to cycle from London to Brighton to raise money for charity.
2 He wants his colleagues to cycle with him.
3 Everybody Dan speaks to agrees to give some money.

2 🔘 2.35–2.39 Listen to the dialogues again. In which dialogue 1–5 does someone …

1 say that they don't have much money at the moment?
2 think that Dan will not complete the ride?
3 give the least amount of money?
4 give 20 pounds?
5 say they have received some good news?
6 say they are extremely busy?
7 say they are unhappy about doing somebody else's work?
8 say they want a cup of tea?

VOCABULARY: *make & do*

1 Find these words and phrases in audioscripts 2.35–2.39 on page 145. Then mark them *make* (M) or *do* (D).

a cup of tea *M*	some work *D*	a donation
the shopping	these accounts	a mess
mistakes	someone a favour	sport

2 Complete the questions with the correct form of *make* or *do*.

1 Who _____ the most mess in your home?
2 Have you ever _____ a donation to charity?
3 How often do you _____ sport?
4 Who usually _____ the accounts in your home?
5 Who was the last person who _____ you a favour?
6 What is the biggest mistake you have ever _____?
7 Who usually _____ the shopping in your home?

3 Work in pairs. Ask and answer the questions in exercise 2.

FUNCTIONAL LANGUAGE: question tags (checking)

Use a question tag after a sentence to check information that you think is true.
  *That was a great film, **wasn't it**?*

Use a negative tag after a positive main verb.
  *It's time to go, **isn't it**?*
Use a positive tag after a negative main verb.
  *You can't speak Japanese, **can you**?*

Make question tags with an auxiliary verb and a pronoun. The voice falls on the tag.

*It's easy, **isn't it**?*
*You're not busy, **are you**?*
*She lives near here, **doesn't she**?*
*We didn't have any homework, **did we**?*

> SEE LANGUAGE REFERENCE PAGE 115

1 Complete the phrases in column A with a question tag from column B.

A		B	
1	You aren't working,	a	aren't you?
2	You can drive,	b	are you?
3	You don't have children,	c	weren't you?
4	You didn't like it,	d	do you?
5	You play tennis,	e	haven't you?
6	You're older than me,	f	did you?
7	You've been to London,	g	don't you?
8	You were a bit tired,	h	can't you?

2 Complete the phrases with an appropriate question tag. Then check your answers in audioscripts 2.35–2.39 on page 145.

1 We can use first names, _____?
2 It's about the photocopying machine again, _____?
3 You're not taking any time off work for this, _____?
4 You said something about that last week, _____?
5 It was just £2, _____?
6 You've got it, _____?
7 She hasn't given much, _____?
8 You'll sponsor me for the cycle ride, _____?

3 Work in pairs. Write six things about your partner that you think are true. Then check the information with your partner. Use question tags.

A: You've got two brothers, haven't you?
B: Yes, I have.

DID YOU KNOW?

1 Work in pairs. Read about the British royal family and discuss the questions.

The British royal family has no real political power. Much of their time is devoted to sport and charity. They hold positions in various sports organizations and they are often asked to present the medals at important events. They also take part in various sports. Horse-riding and polo are traditionally very popular with the royals.

Members of the family are also very involved in work for charity. They work as unpaid patrons of many charitable organizations and help raise money.

• What else do you know about the royal family?
• Is the head of state in your country involved with any sports or charities?

Self-assessment (✓)

☐ I can talk about different ways to raise money for charity.
☐ I can present a group decision and explain the reasons for making it.
☐ I can use question tags to check information.

GRAMMAR
Passive

We use the passive voice ...
- to talk about an action when the agent (the person or thing that does the action) is unknown or unimportant.
  *The captain **was shown** the red card in the second minute of the game.*
- to emphasize what happened rather than who did it.
  *The first World Cup **was held** in Uruguay in 1930.*

If we want to name the agent, we use *by*. We name the agent when it is important or unusual, or because we want to make this information more noticeable.

*The gold medal **was won** by Michael Johnson.*

	active	passive
present simple	They **play** tennis indoors.	Tennis **is played** indoors.
present continuous	They **are holding** the next games in Russia.	The next games **are being held** in Russia.
past simple	They **changed** the rules.	The rules **were changed**.
past continuous	Officials **were showing** them around the city.	They **were being shown** around the city.
present perfect	They've **done** it.	It's **been done**.
future 1 (future plans)	They're going **to cancel** the games.	The games **are going to be cancelled**.
future 2 (*will*)	We'll **finish** it soon.	It'll **be finished** soon.
modal verbs	You **must write** it down.	It **must be written** down.
infinitive	I want you **to help** me.	I want **to be helped**.

Verbs with two objects

Some verbs can have two objects: an indirect object and a direct object.

	indirect object	direct object
She sent	her father	a letter.
	indirect object	direct object
She made	me	a special cake.

With these verbs, we can also put the direct object immediately after the verb. When we do this, we need to use *to* or *for* before the indirect object.

*She sent a letter **to** her father.*
*She made a special cake **for** me.*

Other verbs that can have two objects (and are used with *to*) include: *bring, give, offer, pay, promise, read, send, show, teach, tell, write.*

Other verbs that can have two objects (and are used with *for*) include: *buy, find, get, keep, make, write.*

When we use these verbs in the passive voice, both the direct and indirect objects can become the subject of the sentence.

Active: *They gave him a lot of support.*
Passive 1: ***He** was given a lot of support.*
Passive 2: ***A lot of support** was given to him.*

Causative

We use the causative to talk about an action that you ask someone else to do for you.

*She **has her hair** cut every Friday.*
(= She pays someone to cut her hair.)
*We **had champagne brought** to our room.*
(= We asked room service to bring champagne to our room.)

We do not usually need to say who does the action, because this is usually understood from the context. We use *by* if we want to say who does the action.

*He has his suits made **by** the most expensive tailor in town.*

subject	verb	object	past participle
He/She/They, etc.	has/have is/are having had is/are going to have	the car/ the TV/ it	repaired/ mended/ fixed

FUNCTIONAL LANGUAGE
Questions tags (checking)

We can use tags after a sentence to check information that we think is true.

*Wimbledon is in London, **isn't it?***
*You went there last year, **didn't you?***

We use a negative tag after a positive main verb, and we use a positive tag after a negative main verb.

*You've already given some money, **haven't you?***
*You didn't call me this morning, **did you?***

We use an auxiliary verb in the tag. The auxiliary verb corresponds to the main verb in the opening part of the sentence. We use *do/don't/does/ doesn't* if the main verb is in the present simple. We use *did/didn't* if the main verb is in the past simple.

*I can pay by credit card, **can't I?***
*She isn't waiting for us, **is she?***
*He works with you, **doesn't he?***
*They didn't know, **did they?***

The voice (intonation) falls on the tag to show that we are checking information.

WORD LIST
Sport

amateur *n C/adj* *	/ˈæmətə(r); ˈæmətʃʊə(r)/
athlete *n C* *	/ˈæθliːt/
athletics *n U* *	/æθˈletɪks/
baseball *n U* *	/ˈbeɪsˌbɔːl/
beat *v* ***	/biːt/
boxing *n U*	/ˈbɒksɪŋ/
catch *v* ***	/kætʃ/
champion *n C* ***	/ˈtʃæmpiən/
championship *n C* ***	/ˈtʃæmpiənʃɪp/
coach *n C/v* **	/kəʊtʃ/
competitor *n C*	/kəmˈpetɪtə(r)/
court *n C* ***	/kɔː(r)t/
dive *v* **	/daɪv/
field *n C* ***	/fiːld/
finalist *n C*	/ˈfaɪn(ə)lɪst/
football *n U* ***	/ˈfʊtˌbɔːl/
gym *n C* *	/dʒɪm/
gymnast *n C*	/ˈdʒɪmnæst/

gymnastics *n U*	/dʒɪmˈnæstɪks/
hit *v* ***	/hɪt/
jump *v* ***	/dʒʌmp/
kick *v* ***	/kɪk/
marathon *n C* *	/ˈmærəθ(ə)n/
medal *n C* **	/ˈmed(ə)l/
paraglider *n C*	/ˈpærəˌglaɪdə(r)/
paragliding *n U*	/ˈpærəˌglaɪdɪŋ/
pass *v* ***	/pɑːs/
penalty *n C* ***	/ˈpen(ə)lti/
polo *n U*	/ˈpəʊləʊ/
player *n C* ***	/ˈpleɪə(r)/
race *n C/v* ***	/reɪs/
racket *n C* *	/ˈrækɪt/
rugby *n U* *	/ˈrʌgbi/
run *v* ***	/rʌn/
semi-final *n C* *	/ˌsemiˈfaɪn(ə)l/
serve *v* ***	/sɜː(r)v/
strength *n U* ***	/streŋθ/
throw *v* ***	/θrəʊ/
trampoline *n C*	/ˈtræmpəˌliːn/
triathlon *n U*	/traɪˈæθlən/
volleyball *n U*	/ˈvɒliˌbɔːl/
water polo *n U*	/ˈwɔːtə(r) ˌpəʊləʊ/
wetsuit *n C*	/ˈwetˌsuːt/

Nouns and adjectives (describing people)

agile *adj*	/ˈædʒaɪl/
agility *n U*	/əˈdʒɪləti/
ambitious *adj* **	/æmˈbɪʃəs/
ambition *n C* **	/æmˈbɪʃ(ə)n/
determined *adj* **	/dɪˈtɜː(r)mɪnd/
determination *n U* **	/dɪˌtɜː(r)mɪˈneɪʃ(ə)n/
enthusiastic *adj* **	/ɪnˌθjuːziˈæstɪk/
enthusiasm *n U* **	/ɪnˈθjuːziˌæzəm/
intelligent *adj* **	/ɪnˈtelɪdʒ(ə)nt/
intelligence *n U* **	/ɪnˈtelɪdʒ(ə)ns/
power *n U* ***	/ˈpaʊə(r)/
powerful *adj* ***	/ˈpaʊə(r)f(ə)l/
ruthless *adj*	/ˈruːθləs/
ruthlessness *n U*	/ˈruːθləsnəs/
talent *n C* **	/ˈtælənt/
talented *adj* *	/ˈtæləntɪd/

Make & do

make a cup of tea	/meɪk ə ˈkʌp əv tiː/
a donation	/meɪk ə dəʊˈneɪʃ(ə)n/
a mess	/meɪk ə ˈmes/
a mistake	/meɪk ə mɪˈsteɪk/
do some work	/duː səm ˈwɜː(r)k/
the shopping	/duː ðə ˈʃɒpɪŋ/
the accounts	/duː ði əˈkaʊnts/

someone a favour	/duː ˈsʌmwʌn ə ˌfeɪvə(r)/
some sport	/duː səm ˈspɔː(r)t/

Other words & phrases

acceptance *n U* **	/əkˈseptəns/
achievement *n C* ***	/əˈtʃiːvmənt/
anorexia *n U*	/ˌænəˈreksiə/
bet *v/n C* **	/bet/
bizarre *adj* *	/bɪˈzɑː(r)/
bounce *v*	/baʊns/
casual *adj* **	/ˈkæʒuəl/
charitable *adj* *	/ˈtʃærɪtəb(ə)l/
contribution *n C* ***	/ˌkɒntrɪˈbjuːʃ(ə)n/
cycle *n C* **	/ˈsaɪk(ə)l/
declare *v* ***	/dɪˈkleə(r)/
devote *v* **	/dɪˈvəʊt/
disability *n C* **	/ˌdɪsəˈbɪləti/
discipline *n U/v* ***	/ˈdɪsəplɪn/
donation *n C* **	/dəʊˈneɪʃ(ə)n/
dye *v*	/daɪ/
fed up *adj* *	/ˌfed ˈʌp/
fill in *v*	/ˌfɪl ˈɪn/
foundation *n C* ***	/faʊnˈdeɪʃ(ə)n/
gang *n C* **	/gæŋ/
glory *n U* **	/ˈglɔːri/
host *v* **	/həʊst/
income *n U* ***	/ˈɪnkʌm/
inflatable *adj*	/ɪnˈfleɪtəb(ə)l/
iron *v* *	/ˈaɪə(r)n/
massage *v/n C* *	/ˈmæsɑːʒ/
obstacle *n C* **	/ˈɒbstək(ə)l/
odd *adj* **	/ɒd/
outlook *n C* *	/ˈaʊtˌlʊk/
patron *n C* *	/ˈpeɪtrən/
phenomenon *n C* **	/fəˈnɒmɪnən/
prime-time *adj*	/ˈpraɪmˌtaɪm/
psychological *adj* **	/ˌsaɪkəˈlɒdʒɪk(ə)l/
psychologist *n C* **	/saɪˈkɒlədʒɪst/
relief *n U* ***	/rɪˈliːf/
require *v* ***	/rɪˈkwaɪə(r)/
royal *adj* ***	/ˈrɔɪəl/
sacrifice *n C* *	/ˈsækrɪfaɪs/
shave *v* *	/ʃeɪv/
successive *adj* **	/səkˈsesɪv/
take part *v*	/ˈteɪk ˈpɑː(r)t/
tough *adj* **	/tʌf/
train *v* ***	/treɪn/
trainers *n pl* *	/ˈtreɪnə(r)z/
unpaid *adj*	/ʌnˈpeɪd/
weird *adj* *	/wɪə(r)d/
wheelchair *n C*	/ˈwiːlˌtʃeə(r)/

12A | Basic needs

SPEAKING

1 Work in pairs. Look at the photo below and put these things in order of importance (1 = most important → 7 = least important) for the person.

- ☐ a roof over your head
- ☐ something to eat
- ☐ money in your pocket
- ☐ a steady job
- ☐ friends and family
- ☐ someone to share your life with
- ☐ hope for the future

2 Which of the things in exercise 1 are most important to you?

3 Discuss these questions with your partner.

- Are there many beggars and homeless people in your town?
- Do you ever give them any money? Why or why not?
- Who do you think should be responsible for helping them?

READING

1 Read the first part of the magazine article on this page. How do you think the story ends? Discuss your ideas with a partner.

2 Turn to page 134 and read the second part of the article to see if you were right.

I never thought it would happen to me

Every day on her way to work, Sheila Fletcher, a senior nurse from north London, passed a group of homeless men outside the Underground. She never paid any attention until, one day, she noticed a man who seemed different from the others. 'I don't know why,' said Sheila, 38, 'but I gave him £5. When I gave him the money, he looked so vulnerable, like a little boy.'

Sheila thought about him all day at work and realized that she wanted to see him again. That afternoon, he was there again and he smiled when he saw her. She didn't give him any money, but they talked for a few minutes without saying much. For the next three days, they chatted morning and afternoon and Sheila learnt more about him.

He told Sheila that his name was Akan and he came from Cyprus. He had lost his job in a shoe factory and he had lost his home at that time. He said that his friends didn't want to know him any more and he had been on the streets for eight weeks. He wanted to return to Cyprus, but he thought that he would never have the money.

On the fifth afternoon, Sheila stopped, as usual. 'It was cold and wet,' she says. 'I couldn't leave him in the street. I knew it was crazy to invite a beggar to my home, but I wasn't worried.' At home, they chatted for hours about their families, their lives and their interests. Much later, feeling tired, Sheila told Akan that he could sleep on the sofa, and, before going to her room, she kissed him goodnight.

Suddenly, Akan looked agitated. 'Wait,' he said. 'I have to tell you something. I know it will shock you, but I have to tell you.' With tears rolling down his cheeks, Akan told Sheila that he was a heroin addict. Sheila was angry with herself, thinking she had been stupid to fall in love with an addict. After staying awake all night, she knew that although she loved him, she couldn't let him stay with her.

The next day, Sheila took Akan to a travel agent's and bought him a ticket to Cyprus. She didn't know if she felt happy or sad that he was returning home.

Continued on page 134 …

3 Read the two parts of the magazine article again. Correct the statements about Sheila and Akan.

1 Akan was from London.
2 He had been homeless for years.
3 Sheila gave him money every time she saw him.
4 Akan still had a lot of good friends.
5 Sheila was sad when she found out that Akan was a heroin addict.
6 Sheila thought it was stupid to fall in love with a homeless beggar.
7 Akan waited for a week before phoning Sheila.
8 When she arrived in Cyprus, Akan told her he was going to give up heroin.

4 Work in pairs. Discuss these questions.

● Do you think that Sheila and Akan's relationship will last?
● What kind of problems do you think they will face in the future?

GRAMMAR: reported speech & thought

When we report someone's words or thoughts, the verb forms usually move into the past.

direct speech	reported speech
'My name **is** Akan.'	He said his name **was** Akan.
'I **lost** my job in a shoe factory.'	He said he **had lost** his job in a shoe factory.
'I **will never have** the money.'	He thought he **would never have** the money.
'I **can't** let him stay with me.'	She knew that she **couldn't** let him stay with her.

We also make changes to pronouns and time expressions.
  'I lost **my** home **then**,' said Akan.
  He said *he* had lost **his** home **at that time**.

say and *tell*
Use *tell* + the person you're talking to + reported speech.
  Akan **told Sheila** that he was a heroin addict.
  Not ~~Akan said Sheila that he was a heroin addict~~.
Use *say* + reported speech (do not refer to the person you're talking to).
  He **said** that his friends didn't want to know him.
  Not ~~He said her that his friends didn't want to know him~~.

● SEE LANGUAGE REFERENCE PAGE 124

1 Underline the examples of reported speech and thought in the magazine article.

2 Rewrite the sentences in direct speech or thought. Use these words to help you.

I	me	my	you	your
tomorrow		ago		today

1 'I really miss my family.'

1 He said he really missed his family.
2 She told him she was a nurse.
3 He said he had arrived in London four years before.
4 She told him she couldn't stop thinking about him and his sad story.
5 He said he didn't understand why she wanted to help him.
6 She thought she would book him a flight home the next day.
7 He said his family would be delighted to welcome her to Cyprus.
8 She decided that she was going to fly to Cyprus that day.

3 Report the speech and thought below. Use *told, said, thought* or *decided*. Pay attention to the underlined phrases.

1 She said she really had to get her work done that night.

1 'I'm sorry Sam, I really have to get my work done <u>tonight</u>.'
2 'I can't go out <u>tonight</u>, Bill, I've got some work to do.'
3 'David, I've just typed and printed the report for you.'
4 'I'll never understand why John did that.'
5 'I'm going to tell him what happened first thing <u>tomorrow</u>.'
6 'Jane, I'm really sorry I didn't phone you <u>last night</u>.'

4 Work in pairs. Imagine a situation for each of the sentences in exercise 3. Who is speaking to whom?

5 What was the longest conversation you've had in the last twenty-four hours? Who were you talking to? What did you talk about? Report the conversation to your partner.

I had a conversation with my girlfriend yesterday evening. She said she needed a holiday. I told her I wanted to take some time off, too. We decided to book a week in France.

12B Money

READING & SPEAKING

1 Look at the survey. What is it investigating?

1 people's spending habits
2 how much money people earn
3 people's attitudes to money

2 Answer questions 1–6 in the survey. Then work in pairs and compare your answers.

3 With your partner, complete question 7. Compare your sentence with the rest of the class and choose the best one.

THE MONEY SURVEY

Complete the survey and you could win one of our fabulous prizes.

1 Is money important to you?
- a) Yes, but other things are as important.
- b) Yes, of course. You can't do anything without money.
- c) No, not really, so long as I've got enough to survive.

2 Do you worry about money?
- a) Yes, all the time.
- b) Only at the end of the month.
- c) No, not on the whole.

3 What do you do with your money?
- a) donate it
- b) lend it
- c) enjoy it
- d) save it
- e) invest it
- f) spend it

4 What is your main source of income?
- a) your job
- b) your family
- c) the government
- d) other (please specify)

5 Who or what influences the way you spend your money?
- a) your friends
- b) your family
- c) your bank
- d) information on TV, online or in the papers

6 Which of these prizes would you most like to win?
- a) a holiday for two
- b) a Smart car
- c) £5,000
- d) £1,000 a year for the next ten years

7 In no more than fifteen words, describe your attitude to money*:

_____
_____

*The best answers here may be used as a slogan in an advertising campaign for Western Commercial Bank.

If you want to take part in our prize competition, fill in the information below and send it to us by 30 June.

Name: _____
Address: _____

Age: under 18 ☐   18–25 ☐   25–35 ☐
over 35 ☐

LISTENING

1 🔊 **2.40** Listen to a woman from Western Commercial Bank talking about the results of the survey. Tick the most popular answers for each question on the survey in the Reading section.

2 🔊 **2.40** Listen again and say if the sentences are true (T) or false (F). Correct the false sentences.

1 The people who answered the questions were under eighteen.
2 The survey took place in a café.
3 The woman was surprised by the answers to the second question.
4 A lot of young people give money to charity.
5 Very few young people invest their money.
6 About half of the people in the survey have a job.
7 Most of them share a flat with friends.
8 Newspapers, the internet and the TV influence most people's money decisions.

GRAMMAR: reported questions

To report a *wh-* question …
- move the verb tenses into the past.
- drop the question mark.
- change the word order.
  'What are you saving your money for?'
  He asked me what I was saving my money for.

Note that in *yes/no* questions you also use *if* or *whether* to introduce the question.
  'Do you have a savings account?'
  *She wanted to know **if/whether** I had a savings account.*

Note that you do not need an auxiliary verb (*do/does/did*) to report questions in the present simple or the past simple.
  He asked me whether I saved money regularly.
  Not *He asked me whether I did save money regularly.*

🔘 SEE LANGUAGE REFERENCE PAGE 124

1 Find four examples of reported questions in audioscript 2.40 on pages 145–146.

2 Put the reported questions into direct speech.

1 *'Have you got a job?'*

1 They asked me if I had a job.
2 They wanted to know whether I lived at home.
3 They asked me what I had studied at university.
4 They wanted to know what I was going to do in the holidays.
5 They asked me who my greatest hero was.
6 They asked me if I could speak any other languages.

3 Work in pairs. Choose and discuss eight of these questions.
- Would you like to be a millionaire?
- Do you think money can buy happiness?
- What is your greatest ambition?
- Who do you admire most?
- What makes you feel happy?
- How many bank accounts do you have?
- Are you often in debt?
- Have you ever paid a bill late?
- When did you last read a financial newspaper?
- Do you prefer giving or receiving?
- Have you ever dreamed about money?
- How often do you go on holiday?
- Is it easy for you to save money?

4 Work with a different partner. Tell your new partner about the questions you asked and the answers you received in exercise 3. Use *I asked her/him* …

SPEAKING & VOCABULARY: verb collocations (money)

1 Complete the questions with a verb from the box.

get into	withdraw	write	take out
open	pay	make	buy

1 When was the last time you _____ a bill in cash?
2 How old were you when you _____ your first bank account?
3 Do you prefer to _____ cash from the bank or from a cash machine?
4 How many cheques have you _____ in the last three months?
5 Is it easy for young people to _____ a mortgage these days?
6 Have you considered _____ stocks and shares?
7 What's the quickest way to _____ a million?
8 Do you agree that it's far too easy to _____ debt these days?

2 Work in pairs. Ask and answer the questions in exercise 1.

12c | Sue!

READING

1 Work in pairs. Look at the cartoons A–E. Something is going wrong in each one. What is it?

2 Read the newspaper articles 1–5 below. Match them to the cartoons in exercise 1.

3 Read article 1 again and find words that match these definitions.

1 a person who takes another person to court
2 a financial agreement
3 asking a law court to change its decision
4 taking a person to court to get money from them because they have done something bad to you
5 money that is paid because you have done something bad to another person
6 extreme unhappiness

1 **A grandmother** from Kansas City is suing a Florida theme park because she says that one of the attractions is too frightening. The plaintiff, Mrs Darlene Joel, refused the offer of a small out-of-court settlement. She has asked for $15,000 in damages for the emotional distress she suffered. However, the court is expected to turn down Mrs Joel's claim in the judgment later today. Her lawyers are already planning an appeal.

2 **In March 2003, Mr Merv Grazinski of Oklahoma City bought a new 10-metre Winnebago motor home.** On his first trip, he set the cruise control at 70 mph and went into the back of the vehicle to make himself a cup of coffee. Within minutes, the motor home had crashed. Mr Grazinski was not hurt, but he wanted his money back. In court, he insisted that he was not responsible. He pointed out that the instruction manual did not tell him to stay in the driver's seat when he was using cruise control. The manufacturers denied responsibility and asked the judge to throw out the claim.

3 **At an Elton John concert** in a San Diego stadium, Robert Glaser needed to go to the men's room. However, when he got to the toilet, he was surprised to find a woman using it. When he asked a stadium official to show him to another men's room, he was informed that all the toilets in the stadium were unisex. Too embarrassed to share a toilet with a woman, Glaser had to wait until the end of the concert, four hours later. He complained that he had suffered emotional distress and sued the stadium for $5.4 million.

4 **Cheryl Vandevender, a shop worker in West Virginia, seriously injured her back at work after opening a jar of pickles.** Her doctor told her to take some time off work. Her manager warned her that she would lose her job if she did not return to work within twelve months. Nearly a year later, she returned to the shop and her manager told her to fill up a fridge. After only twenty minutes, her back was injured again. This time, Ms Vandevender decided to sue the company, Sheetz Inc.

5 Veronica Martin and her husband were eating hamburgers from a fast-food chain when a hot pickle fell out of the burger and burnt Veronica's chin. Her lawyers have asked a court in Knoxville, Texas, to award $110,000 in damages for medical bills, loss of earnings and emotional distress. Her husband, Darrin, has claimed that he lost the 'services and companionship' of his wife and is also suing for $15,000. A company spokesman said that all its products were safe.

4 Now read articles 2–5 again. What do you think the judge decided in each case?

5 Match the articles 2–5 to the judges' decisions a–d.

a In order to avoid legal costs, the company reached a secret settlement with the couple, but refused to discuss details or to accept any responsibility.
b The judge, however, agreed with the plaintiff and ordered the company to pay $1.75 million in damages and replace the vehicle.
c But the real emotional distress came later when the judge said the claim was not serious, and the Supreme Court refused to hear an appeal.
d The court decided that the company had acted in an illegal and unfair way towards its employee and ordered it to pay over $2 million in damages.

6 Work in pairs. Discuss these questions.

- Do you think that Mrs Joel (article 1) was right to sue the theme park? Why or why not?
- For what reasons do people sue in your country?
- Can you think of any recent examples?

7 All five of the stories you read in exercise 2 were reported in newspapers in the United States. Later it was discovered that one of the stories was untrue. Which one, do you think? Explain your reasons.

GRAMMAR: *tell* & *ask* with infinitive

You can use *tell/ask* + object + *(not) to* + infinitive to report instructions, orders or requests.

direct speech	reported speech
'Can you show me the men's room?'	He **asked an official to show** him the men's room.
'Don't go back for three weeks.'	Her doctor **told her not to go back** for three weeks.

> SEE LANGUAGE REFERENCE PAGE 124

1 Put the sentences into reported speech.

1 'Can you describe the attraction?' the judge asked her.
2 The instruction manual told drivers: 'Use cruise control for long-distance trips on the freeway.'
3 'Stop wasting the court's time!' the judge told him.
4 'Don't interrupt me when I'm speaking,' she told her son.
5 'Could you give me the name of a good lawyer?' she asked her friend.
6 'Can you call an ambulance?' she asked her husband.

2 Write five sentences about things that your teacher has recently told or asked you to do.

She asked me to do some grammar exercises.
He told me to listen to the news on BBC radio.

VOCABULARY: reporting verbs

1 Match the highlighted verbs in the newspaper articles to the definitions 1–6.

1 gave someone some information
2 continued saying that something was true
3 said that something was not true
4 said that something was true, although you knew that other people may not agree
5 said you were not happy about something
6 told someone that something bad may happen

2 Match the sentences to the reporting verbs in exercise 1.

1 'It's not true that the attractions in our theme park are dangerous.'
2 'Danger! This attraction is not suitable for people with a heart condition.'
3 'Please, Gran. I really, really, really want to try it.'
4 'The park will close in 45 minutes.'
5 'This is the best theme park in the world.'
6 'We had to wait far too long for some of the attractions.'

SPEAKING

1 Work in groups. Read the information below and decide how much money the woman should receive.

A woman went to a fast-food restaurant and bought a cup of coffee. She placed the cup between her knees and as she was taking the lid off the cup of coffee to add cream and sugar, she spilled the coffee, which burned her legs. She decided to sue the company that owned the restaurant and she found a lawyer who agreed to help her.

2 Compare your ideas with other groups and explain your reasons.

Now turn to page 126.

12D | Golden moments

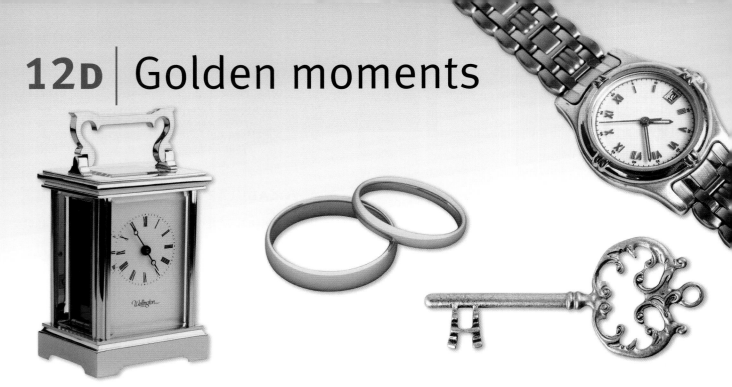

SPEAKING

1 Work in pairs. Discuss these questions.

- Do you know anyone who …

a) has got engaged?
b) has graduated from university?
c) has had their golden (50th) wedding anniversary?
d) has moved to a new home?
e) has retired?
f) has been promoted to a top job?
g) has worked for the same company for 25 years?

- Did these people do anything to celebrate these occasions?
- What would you do to celebrate these occasions?

2 Choose three occasions from the list in exercise 1 that you think are the most important in a person's life.

Now choose an appropriate present for each of these occasions. Explain your reasons.

PRONUNCIATION: intonation (social expressions)

1 🔘 **2.41** Listen to the recording. Who sounds more friendly, the man or the woman?

2 Practise saying the words and phrases in a friendly way.

1	Thank you very much.	5	Take care.
2	Sorry.	6	Have a nice day.
3	See you soon.	7	Excuse me.
4	Well done!	8	Pardon?

FUNCTIONAL LANGUAGE: social expressions

1 Match the comments 1–8 to the best response a–h.

1 Bad news, I'm afraid. I didn't get the job.
2 Excuse me, would you mind taking a photo of us?
3 Good luck for the big day tomorrow.
4 Guess what! We've decided to get married.
5 I'm afraid I can't come out for dinner this evening.
6 Thank you so much. It was really kind of you.
7 We'll really miss you.
8 Well, I must be going. The plane leaves in half an hour.

a Excellent news! Congratulations!
b Not at all. My pleasure.
c Of course. Are you ready? Say 'cheese'.
d Oh well, never mind. Another day, maybe?
e Oh, what a shame. That's really bad luck.
f OK. Have a safe journey and all the best.
g The same to you. I'll keep my fingers crossed.
h We'll miss you, too. Keep in touch, OK?

2 🔘 **2.42** Listen to the recording to check your answers.

3 Choose an appropriate response from exercise 1 for each of these situations.

1 A friend tells you that she has broken her leg, and so she can't come to your party at the weekend.
2 A friend tells you that she has just got engaged to her boyfriend and is going to live at the other end of the country after the wedding.
3 A friend tells you that she has got a very important interview for a new job tomorrow.
4 A friend thanks you for lending her your car last week.
5 An American friend tells you that her mother is ill and that she must return to New York tomorrow.

LISTENING

1 Work in pairs. Discuss these questions.

- When was the last time you announced some important news to your family or friends?
- What was the news?
- How did they react?

2 🔘 **2.43–2.44** Listen to two telephone dialogues. In each dialogue, what are the two important events that are discussed?

3 🔘 **2.43–2.44** Listen to the dialogues again and complete the sentences.

Dialogue 1

1 Karen can't go to dinner at her father's because _____.
2 She has not fixed a date for the 'big day' because _____.
3 She will probably get married in Sweden because _____.
4 She finished the conversation because _____.

Dialogue 2

5 Jeff sent his grandparents a present because _____.
6 He is leaving England because _____.
7 He thanks his grandparents because _____.

4 Look at audioscript 2.43–2.44 on page 146 and find expressions which mean …

1 you were not quick to do that.
2 if everything is the way I want it.
3 there's nothing we can do to change the situation.
4 I'm sure you understand my situation.
5 when do you leave?
6 it wasn't necessary.

5 Work in pairs. You are two old friends. Think of two important pieces of news to tell your partner. Then practise the dialogue.

DID YOU KNOW?

1 Work in pairs. Read about the US Congressional Gold Medal and discuss the questions.

The US Congressional Gold Medal is an award that is given to individuals and institutions to honour special achievements. The first person to receive the medal was George Washington and other winners include Nelson Mandela and Mother Teresa of Calcutta. The medal is also awarded for achievements in the arts (Walt Disney, Frank Sinatra, John Wayne), sport (the runner, Jesse Owens and the boxer, Joe Louis) and the sciences (Thomas Edison).

- Who would you give a Congressional Gold Medal to? Give your reasons.
- Does your country give medals for special achievements?
- Who has won medals and what were their achievements?

Self-assessment (✓)

- ☐ I can talk about important life events.
- ☐ I can give an appropriate response to someone telling me their news.
- ☐ I can use friendly intonation in social situations.

GRAMMAR
Reported speech & thought

We use reported speech to report someone's words or thoughts.
Direct form: *'I'm very tired,' she said.*
Reported form: *She said she was very tired.*
Direct form: *'It's boring,' he thought.*
Reported form: *He thought it was boring.*
We usually change the verb forms into the past in reported speech and thought. However, this is not always necessary.

direct form	reported form
'I work ...'	*She said she worked ...*
'I'm working ...'	*She said she was working ...*
'I've worked ...'	*She said she had worked ...*
'I worked ...'	*She said she had worked ...*
'I was working ...'	*She said she had been working ...*
'I'll work ...'	*She said she would work ...*
'I'm going to work ...'	*She said she was going to work ...*
'I must work ...'	*She said she had to work ...*
'I can work ...'	*She said she could work ...*

When we are reporting, we often need to change pronouns and time expressions.

Direct form: *'I'm going to see my doctor tomorrow.'*
Reported form: *She said she was going to see her doctor the following day.*

Because the time of the reporting may be different from the time of the direct speech or thought, we may need to change the expression to make the meaning clear.

Direct form: *'I'll do it now.'*
Reported form: *She said she'd do it immediately.*

Other time expressions that may change include the following: *now (immediately), today (that day), yesterday (the day before), tomorrow (the following day), this (that), last (the ... before), next (the following ...).*

Two very common verbs for reported speech are *say* and *tell. Say* is followed immediately by the reported speech. We do not refer to the person we were talking to. *Tell* is followed by an object (the person we were speaking to), and then the reported speech.

> *He said (that) he loved her.*
> Not ~~He said her that he loved her~~.
> *He told her (that) he loved her.*
> Not ~~He told that he loved her~~.

Reported questions

When we report questions, we ...
- also move the verb form into the past.
- drop the question mark.
- change the word order.

Direct form: *'What's the time?'*
Reported form: *She asked what the time was.*

In the reported form, we put the subject before the verb, so we do not need to use the auxiliaries *do/does/did* in the present and past tenses.

Direct form: *'Where do you live?'*
Reported form: *She asked me where I lived.*
Not *'~~She asked me where I did live~~.'*

With *yes/no* questions, we use *if* or *whether* to introduce the question.

Direct form: *'Do you read the financial newspapers?'*
Reported form: *He asked me if/whether I read the financial newspapers.*

Tell & *ask* with infinitive

To report instructions, orders or requests, we can use *tell/ask* + object + *(not) to* + infinitive.

Direct form: *'Can you hurry up?'*
Reported form: *She told/asked me to hurry up.*

Direct form: *'Don't be late'.*
Reported form: *I told/asked them not to be late.*

FUNCTIONAL LANGUAGE
Social expressions

All the best.
Another day/time, maybe.
Bad news, I'm afraid.
Congratulations!
Excellent news!
Good luck for …
Guess what?
Have a safe journey.
I must be going.
I'll keep my fingers crossed.
Keep in touch.
My pleasure.
Never mind.
Not at all.
Say 'cheese'.
The same to you.
What a shame.

WORD LIST
Money

bank account *n C* *	/'bæŋk ə‚kaʊnt/
cash machine *n C*	/'kæʃ mə‚ʃiːn/
dependent *adj* ***	/dɪ'pendənt/
earnings *n pl* **	/'ɜː(r)nɪŋz/
financial *adj* ***	/faɪ'nænʃ(ə)l/
financially *adv*	/faɪ'nænʃəli/
get into debt	/‚get ɪntə 'det/
invest *v* ***	/ɪn'vest/
investment *n C* ***	/ɪn'ves(t)mənt/
make money	/‚meɪk 'mʌni/
open an account	/‚əʊpən ən ə'kaʊnt/
pay a bill	/‚peɪ ə 'bɪl/
save *v* ***	/seɪv/
savings account *n C*	/'seɪvɪŋz ə'kaʊnt/
share *n C* ***	/ʃeə(r)/
stock *n C* ***	/stɒk/
take out a mortgage	/‚teɪk aʊt ə 'mɔː(r)gɪdʒ/
withdraw *v* **	/wɪð'drɔː/
write a cheque	/‚raɪt ə 'tʃek/

Reporting verbs

claim ***	/kleɪm/
complain ***	/kəm'pleɪn/
deny ***	/dɪ'naɪ/
inform ***	/ɪn'fɔː(r)m/
insist ***	/ɪn'sɪst/
warn ***	/wɔː(r)n/

Other words & phrases

agenda *n C* **	/ə'dʒendə/
agitated *adj*	/'ædʒɪ‚teɪtɪd/
appeal *n C* ***	/ə'piːl/
astonishing *adj* *	/ə'stɒnɪʃɪŋ/
attract *v* ***	/ə'trækt/
beg *v* **	/beg/
beggar *n C*	/'begə(r)/
bug *n C* *	/bʌg/
campaign *n C* ***	/kæm'peɪn/
cheek *n C* **	/tʃiːk/
chin *n C* **	/tʃɪn/
companionship *n U*	/kəm'pænjənʃɪp/
cruise *v* *	/kruːz/
damages *n pl*	/'dæmɪdʒɪz/
delighted *adj* **	/dɪ'laɪtɪd/
distress *n U* **	/dɪ'stres/
edition *n C* **	/ɪ'dɪʃ(ə)n/
emphasis *n C* ***	/'emfəsɪs/
freeway *n C*	/'friː‚weɪ/
heroin *n U*	/'herəʊɪn/
homeless *adj* *	/'həʊmləs/
honour *v* **	/'ɒnə(r)/
investigate *v* ***	/ɪn'vestɪgeɪt/
lid *n C* **	/lɪd/
limited *adj* ***	/'lɪmɪtɪd/
manual *n C* **	/'mænjʊəl/
manufacturer *n C* ***	/‚mænjʊ'fæktʃərə(r)/
men's room *n C*	/'menz ‚ruːm/
motor home *n C*	/'məʊtə(r) ‚həʊm/
multiplex *n C/adj*	/'mʌltɪ‚pleks/
pickle *n C*	/'pɪk(ə)l/
plaintiff *n C*	/'pleɪntɪf/
predictable *adj* *	/prɪ'dɪktəb(ə)l/
reflect *v* ***	/rɪ'flekt/
report *n C* ***	/rɪ'pɔː(r)t/
responsibility *n C* ***	/rɪ‚spɒnsə'bɪləti/
roll *v* ***	/rəʊl/
settlement *n C* **	/'set(ə)lmənt/
shock *v* **	/ʃɒk/
source *n C* ***	/sɔː(r)s/
specify *v* **	/'spesɪfaɪ/
steady *adj* **	/'stedi/
student union *n C*	/‚stjuːd(ə)nt 'juːnjən/
sue *v* **	/suː; sjuː/
suitable *adj* ***	/'suːtəb(ə)l/
survey *n C/v* ***	/'sɜː(r)veɪ/
tear *n C* **	/teə(r)/
theme park *n C*	/'θiːm ‚pɑː(r)k/
turn down *v*	/'tɜː(r)n ‚daʊn/
unfair *adj* **	/ʌn'feə(r)/
unisex *adj*	/'juːnɪ‚seks/
vast *adj* **	/vɑːst/
vehicle *n C* ***	/'viːɪk(ə)l/
vulnerable *adj* **	/'vʌln(ə)rəb(ə)l/

Communication activities

1A Grammar exercise 3   page 7

Student A

1A Speaking exercise 1   page 7

I come from …	I have …	I'm feeling …
I live in …	I really like …	I always …
I work for …	I am looking for …	

1C Speaking exercise 1   page 11

Grammar exercise 2

1 a) about five million b) about 25 million
   c) about 50 million
2 a) Queen Elizabeth II was born.
   b) The Normans invaded England.
   c) England won the World Cup.
3 a) never, at least not in theory
   b) on the Queen's birthday
   c) when you are at a demonstration
4 a) the Campaign for the Real Europe
   b) the Commission for Racial Equality
   c) the Committee for the Revolution in England
5 a) 100 b) 911 c) 999
6 a) most immigrants from India and Pakistan
   b) some people in Cornwall
   c) some people in London

Grammar exercise 3

1 a) Queen Elizabeth II b) Diana Spencer
   c) Margaret Thatcher
2 a) the Conservatives b) the Labour Party
   c) the Liberal Democrats
3 a) It is a famous nightclub.
   b) It is the headquarters of the Secret Service.
   c) The prime minister lives there.
4 a) People eat chocolate eggs.
   b) People have a day off work.
   c) People watch firework displays.
5 a) 1918 b) 1938 c) 1968
6 a) Henry I b) Henry V c) Henry VIII

2B Vocabulary exercise 5   page 19

Student A

1 Complete the questions with some of the phrasal verbs from page 19.

1 When was the last time you had to solve a difficult problem? What was it? How did you _____ it _____?
2 When was the last time you _____ someone _____ at an airport? Who was it? Where were they going?
3 Have you ever _____ any money in the street? What did you do with it?

2 Discuss the questions with your partner.

12C Speaking exercise 2   page 121

This was not the first time that the company had received complaints about their hot coffee. Company documents showed that they had received at least 700 complaints in the previous ten years. In some of these cases, the company had made a settlement with the plaintiff before the case went to court. In one case (of a woman who suffered similar burns), the company paid $230,000.

How much money should the woman receive? Does this information change your opinion?

Compare your ideas with the ideas of other groups and explain your reasons.

Now turn to page 129.

3D Functional language exercise 7   page 33

Student A

You've only just met. You haven't been to your friend's house before. Your friend is still in the kitchen preparing the food when you arrive. You really enjoy the evening. Your new friend is a great cook and a really interesting person. You'd like to get to know him/her better.

Think of four requests using the verbs in the box.

close	give	have	leave	open	call
pass	put	smoke	take	use	do

If you refuse a request, give a reason.

4D Speaking exercise 1   page 43

Student A

Ask questions to find out the missing information in the text.

Who is the second president?

There are a number of strange coincidences that link American presidents _____ and Kennedy. Both of them have seven _____ in their _____ and Lincoln had a secretary called _____ , while Kennedy's secretary was called Lincoln. Lincoln was _____ in 1860 and Kennedy one hundred years later in 1960, and the next president, in both cases, was called Johnson. Both men were _____ on a Friday, and both times, the men were with their wives. John Wilkes Booth shot Lincoln in a _____ and then ran to a warehouse; Lee Harvey Oswald shot Kennedy from a warehouse and then ran to a _____. Both killers have fifteen letters in their names.

5C Speaking exercise 1   page 51

Student A

> **The boss**
> A party is good for the staff because it is an opportunity for people to get to know each other better. For this reason, you don't mind paying as long as it isn't too expensive. You think that it is important that the staff decide what kind of party they want, but the final decision is yours.

6B Speaking exercise 2   page 59

Group A

> - interested in water sports
> - would like a babysitter a few evenings a week
> - the younger children love anything to do with animals

6A Reading exercise 2   page 56

What kind of holiday person are you?

Mostly As

You are obviously hyper-organized and you like to make sure that you have everything under control months ahead of time. But have you ever thought that maybe you're a bit too organized? Sometimes it can be fun to make decisions at the last minute.

Mostly Bs

You know that planning ahead makes sense, and you like to make sure that the big decisions have been taken in plenty of time. But you still leave some space for flexibility and you are quite happy to change your plans if something better comes along.

Mostly Cs

You love to leave everything till the last minute. You think that way you can make the best of every opportunity that comes your way. But you may be missing out by letting fate and last-minute bargains make your decisions for you. Why not try making your own decision for a change? You may like it!

6A Speaking exercise 1   page 57

Student A

> You're on holiday with a friend, but he/she isn't feeling well and has decided to stay in bed this morning. You'd like to wander around and explore the resort. You also want to do a bit of shopping. It would certainly be more fun with some other people. If your friend isn't feeling better later, you think you'll find out if it's possible to do some water-skiing.

7B Speaking exercise 2   page 69

LIFE CHANGES

You have recently:

★ started work as an early morning newsreader.
★ gone back to college to train to be a nurse.
★ become a ski instructor.
★ opened a beach bar on a tropical island.
★ married a millionaire.
★ signed up at circus school to train to be a clown.
★ been chosen to star in a Hollywood movie alongside a very famous actor/actress.
★ had five children (quintuplets).

7c Reading exercise 4   page 71

Student A

1 Where does Florrie live? How long has she lived there?
2 What preparations have her family and friends made for her party?
3 What did her husband do?
4 How many grandchildren and great-grandchildren has she got?

7c Speaking exercise 1   page 71

Group A

1 How has your town changed in your lifetime? Is it a lot bigger?
2 Have a lot of immigrants moved into your town? If yes, from where?
3 Have a lot of new houses been built? If yes, where and what kind of houses?
4 What other new buildings are there?
5 Have the shops and shopping areas changed?
6 Can you think of any other changes?

7d Listening & functional language exercise 6 page 72

Student A

You have won a holiday for two in Venice. You don't know whether to take your mother or your boyfriend/girlfriend with you. Tell your friend the following facts one by one:
- You have won a holiday for two in Venice.
- You're thinking about taking your mother with you to celebrate her 60th birthday.
- She's been having a hard time recently and she needs a break.
- You know your girlfriend/boyfriend will be jealous.
- It's your second anniversary at the same time, so it would also be nice to use the holiday to celebrate that.

10c Speaking exercise 2   page 101

Group A

The man was staying in a motel with his wife, who was deaf. He went outside to get something from his car, but then forgot which room was his. He hooted loudly on his horn. The other guests opened their doors or looked out of their windows to find out what was happening. However, his wife was deaf so she didn't hear him. She didn't look out of the window or open the door, so he knew which room was his. He was then able to return to his room.

8b Speaking exercise 2   page 79

Student A

New road endangers wildlife says report
A report published today says that the new Arne Valley road will endanger local wildlife. According to the report, the new bridge over the River Arne will destroy an area of outstanding natural beauty. The Arne Valley is home to the Arne orchid and three species of very rare butterflies. The report says that these vulnerable species may disappear completely as a result of the building of the new road. The spokeswoman for the Ministry of Transport was unavailable for comment.

6b Speaking exercise 2   page 59

Group B

- *want somewhere warm and sunny*
- *don't want to be based in a town*
- *love camping*

8a Speaking exercise 1   page 77

Group A

1 A factory is going to close in the north of your country and 800 people are going to lose their jobs.
2 A man has killed a policeman. He says he got the idea after watching a recent violent Hollywood thriller.
3 The fifteen-year-old daughter of an important politician in the government is going to have a baby with her seventeen-year-old boyfriend.
4 The most famous footballer in your country has announced that he is going to retire next year.
5 The police have arrested a well-known pop star after finding drugs and a gun at his house.

11D Speaking exercise 2 page 112

Student A

The **British Wheelchair Sports Foundation** can play an important part in the lives of people with disabilities. For some people, it can help them to build confidence and a positive outlook on life. For others, it can help them to stay healthy and to explore new talents. For everyone, sport can provide a sense of achievement. The British Wheelchair Sports Foundation organizes sports camps and sports events for both adults and children of all ability levels.

1C Speaking exercise 2 page 11

Student B

1   Margaret Thatcher was the first woman prime minister. Diana Spencer was the Princess of Wales, who died in a car crash in Paris in 1997.
2   The colours used by the three main political parties in England are the Conservatives (blue), the Labour party (red) and the Liberal Democrats (yellow/orange).
3   The photo shows No. 10 Downing Street, the official home of the prime minister.
4   Every year, on 5 November, people celebrate Guy Fawkes' Night with large fires and fireworks. It is not a national holiday. Chocolate eggs are a tradition at Easter.
5   Women who were aged 30 or over were first allowed to vote in 1918. Ten years later, in 1928, women had the same rights as men and could vote when they were 21. Eighteen became the voting age for men and women in 1969.
6   King Henry VIII, who was king from 1509–1547, married six times.

6A Speaking exercise 1 page 57

Student B

You're staying in the hotel on business. You have a conference tomorrow, but today is free. You know the resort well. When you have free time, you often hire a speedboat, but it isn't much fun on your own. You also like windsurfing. But, first of all, you need to go to the shops to buy a new battery for your laptop.

11A Grammar exercise 3 page 107

1 Athens   2 three   3 300   4 the United States   5 28
6 1960   7 4.7 billion   8 beach volleyball   9 1920

2B Vocabulary exercise 5 page 19

Student B

1   Complete the questions with some of the phrasal verbs from page 19.

1   What's the best way to help someone _____ a disappointment?
2   Do you ever _____ hitchhikers _____ in your car? Why or why not?
3   When was the last time someone _____ you _____ outside your house? Why were you in their car?

2   Discuss the questions in pairs.

8C Speaking exercise 2 page 80

Student A

Clyde: This is a hold-up. Give me all your money and you'll be OK.
Clerk: _____
Clyde: You heard me. The money. I don't wanna have to use this.
Clerk: _____
Clyde: I am in a bank, right?
Clerk: _____

12C Speaking exercise 2 page 121

The restaurant's coffee was served at 82.2°C, which is more than 10% hotter than some other restaurants. According to one of the company's executives, the company knew that the coffee sometimes caused serious burns. However, the company had decided not to warn customers about the danger and did not plan to change the way it served coffee.

A few days before the case began in court, the judge asked the company and the woman's lawyer to come to a meeting. At the meeting, the judge said that he thought the restaurant should pay $225,000. However, the company continued to deny responsibility, arguing that the woman should not have put the coffee between her legs and claimed that her injuries were more serious because she was old.

How much money should the woman receive? Does this information change your opinion?

Compare your ideas with the ideas of other groups and explain your reasons.

Now turn to page 131.

5C Speaking exercise 1   page 51

Student C

The gossip
You think a party is a great idea. A disco would be nice and you have lots of friends who would like to come. You know some very good clubs in the centre of town and you think that everyone would like them. These clubs are often closed on Monday and Tuesday nights, so the company could rent one. It could be a fantastic night out.

1C Speaking exercise 2   page 11

Student A

1 The population of Scotland is approximately five million. The total population of the United Kingdom is about 60 million.
2 In 1066, the Normans successfully invaded England. Their leader, William the Conqueror, became king. It was the last successful invasion of England.
3 According to the law, the police cannot arrest anybody without a good reason.
4 The CRE is the Commission for Racial Equality, an organization that fights racism.
5 In the UK, you telephone 999 for police, fire or ambulance. You dial 100 for the operator. 911 is the number for the emergency services in the United States.
6 Cornish is spoken by some people in Cornwall, in the south-west of England.

7D Listening & functional language exercise 7   page 72

Student A

You know the following things about your friend:

- Your friend is a really good student.
- Your friend is doing well on his/her course.
- He/She always gets good marks.
- Your friend works too hard, he/she needs to get out more.
- He/She is pretty serious about his/her new boyfriend/girlfriend.

Listen to his/her dilemma and try to help.

10A Speaking exercise 1   page 97

Group A

The self-tying handkerchief
- To do this trick you need a handkerchief with a knot tied in one corner. Put the handkerchief in your right pocket.
- Tell your partner that you're going to tie a knot in a handkerchief using only one hand. Pull the handkerchief out of your pocket with your right hand, keeping the knot hidden in your hand (see picture A).
- Pick up the opposite corner of the handkerchief with your left hand, and put it into your right hand (see picture B).
- Pretend the trick is difficult. (You succeed on the third attempt!) Drop the end of the handkerchief without the knot out of your right hand with a snap. Pick up the other end with your left hand as before and repeat, again letting go of the end without the knot.
- On the third try, let go of the knotted end instead of the expected corner (see picture C) and there you are: a one-handed knot!

4D Speaking exercise 1   page 43

Student B

Ask questions to find out the missing information in the text.

Who is the second president?

There are a number of strange coincidences that link American presidents Lincoln and _____. Both of them have seven letters in their names and Lincoln had a secretary called Kennedy, while Kennedy's _____ was called Lincoln. Lincoln was elected in 1860 and Kennedy one hundred years later in 1960, and the next president, in both cases, was called _____. Both men were assassinated on a Friday, and both times, the men were with their _____. John Wilkes Booth shot Lincoln in a theatre and then ran to a _____; Lee Harvey Oswald shot Kennedy from a _____ and then ran to a theatre. Both killers have fifteen _____ in their _____.

8A Speaking exercise 1   page 77

Group B

1 A photographer from your newspaper has taken nude photos of a famous TV presenter in your country.
2 A top Hollywood film star has separated from his girlfriend after three years together.
3 Medical scientists have developed a powerful new drug for heart disease.
4 The government has announced that they are going to increase the tax on cigarettes by 6%.
5 Thieves have stolen a valuable painting from the home of a famous businessman in your country.

8B Speaking exercise 2   page 79

Student B

Local residents promise to fight new road
Arne Valley police have arrested a man who threw an egg at the Minister for Transport outside the Houses of Parliament today. The man was protesting against plans to build a new road in the Arne Valley. The man, from the village of Arneford, is from one of 24 families in the area who will lose their homes when the road is built. In a statement to the press, the man's solicitor said that this was only the beginning of the protests. 'The road will completely destroy the historic village of Arneford,' he said. 'All the local residents are against the project and have promised to fight the new road.'

3D Functional language exercise 7   page 33

Student B

You've only just met. Your friend hasn't been to your house before. Your friend arrives early. You're still in the kitchen preparing the food when he/she arrives. You don't really enjoy the evening. Your new friend is a bit boring. You haven't really got a lot in common.

Think of four requests using the verbs in the box.

close	give	have	leave	open	call
pass	put	smoke	take	use	do

If you refuse a request, give a reason.

7C Speaking exercise 1   page 71

Group B

1 How have people's lifestyles changed in your country during your lifetime?
2 Do people still do the same kind of jobs?
3 Have any new industries developed? Have any old industries disappeared?
4 Has family life changed?
5 Do people still do the same kinds of things in their free time? Do they spend their money on the same things? Are their hopes and dreams the same?
6 Can you think of any other changes?

9B Speaking exercise 2   page 89

Group A

You represent a youth association. You believe that it is very important to offer teenagers a variety of free time activities. You want to see the shopping area offering much more than just shops and cinemas. It's very important that the centre has good public transport because most teenagers do not have their own car.

12C Speaking exercise 2   page 121

The woman was 79 years old and the burns were extremely serious. She needed to spend seven days in hospital. Apparently, she only decided to sue the company when they refused to pay $800 for her medical bills.

How much money should the woman receive? Does this information change your opinion?

Compare your ideas with the ideas of other groups and explain your reasons.

Now turn to page 133.

7C Reading exercise 4   page 71

Student B

1 Where is Florrie going to celebrate her birthday?
2 When did she get married?
3 How old was she when she finally moved into a nursing home?
4 How many children did she have? Are any of them still alive?

11D Speaking exercise 2   page 112

Student B

FARE is based in one of the poorest parts of Glasgow, where more than 50% of children are living in poverty. The area is controlled by gangs that come together to fight, often in a local sports ground, that is known as the 'killing fields'. Children grow up with fear and violence as part of their lives. FARE organizes a programme of sports (including football, basketball and tennis) that brings these children together, helps them to build new relationships and to break the cycle of violence in this part of the city.

10c Speaking exercise 1   page 101

Group B

The woman worked in a circus and she was the assistant in a knife-throwing trick. The new shoes that she bought had higher heels than her usual pair. When she went to work, she forgot to tell her colleague about her new shoes. She was now four centimetres taller. Unfortunately, the first knife killed her.

8c Speaking exercise 2   page 80

Student B

Clyde: _____

Clerk: I'm sorry, sir?

Clyde: _____

Clerk: But we don't have any money. It's all gone.

Clyde: _____

Clerk: No, sir. We're closed. We've been closed down for six weeks.

5c Speaking exercise 1   page 51

Student D

The lazy worker
You don't really want to go out with people from work on a Friday night or at the weekend – you've got better things to do. But if the company is going to pay for an expensive meal in a restaurant or a good party, you don't mind. In fact, you don't mind organizing everything – booking a place and making other arrangements. It would be a nice change from your usual boring job.

11d Speaking exercise 2   page 112

Student C

SportsAid is a national organization that provides financial help to sportsmen and women between twelve and eighteen years old. These young sports people have already shown a special talent in their sport, but they come from families who do not have enough money to support their children's sporting ambitions. The money will help to pay for training, equipment and for travel to competitions. Without this help, these young people will turn their backs on sport. With help from SportsAid, they will have the chance to become international stars in their chosen sport.

7d Listening & functional language exercise 7   page 72

Student B

You have been invited to meet your new partner's parents. This means going away for the weekend. You really want to go but you have an important exam next week and you should really spend the weekend studying for it. Tell your friend the following facts one by one:
- You've been invited to your partner's parents' house for the weekend next weekend.
- You've got a really important exam next week.
- You haven't done enough studying for the exam – you know you won't pass if you don't study more.
- It's really important to your partner that you go.
- You really don't want to offend him/her or his/her parents.
- It's a four-hour train journey to get there.

6b Speaking exercise 2   page 59

Group C

* good beaches very important
* like to visit markets and buy souvenirs
* want lots of night life

9b Speaking exercise 2   page 89

Group B

You represent an old age pensioners' association. You want to see cheap and easy public transport to the shopping area. This would probably be easier if the shopping centre was near the centre of town. You also want to make sure the centre is easily accessible for wheelchair users. You would also like to see cultural activities that will appeal to older people.

12c Speaking exercise 2   page 121

After seven days of listening to the evidence, the jury decided that the restaurant was responsible. The jury decided that the company should pay $160,000 in compensatory damages and an additional $2.7 million in punitive damages. The trial judge later reduced the amount of punitive damages to $480,000.

Do you think the court's decision was fair?

10A Speaking exercise 1   page 97

Group B

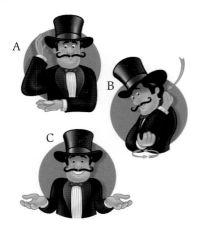

The vanishing coin

- Show your partner a coin in your left hand, then rub it in your right elbow (see picture A). Tell your partner that you are going to make the coin disappear!
- After a few moments drop the coin onto the table and say it usually works better with the right hand. Pick the coin up and pretend to put it into your right hand, but in fact leave it in your left hand.
- Then pretend to rub the coin into your left elbow with your right hand. At the same time, lift your left hand, which is still holding the coin, up behind your ear (see picture B).
- Drop the coin into the back of your shirt collar, and then show that the coin has vanished, and both hands are absolutely empty!

2c Speaking exercise 3   page 20

Uluru – also known as Ayers Rock – is a large sandstone rock formation in central Australia. It stands more than 200 miles south west of the nearest large town, Alice Springs. It is of particular importance to the local Aboriginal people, the Anangu, who believe it is sacred. There are many caves with prehistoric cave paintings which are almost 10,000 years old. The Rock was declared a World Heritage Site in 1987.

9c Reading exercises 2 & 3   page 90

Match the descriptions to three of the stores on the Eezeemall home page.

1 Posters, reviews, memorabilia and of course ... hundreds upon hundreds of films. Take our word for it, there are enough DVDs and screenplays to keep the keenest film buff happy for a long, long time! This month's special star is Clint Eastwood. Check out the special prices on all his films, take a look at some of the scenes that were not included in the movies (outtakes), and there's even a chance for a few lucky customers to win a trip to Almería, the Spanish home of spaghetti Westerns.

2 The first stop for all children, no matter how old. Whether you're looking for that special first toy for a recent arrival or shopping around for an unusual gift for the person who's got everything – you've come to the right place. Not many other shops can offer the incredible range we offer. From bikes and trikes to a ride in a Formula One car. From educational toys to once in a lifetime experiences (check out this month's special offer – a champagne ride in a hot-air balloon), we've got exactly what you're looking for. There's almost too much choice!

3 Flowers, plants, herbs, spices and so much more! Take our advice. Don't waste precious time travelling out to your local garden centre, where there are too many people and too little choice to find exactly what you're looking for. Make all your gardening decisions in the comfort of your own home! And with the expert help of the country's best-known landscape gardeners. Email your queries to the experts, or take a look at a couple of their favourite designs.

7D Listening & functional language exercise 6   page 72

Student B

You know the following things about your friend:

- His/Her mother loves Italy.
- Your friend spends a lot of time with his/her mother and they are very close.
- Your friend's partner is very much in love with him/her, but is sometimes quite jealous.
- Your friend and his/her partner don't spend much time together because they work different hours.

Listen to his/her dilemma and try to help.

12A Reading exercise 2   page 116

A week later, Sheila went with Akan to the airport. 'We kissed goodbye and I thought I would never see him again,' says Sheila. 'But I knew that he was sad to be leaving me, too. He promised that he would phone.'
5 Sheila went back to her work at the hospital and didn't hear from Akan for over two months. Then, one day, the phone rang. Akan explained that he missed Sheila and that he thought about her all the time. He said that he had given up heroin and that he had found a job. He
10 begged her to come and visit him.
Sheila asked her friends for advice and they all thought it was astonishing that she was even thinking of seeing him again. But Sheila couldn't imagine life without him and a few months later, she flew to Cyprus. Akan met
15 her at the airport, and she couldn't believe how much his appearance had changed. He looked tanned and healthy, and had put on weight, so different from the homeless man she had seen outside the Underground station. He told her that she had inspired him to change
20 his life, that he was a new man.
Sheila and Akan were married four weeks later. 'I never thought it would happen to me,' she says. 'But it goes to show that you find true love where you least expect it.'

9B Speaking exercise 2   page 89

Group C

You represent a local parents' association. You think that it is very important that the shopping area offers plenty of facilities for families with young children, including parks, playgrounds and indoor play areas. You would prefer to see the area outside the town, away from traffic and noise.

8B Speaking exercise 2   page 79

Student C

New road will cut journey times by twelve minutes
The government has announced plans for a new road in the west of the country. The new fourteen mile road, which will cross the Arne Valley, will provide a new connection between the A40 and the M5. A spokeswoman for the Department of Transport said that the journey time between the Arne Valley and Birmingham will be reduced by about twelve minutes. The project will cost £67 million and work will start within two years. At a press conference earlier today, the spokeswoman said that the new road will reduce heavy traffic on the A40. 'This is good news for local businesses and local residents. The area has needed decent road connections for a long time,' she said.

6A Speaking exercise 1   page 57

Student C

You're on holiday on your own because you think it's a good way to make new friends. You want to go into town to find out about hiring a car. You have read that there is a very interesting old town about 40 kilometres from your resort, and you would like to visit it. With a car you could also visit the most beautiful beaches which are further along the coast.

1A Grammar exercise 3   page 7

Student B

9A Pronunciation exercise 4   page 86

5C Speaking exercise 1   page 51

Student B

The workaholic
You're not very keen on parties and you hate dancing, but a meal in a restaurant would be a good opportunity to talk to people from other departments. You certainly don't want a late night, because you like to get up early in the morning.

Audioscripts

1B Listening exercises 3 & 5
 1.1

My choice for *Pick of the Week* this week is the BBC2 archive documentary *How Michael Portillo Became a Single Mum*. I think this is one of the best reality TV shows of all time. For those of you who haven't seen it, Michael Portillo volunteers to step into the shoes of working mum, Jenny Miner, for a week, and look after her kids and her house and take over at her two part-time jobs.

He is obviously used to a very different lifestyle. He never cooks or cleans or does the shopping – he pays someone else to do that for him. And he doesn't have any children. Life as a single parent is going to be a real eye-opener for him.

Jenny has four children, the oldest is eleven and the youngest is eight. Every day, Monday to Friday, she drives the kids to school, and then she goes to her two part-time jobs, one as a classroom assistant and one as a supermarket cashier – and she doesn't pay anyone to do her housework for her!

1B Listening exercise 4 & 5
 1.2

I always thought of Portillo as an arrogant and self-important man, but in this programme, Portillo comes across as very different. Very modest, very friendly, very likeable. He had a lot to learn in his week as a single mum. He had problems, and he wasn't afraid to admit it, but he never lost his sense of humour – and he even seemed to be enjoying himself at times.

At one point, Tasha, the eldest of the children, is having a karaoke party for her friends and Portillo is obviously having a good time. Tasha's friends are impressed by him and think he looks like George Clooney! It's one of the high points of his week.

In another clip, Portillo is working behind the cash till at the supermarket. He doesn't pretend to enjoy the work, but he says that the atmosphere is much nicer than in the Houses of Parliament.

His second job, in the primary school, is more difficult and, at the beginning, it looks as if he's bitten off more than he can chew. We see him in the classroom where he is working as a classroom assistant. At one point, he's having problems with some eight-year-olds. He's trying, and failing, to explain a maths problem to them. But he listens patiently to the teacher and by the middle of the week he's doing much better.

His greatest challenge is little Ellie, the youngest child. She's eight years old and very stubborn, and she's going through a very rebellious phase. She flatly refuses to listen to him and you can see that all his lessons in political diplomacy will get him nowhere. In one typical situation, Portillo is trying to persuade Ellie that it's bedtime, but she's being particularly difficult. Although you can see she's really tired and really wants to go to sleep, she's refusing to go.

I think in the end Ellie is my favourite character in the programme – but Portillo definitely came a close second.

1D Listening exercises 2 & 3
 1.3

W1 = woman 1   **W2** = woman 2

W1: So, did she come round?
W2: Who, the new flatmate? Yes, she did, this morning.
W1: And?
W2: And what?
W1: Well, what's she like? Is she going to fit in do you think?
W2: Well ... she's quite a bit older than the rest of us ... she's doing a Master's, I can't remember in what. I think she's about 35, maybe younger. She looks nice enough. She's smiley, chatty, friendly – and quite trendy. She looks like Tan, actually.
W1: Tan?
W2: Yeah, you know, she's got long dark hair and blue eyes, she was wearing make-up and her clothes looked kinda smart, she looked more like a businesswoman than a student.
W1: Mmm ... I'm not sure that's good ... Did she like the flat?
W2: Well ... I think she thought it was OK. I showed her the kitchen, the living room, the bathroom, her bedroom and the bedrooms. I think she likes the bedroom. I mean it's the biggest one, isn't it? I don't think she liked the wallpaper or the furniture though.
W1: Yeah, it does look a bit like an old granny's room.
W2: Yeah, and those horrible pink curtains! But I suppose she can change it, make it look a bit nicer.
W1: So is she going to move in?
W2: I don't know, she said she had to talk to the landlord and she'd let us know tomorrow at the latest.
W1: So, what do you think? Did she look as if she was going to say yes?
W2: Who knows! I guess, yes. She looked as if she was desperate to find somewhere as fast as possible, actually. She said she's living in a guest house at the moment. She said she'd let us know by tomorrow.
W1: OK, then I guess we'll just have to wait and see ...

1D Pronunciation exercise 1
 1.4

the kitchen, the living room, the bathroom, her bedroom and the bedrooms

1D Pronunciation exercise 3
 1.5

1   Monday, Tuesday, Wednesday and Thursday
2   who, what, where, when and why
3   Sue, Nick, Beth, John and me

2B Listening & reading exercises 1, 2 & 4   **1.6–1.8**

1   A Swedish pizza deliveryman has broken the record for the longest solo Vespa journey across Europe. Tommy

Kallstrom, from Stockholm, arrived in Athens last week, after a four-month trip. Tommy visited fifteen countries on the way, including the principalities of Monaco and Liechtenstein. He kept a diary of his trip and, using his laptop computer, posted details and photos of his journey on his personal website. Tommy almost gave it all up when he had mechanical problems with his Vespa during a storm in the Swiss Alps. Fortunately, he was rescued by a farmer in a tractor who picked him up and took him to the nearest town, where he sorted the problem out. He eventually arrived in Athens on July 1st. Just in time to celebrate his 21st birthday! Tommy's website has won this year's Web Travel Site of the Year.

2   On TV later this week, you can see a documentary film of another incredible journey. Italian TV journalist Chiara Colucci and her husband, Luca, a wildlife cameraman, spent six months driving across Siberia in a Land Rover to make the film. They were looking for the rare Siberian tiger, of which only about two hundred still exist in the wild. However, the star of the film is a baby bear cub called Tizio that they came across near the River Amur. Tizio had been injured and the Coluccis took him with them so they could look after him. When Tizio got over his injury, he didn't want to leave the Coluccis, and the three became close friends. It's an extraordinarily beautiful film and you will not be able to stop crying when the Coluccis finally say goodbye to Tizio at the end of their journey in Vladivostok.

3
A: Hey, have you seen this?
B: What?
A: Here, look: 'University students hitchhike for charity'.
B: It's Alex and Isabelle! So what's the story?
A: Well, apparently they were part of a group of students who have hitchhiked from Land's End to John O'Groats to raise money for charity.
B: That's a long way to hitch ... and what charity was it?
A: Let's see ... yeah, a local children's hospital ... yeah, and it seems although ten of them set out together, only four of them actually arrived.
B: What do you mean, only four of them arrived? Did the others get lost or something?
A: No, the thing was they had a time limit; they had to get to John O'Groats in less than two days. See, there's a photo here of their friends and families seeing them off from Land's End last Friday, and it says here that they had to get to John O'Groats by midday on Sunday.
M: And they made it there in time?
F: Yeah, not only that, they broke the record, too ... it only took them ten hours and 20 minutes.

M: Ten hours? What did they do? Hire a helicopter or something?

A: Well, it says here that they were really lucky with their first lift. A van picked them up after only five minutes and took them almost all the way. It dropped them off just 20 minutes' walk from the finishing line.

B: And what happened to the others, then?

A: Looks like they gave up and turned for home.

2B Pronunciation exercise 1
1.9

1 arrived in Athens
2 gave it all up
3 film of another incredible
4 still exist in
5 it's Alex and Isabelle
6 part of a group

2B Pronunciation exercise 3
1.10

1 perform as a clown
2 lie in an office
3 set out on his adventure
4 hitchhike around Ireland

2D Listening exercises 2 & 3
1.11–1.13

1 **D = driver   L = Linda**

L: Hi. Does this bus go to the town centre?
D: Sorry, what was that?
L: Are you going into the centre?
D: Yeah, we go there.
L: Er, a single to the town centre, please.
D: That'll be one twenty, please.
L: Er, yeah. Er, sorry, have you got change for a ten-pound note?
D: No, sorry. Exact change only.
L: OK, just a second … erm … I don't think I've got it … oh yes, I have … .
D: Here you are.
L: Erm, I'm going to Bridge Street. Could you tell me when we get to the bridge, please?
D: Yup. I'll let you know.
L: Thanks.

2 **A = male 1   B = male 2**

A: How are you getting home? Have you got your car?
B: No, I didn't bring it … I'm going to get a cab. You live my way. Do you want to share one?
A: Well, OK, thanks, why not … I was going to get the bus, but, why not, if we're sharing …
B: Hello? Yes, I'd like a cab for the Pizzeria Roma, please. On West Road. Yes, on West Road. Er, as soon as possible, please. Five minutes? Perfect. Yes, the name is Harding. Yes, thanks, bye.

3 **SA = Station Announcer
   C = Camilla   I = Information Clerk**

SA: Platform 14 for the 11.45 train to Brownsville. Platform 14 for the 11.45 train to Brownsville.
C: Excuse me, has the 11.40 for North Park left yet?
I: Not if you hurry, it's still at the platform, platform 10. It's running a bit late, you

might catch it if you run … oh, no, that's it pulling out now.
C: Rats! Can you tell me the time of the next train to North Park?
I: The next one's at 2.35, madam.
C: 2.35! Oh no. I'm going to be so late. Can I get a taxi anywhere round here?
I: Yes, madam. There's a taxi rank at the front of the station. But you'll probably have a bit of a wait at this time of day.
C: Thanks, thanks.

3A Reading exercises 4 & 5
1.14–1.18

1 Disadvantages? I can't think of any, really. Maybe the monthly meetings that you have to go to. Some people never stop talking, and you have to sit there listening to people for hours. Er, I can't really think of anything else.

2 We're very happy here, but sometimes, yeah, I guess sometimes, it feels very small. I mean, everybody knows everything about everybody else. Sometimes it gets a bit too much.

3 We all have to help with repairs and things like that, but some folks do a lot more than others. The work isn't always divided very fairly. You know, it seems some families don't have to do as much as other families.

4 Every now and then, someone cooks a really horrible meal. You can't say anything. Well, you can, but nobody ever does. We all sit there and eat it and smile.

5 I think that most of us agree that one or two of the children are a problem. You know, just difficult kids, but their parents never do anything about them. They're allowed to do anything. But it's no big deal.

3B Listening exercises 2 & 3
1.19–1.21

1
A: The best thing? The sense of freedom, I guess. The fact that we can decide to go where we want when we want … if we get bored, we go somewhere new.
B: And the worst?
A: When the police or the local authorities make us move on. I mean, when we find somewhere where we want to stop, and we set up camp and make everything really nice and comfortable and then the police or the farmer or the local people don't let us stay. That happens quite often.
B: Do you have a favourite place to stop?
A: Yes, we've got two or three places we go back to every year, where we've got friends, where the farmers are happy to let us stay on their land. We usually go to pick fruit or do other odd jobs … .

2
A: The best thing? The views – no doubt about that. They're spectacular. And I love getting up to the sound of the sea. I particularly love the sea in winter, when the waves are enormous, and come crashing down on the rocks around

the house. What other job lets you live somewhere so dramatic?
B: It certainly is dramatic, but doesn't it get a bit lonely out here sometimes?
A: Yes, that's the worst thing, it can get quite lonely. I usually spend three weeks here on the island and then I have three weeks off while my partner takes over. I love going home to see my friends and family. I miss them a lot! They don't allow us to have visitors, but the job keeps me pretty busy. And they let us keep pets. I've got three dogs, they keep me company!

3
A: Do you live here all year round?
B: No! It's a holiday home really. We usually spend a month or so here in the summer.
A: Isn't it a bit dangerous living halfway up a tree?
B: Obviously the biggest drawback of living in a tree is the danger of falling off! To start with, we were quite worried about it, especially when visitors came to stay … but nothing's happened yet. We don't let little kids come up on their own and we make dog owners leave their pets in the garden! And the other problem, of course, is fires … that really does worry us … so we don't allow any smoking.
A: It looks pretty small, too. Why on earth did you choose this as a holiday home?
B: Well, we wanted something different, but what we really like most of all is the idea … the feeling of, you know, of being part of nature. Hearing the birds, seeing all the animals …

3D Listening exercises 2 & 3
1.22–1.25

1 **W = woman,   M = man**

W: Hello. Come in, come in … .
M: Thanks … erm … these … are for you.
W: Oh, flowers … thank you, you shouldn't have. They're lovely! Come into the kitchen, I'm just finishing something …

2
M: Can I help with anything?
W: Oh, yes, please can you put these flowers in some water for me? Thanks.
M: No problem.
W: Can I get you something to drink? Some fresh lemonade maybe, I made some earlier this morning.
M: Erm … yes, yes thank you. That sounds great – just what I need, it's so hot today! Is it OK if I go out into the garden?
W: Sure thing, be my guest. I thought we'd eat out there, actually. The table needs laying, could you take these plates out for me?
M: Do you want me to take the glasses and the lemonade, too?
W: Yeah, thanks.

3
W: Are you alright sitting in the sun?
M: Yeah … it is hot though! Would you mind if I moved the sunshade a little?
W: Feel free, do you need any help?
M: No, thanks, I think I can do it. There … that's better – wow, this is great, I love your flat, and this garden, it's just perfect.

W: Thank you, yes, I was really pleased when I found it ... Would you mind passing the salad? Thanks!

M: How long have you been here?

W: Well, I moved in ...

4

M: Thank you so much ... that was great ... hey, do you fancy going to the cinema later? That new Italian film's on ... you know the one.

W: I'd love to, thing is, I've got to do some work. Do you think I could do that first?

M: Yes, that's fine, do whatever you need to do.

W: It'll only take me an hour or so. I mean, do you mind waiting?

M: No worries, that's fine, could I wait here ... ?

W: Of course! Make yourself at home! And help yourself to whatever you want ... Oh yes, do you think you could clear the table? Thanks!

M: Sure thing, and I'll do the dishes.

3D Functional language exercise 3
1.26

A = woman,   B = man

1

A: I've got to do some work. Do you think I could do that first?

B: Yes.

2

A: Is it OK if I go out into the garden?

B: Yes.

3

A: Do you mind waiting? It'll only take me an hour or so.

B: No.

4

A: Would you mind if I moved the sunshade a little?

B: No.

3D Functional language exercise 4
1.27

A = woman,   B = man

1

A: I've got to do some work. Do you think I could do that first?

B: That's fine, do whatever you need to do.

2

A: Is it OK if I go out into the garden?

B: Sure thing, be my guest. I thought we'd eat out there, actually.

3

A: Do you mind waiting? It'll only take me an hour or so.

B: No worries, that's fine. Could I wait out here?

4

A: Would you mind sharing if I moved the sunshade a little?

B: Feel free, do you need any help?

3D Functional language exercise 5
1.28

Could you take these plates out for me, please?

4A Pronunciation exercise 1
1.29

A: Was that man standing under the tree again?

B: Yes, he was. He was with a friend this time.

A: What do you think they were doing?

B: I asked them. They said they were waiting for a bird.

A: A bird! I find that hard to believe.

B: They were! They said it was a lucky bird.

A: I knew he was a bit crazy!

4B Listening exercises 3 & 5
1.30

Part 1 There's a great story in the news today about a 74-year-old retired teacher, Frane Selak. The headlines are calling him the luckiest man in the world – and it may well be true. Many of us buy our weekly lottery tickets and never win anything, but Selak recently won more than $1 million with the first lottery ticket he had bought in forty years. With the money, he bought a new house, a car, a speedboat and married his girlfriend.

4B Listening exercises 4 & 5
1.31

Part 2 But that's not the only reason why Selak is thanking his lucky stars. He is also lucky to be alive. A few years ago, he was driving his car in the mountains, when he saw a truck coming straight towards him. His car crashed off the road through the forest for a hundred metres, ploughed into a tree and exploded. Fortunately, Selak had jumped out. But this was not the first of his lucky escapes. In fact, Selak has become the master of lucky escapes. Back in 1962, he was travelling from Sarajevo to Dubrovnik when the train came off the rails and fell into an icy river. Rescue workers found seventeen corpses in the water, but Selak had swum to safety, suffering only shock, bruises and a broken arm. A year later, he was involved in a plane crash in which nineteen people died. But before the crash, Selak had jumped out of the plane and fallen in a haystack. Again, the only injuries were cuts and scratches and the usual shock. His next disaster was a bus accident when four people died. The bus left the road and Selak again found himself in a river. But he was becoming something of an expert at this sort of situation and again swam to safety. By this time, said Selak, his friends had stopped visiting him. A few years later, he suffered burns – and lost a lot of his hair – when his car caught fire at a petrol station. The petrol pump was old and had sprayed petrol all over the hot engine of his car. Then, in 1995, he was in hospital again. Another bus had knocked him over. And what does Selak think of all this good luck? He's just glad that he's been able to live long enough to enjoy his million-dollar lottery win.

4B Grammar exercise 2   1.32

Lucky Luciano was one of America's most famous gangsters and, for a time, he was even more powerful than Al Capone. He got his name when he was a young man because he had been so successful at choosing horses at the horse races. People recognized him immediately because he could not control one of his eyes. In 1929, rival gangsters had kidnapped him and cut his face with a knife. His eye never recovered. In the 1930s, Luciano became famous. He had made so much money that he could go anywhere and do anything. People were frightened of him, but everyone wanted to be his friend. Not surprising when you think that he had been responsible for the murders of about 500 people. In 1940, the Americans joined the Second World War, but Luciano did not have to fight. The police had arrested him four years earlier and he was in prison. He stayed there for ten years. Then, in 1946, he was put on a boat for Italy. The Governor of New York had given him his freedom – on condition that he left the country. Luciano stayed in Italy until he died in 1962.

4D Listening exercises 1 & 2
1.33

C = Clive   L = Linda

C: There you go.

L: Thank you – that should keep me busy for the rest of the afternoon! Hey Clive, were you at that new White Rose leisure club last night?

C: Yeah, why? Were you there too?

L: I thought it was you – you were in the car park, I shouted and waved and sounded the horn, but you didn't see me.

C: Really? Sorry about that.

L: So what do you think of it?

C: The White Rose? Not bad, the gym's pretty good. Pretty expensive but it's worth it. I mean, you have to keep fit, don't you? Are you a member?

L: Yeah, I joined last week. I signed up for the free squash lessons.

C: Really? You didn't! Me, too. Bit of a coincidence that, innit? Have you had your first lesson yet?

L: No, not yet.

C: No, me neither – not yet. I'm going tomorrow.

L: Really, so am I! At half seven.

C: Me, too!

L: With Jeff?

C: Yeah, that's right.

L: Do you think we'll be in the same class, then? I thought it was women only. We'll be in the same class.

C: No, no, it's all mixed. Anyway, so ... Amazing! What a coincidence! So how did you find out about the club, it's a bit out of your way, innit? Don't you live the other side of town?

L: We did, but we moved last week. We live just round the corner now.

C: Yeah? So do we. Me and my wife I mean. Whereabouts?

L: Harlech Crescent.

C: You're kidding! You live in Harlech Crescent!

L: Yes, why?

C: Well, so do we. We do, too. I mean, we live there, too. What number?

L: 48. Why?

C: Number 65, us. We live in 65.

L: Mm. No way! Small world. I didn't know we were neighbours!

C: Neither did I!

L: Hey, we'll have to get together some time. So you must be a regular at the Robin Hood?

C: That's right – it's my local. Not a bad pub, is it?

L: No, it's really nice. We've had a bit of a look around and it's definitely the best pub in the area.

C: So we'll be seeing you there then? Do you like pub quizzes?

L: Yes, from time to time – and Mark absolutely loves them. He went to the one last Monday.

C: Did he? Me, too. Me and some mates, we go every week. Who was he playing with?

L: I've no idea, I didn't go.

C: Neither did my wife – she wanted to see the film on TV.

L: *Titanic*?

C: Yes, that's it. You, too?

L: Yeah, me, too! It's a great film.

C: Listen, you'll have to ... Why don't you come round one evening? Maybe we can get a takeaway in and a video. What do you reckon? Do you like Chinese?

L: Yeah, I love it. That place on the green is pretty good, isn't it? We had a meal from there last night.

C: You're not going to believe it, but so did we! We always do on Wednesdays.

L: Well, we'll have to do it together next time.

C: OK, I'll mention it to Joan, she'll love the idea. Right, got to go ... no rest for the wicked and all that. See you around then ... neighbour ...

5B Listening exercises 3 & 4
 1.34

J = Jones   S = Salesperson

J: Jones here,

S: Good morning, Mr Jones. My name's Michael Everest and I'm calling from Spark Financial Services. I'm sure you're a busy man, but I wonder if I could have a few minutes of your time, if it isn't too inconvenient ...

J: Er, well I'm quite busy at the moment act ...

S: We're doing a market research survey to find out more about people's credit card habits and I have a few questions that we would like to ask you. It'll only take a few minutes.

J: Er, well, OK; so long as it doesn't take too long.

S: Of course, if this is inconvenient, I could always call you back later.

J: Um, er ...

S: That's very kind of you, Mr Jones. I appreciate your time.

J: Er ...

S: Well, could I ask you first if you have heard of the new Spark Gold Card?

J: Er, no ... I'm not really interested in a new credit card ...

S: Ah well, if I may give you just a little bit of information, I'm sure you'll be as excited about the new Spark Card as we are. You may, for example, be interested to know that the interest rates with the new Spark Gold Card are not as high as most other cards. In fact, right now with the Spark Gold Card, the interest rate is an amazing three point seven per cent.

J: That sounds quite good actually ...

S: What's more, if you transfer your balance from your other cards, as a new customer, we will give you nine months' free credit. That's nine months with no interest charges at all.

J: No interest charges?

S: No, none at all. Our market research shows us, too, that many people are dissatisfied with the credit limits on their cards. May I ask you if you sometimes find your credit limit is insufficient for your needs?

J: Er ... well, no, not really ... I'm quite happy with my card at the moment ...

S: But we will take the credit limit on your existing card and double it. The maximum credit limit is twenty thousand pounds – much higher than most other card companies.

J: Oh, right, er ... but I don't think I really need ...

S: I wonder if there are any other reasons why you are unhappy with your present card. Did you know that the new Spark Gold Card also offers you reward points? For every £100 you spend with your card, we will give you five reward points. Isn't that just unbelievable?

J: Er, yeah, sounds good, I suppose. But it's very similar to what I've got already.

S: That's impossible! There are no other credit cards out there that can compete with the Spark Gold Card! Do you think you might be interested in having a new Spark Gold card? Are you sure I can't persuade you to try it out?

J: Er, well, no, not really ... thanks.

S: But this offer is only available until the end of the month.

J: No, thanks a lot, but I'm just not interested. Goodbye

S: Well, maybe I could just take down a few details. It's Mr T Jones, is that correct?

J: Yes, that's right. T for Thomas. Tom Jones. The same as the singer.

S: You're a singer?

J: No, no, I said my name is the same as the singer. You know, er, Tom Jones.

S: Ah yeah, of course. And what do you do for a living, Mr Jones?

J: I'm, er, between jobs.

S: Between jobs?

J: Yes, you know, er, unemployed. That's not a problem, is it?

S: Er, no, no. Could you tell me which card you're using at the present time?

J: Oh, I haven't got one at the moment. But your Spark Card sounds exactly what I need. Could you perhaps send me two or three? Or four maybe? With different names on them?

S: I'm afraid that's impossible, sir, you can't hold a card in a different name.

J: Well, you don't need to tell anyone, do you? It could be our little secret.

S: I'm sorry, sir, but ...

J: No, listen, you send me a pile of credit cards, all with different names – not with my name, of course, but names that are similar to mine. I'll take out lots of cash with them, right up to the credit limit. And then we divide the money between us. It's as easy as that. What do you say? Hello, anyone there? Hah! That got rid of him!

5B Pronunciation exercise 1
 1.35

Whizzo is the most popular washing powder in Scotland!

5B Pronunciation exercise 2
 1.36

/s/ bus; certain; class; course; person; send
/z/ amazing; easy; raise; thousand; times; using
/ʃ/ cash; efficient; mention; shop; sure; wash

5B Pronunciation exercise 3
 1.37

business, citizen, commercials, delicious, insufficient, salesman, surprise, stylish

5D Listening exercises 1 & 2
 1.38

P = Pippa   D = Dave

P: Hello? Good morning.

D: I'd like to place an order, please.

P: Yes, sir. Can I take your name, please?

D: Er, yes, it's Dave. I'm calling from the IT department.

P: Could I have your surname as well, please?

D: My surname? Yes, sure, but you won't need it. I'm the only Dave around here.

P: Sorry, but that's what it says on the form and the computer won't process it if any of the boxes are left blank.

D: Really? Must be a new procedure.

P: Yes, something to do with cutbacks I think.

D: Oh, right, yes, well, that would explain it.

P: So?

D: Oh, yes, er, sorry, it's Blackman.

P: Blackman? Can you spell that please?

D: Yes, of course. B-L-A-C-K-M-A-N.

P: Thank you. And can you tell me your department code, please?

D I'll see if I can find it. Can you hold on a sec?

P: Yeah, sure.

D: Oh, yes, here it is. IT-007.

P: Thanks.

D: I just wanted six packs of paper for the printer and er, a couple of ink cartridges, colour.

P: Two colour cartridges.

D: Er yeah, that's it. The KS7.

P: Oh. I'm really sorry, but you can't order more than one colour cartridge at a time.

D: You're joking! OK, it'll have to be one then, and I'll just place another order tomorrow.

P: And the paper?

D: Er, yeah, six packs of laser paper, please.

P: I'm really sorry, but we haven't got any laser paper. We've only got the ordinary paper.

D: I'll er, just get some photocopying paper instead, then, thanks. Two packs of A4.

P: OK, so, a KS7 ink cartridge and two packs of white A4 paper. Anything else?

D: No, no, that's it thanks.

P: You're welcome. Bye.

5 D Functional language exercise 3

1.39

1
A: Can I ask who's calling, please?
B: Yes, the name's Bond. James Bond.

2
A: Can I leave a message, please?
B: Yes, of course. I'll just get a pen and some paper.

3
A: Could you tell him I called, please?
B: Yes, I'll tell him as soon as he gets back.

4
A: Could you give her a message, please?
B: Yes, but I don't think she'll be in the office until tomorrow morning.

5
A: Can I call you back later?
B: Yes, OK. In about half an hour. Is that OK.

6
A: Could you speak up, please?
B: Yes, I'm sorry. It's a bad line, I think.

6 B Listening exercises 2, 3 & 4
1.40–1.45

1 R = reporter   T = Tourist
R: Hello, can I ask you a quick question?
T1: Yeah, sure, go ahead.
R: Are you off on holiday?
T1: Yup, certainly am ... at last!
R: What are you most looking forward to?
T1: Oh, the windsurfing, definitely. I mean that's what everybody goes for, isn't it? We're planning to surf all day, every day. I mean, we're only going for a week and we have to make the most of what the Canaries have got to offer.
R: Sounds like you're going to need a holiday to get over your holiday – you're going to be exhausted with all that windsurfing.
T1: Yeah, probably! But we'll have plenty of time to catch up on our sleep when we get back home.

2
R: Hello, are you off on holiday today?
T2: Yeah, we are, well sort of ...
R: Do you mind if I ask you a quick question?
T2: Er, no, no, not at all.
R: What are you most looking forward to?
T2: Well, you see, we're off on our honeymoon ...
R: Congratulations!
T2: Thanks ... yeah, so I reckon what I'm most looking forward to is the romantic walks along the beaches. They say that Mauritius has got some of the most beautiful beaches in the world. And during the two weeks we're there we're planning to visit every one!
R: Well, I hope you have a great time.
T2: Thanks a lot, I'm sure we will!

3
R: And you, sir, what are you most looking forward to?
T3: The people-watching, I think.
R: The people-watching?

T3: Yes, you know, sitting in a street cafe watching the world go by.
R: Ah?
T3: Yeah, love it. And the women! You can't beat Italian women. Stunning. Gorgeous. Absolute knockout. And what better place to see them than in the capital?
R: Is that all you're planning to do during your holiday?
T3: More or less – unless I get lucky ... and a bit of sightseeing, too, of course: the Coliseum, the Vatican, that kind of thing. But I'm only going for the weekend, so there won't be much time to do anything else.

4
R: Can I ask you what you're most looking forward to on your holiday?
T4: Er ... I don't know really ... We've never been to Madrid before, so lots of things ... the city, the people, the sights, ... oh yeah, I do know what I'm looking forward to most – the football.
R: The football?
T4: Yeah, we've got tickets for the match on Sunday and that's definitely going to be the highlight of the four days.
R: And who are you travelling with?
T4: My mother ...
R: Your mother? And is she looking forward to the football, too?
T4: Yes, definitely ... she's more of a fan than I am! She really likes their goalkeeper.

5
R: And where are you off to, sir? Madam?
T5: We're off to New York.
R: On holiday or on business?
T5: Holiday.
R: What are you most looking forward to?
T5: The shopping! We've been to New York quite a few times, so we've done the sights. We go for the shopping. Best place for shopping in the world.
R: Are you looking for anything in particular?
T5: Well, the first thing we're going to buy is two large suitcases. To put everything else in that we buy.
R: That sounds like serious shopping!
T5: Yeah, definitely. We've got about er, £5,000 between us.
R: And you're going to ...
T5: Yes, we're going to spend all of it over the weekend. Every single penny.
R: On anything in particular? Apart from the suitcases, of course.
T5: No, no. Whatever bargains we find, you know, electronic equipment, clothes, cowboys boots ...
R: Well, happy shopping!
T5: Thanks!

6
R: And what are you most looking forward to on your holiday?
T6: Well, we're not actually going on holiday. We're going to visit my husband's parents in Melbourne for ten days.
R: Australia? That's a long way to go for ten days ...
T6: Yes, it is, but we're going over to break some good news to the family ...
R: Oh, yes ... ?

T6: Yes, we're going to be parents. I'm expecting a baby in June.
R: Congratulations! And you haven't told them yet?
T6: No, we haven't. We wanted to break the news in person.
R: So that's obviously what you're most looking forward to ...
T6: Yes, that, and the weather. It's summer over there and it looks like it's going to be cold and wet here.
R: It certainly does! Well, enjoy your trip and congratulations again on the good news!
T6: Thanks.

6 B Grammar exercise 2
1.46–1.47

1 G1 = Girl 1   G2 = Girl 2
G1: Have you seen that bloke over there?
G2: The one sitting at the table?
G1: Yeah, not bad looking, is he?
G2: Yeah, and he's looking over.
G1: Do you think he's going to come over?
G2: No, he looks too shy ... pity ... .
G1: Yeah, real pity ... .
G2: You're not going to go over and talk to him!
G1: Yeah, why not, let's give it a try ...

2 B = Boy   G = Girl
B: So, what do you think? Which one do you like?
G: Well, I like that one, but it looks really expensive.
B: Well, it's a special occasion; I don't think expense counts ...
G: No, I suppose not. OK, that one, then. He'll love it!
B: Yeah, I think your dad's going to be really happy with his 60th birthday present.

6 D Listening exercises 1, 2 & 4
1.48

J = June   A = Avril
J: Good morning. T&A travel, how can I help you?
A: Hello, June, it's Avril here.
J: Avril! How are you? How was your weekend away?
A: Well, you know what the weather was like. Absolutely horrible. Awful. But the hotel was superb, and it was good for both of us to get away from that dreadful new woman at work. We had a lovely time, actually.
J: So, you're planning another bargain break weekend away?
A: No, wish I was. No, I'm making some enquiries for Derek my boss, actually.
J: Ah-ha. Derek, eh? What, is he off on a business trip or something?
A: Yes, something like that ...
J: So where's he going this time?
A: Japan. But you mustn't tell anyone.
J: Japan? That's a long way to go for a business meeting. When's he going?
A: Well, he doesn't know yet ... it's all very up in the air. No, he'd just like to know how much it costs for the moment. He isn't going for a business meeting actually, his son's getting married out there.
J: Really? When?

A: Next month.

J: OK. Do you know if he wants to go direct?

A: I think he's more interested in the cost, actually, at the moment. Do you think you could tell me what the cheapest options are? And then maybe we can look at the direct flights and compare costs.

J: OK. So, let's see. Do you know where he wants to fly to?

A: Yes, Tokyo.

J: OK, so leaving from London, arriving Tokyo. Let's see what we've got. OK, I've got a Finnair flight here for £650 return. There's a stop off at Helsinki.

A: Can you tell me how long that takes?

J: Yes, just a minute, here we are. As I said, it's via Helsinki and it takes … er … just over fourteen hours, fourteen hours and fifteen minutes to be precise.

A: Well, that doesn't sound too bad. What about direct flights, can you find out how much a direct flight costs?

J: Right, hold on a sec, here we are, there's a Japan Airlines flight at £884.80 – that takes eleven hours and 45 minutes.

A: Mmm … it's a big difference in price for a relatively small difference in time.

J: Hold on, there's another one coming up on the screen now … a Virgin Atlantic direct flight at £750 … Does that sound OK?

A: Maybe. Could you tell me how long it takes?

J: Well, the flight time's more or less the same, a little bit longer – twelve hours.

A: OK, so let me just check I've got that right. Finnair at £650 via Helsinki and Virgin Atlantic direct at £750. Can you tell me how long those two flights take again, please? Sorry, I forgot to write it down!

J: Yes, of course, fourteen hours fifteen minutes for the Finnair flight and twelve hours for the Virgin Atlantic direct.

A: OK, great, got that, thanks.

J: No problem.

A: Listen, I have to go now, see you over the weekend sometime?

J: Yeah, I'll give you a call. Bye.

A: Bye, but how about coming over for dinner at the weekend? My brother's going to be there, too.

J: Lovely. Are you going to introduce me to your mystery man?

A: Really, June! He's not a mystery man; it's just that we both want to be a little discreet. But yes, Derek will be there.

J: Well, I'd love to. That sounds lovely. I think it's fantastic that you two are, you know, er …

A: Yes, well, OK, I'll give you a call tomorrow. Must rush.

J: OK. Speak to you tomorrow. Bye.

6D Vocabulary & pronunciation exercise 1 💿 1.49

1   **J = June   A = Avril**

J: It's via Helsinki and it takes, er, just over fourteen hours, fourteen hours and fifteen minutes to be precise.

A: Well, that doesn't sound too bad.

2

J: There's another one coming up on the screen now. A Virgin Atlantic direct flight at £750? Does that sound OK?

3

J: Well, I'd love to. That sounds lovely.

6D Vocabulary & pronunciation exercise 4 💿 1.50

1

A: Where did you go last summer?

B: We went camping. It was superb. We loved it.

2

C: What was the weather like?

D: Absolutely awful.

3

E: You know what? We had a car crash on the first day of our holiday.

F: Oh, you poor thing! That sounds dreadful!

4

G: We took a yacht round the Mediterranean last summer.

H: Really? That sounds amazing! I'd love to do that.

5

I: What did you think of Prague?

J: Fantastic! The kids enjoyed it, too.

6

K: You look brown! Where have you been?

L: The Algarve. It was excellent. Really, really good.

7

M: You have a good time in England?

N: No, not really. The food was horrible!

8

O: So, how was the skiing?

P: Terrible. There was no snow.

7A Vocabulary exercise 1 💿 2.1

1

A: I love travelling and I'm quite happy living out of a suitcase.

2

B: I don't need much money to live on – just enough for food and basics.

3

C: I can't understand people who live for their work – there are more important things in life.

4

D: You haven't really lived if you haven't lived through difficult times.

5

E: I want to live my own life. I'm not interested in living up to my parents' expectations.

6

F: There's no point working if you can live off social security.

7B Vocabulary exercise 1 💿 2.2

The Road goes ever on and on
Down from the door where it began.
Now far ahead the Road has gone
And I must follow if I can
Pursuing it with eager feet
Until it joins some larger way
Where many paths and errands meet.

7B Vocabulary exercise 4 💿 2.3

Viggo Mortensen spent his early childhood on a farm in Argentina, but, at the age of eleven, his life took an unexpected turn. His parents decided to go their separate ways and Viggo went to New York with his mother. After graduating from university, Viggo's life was at a crossroads. He chose to go to Europe, but after two years, he decided it was time to move on again. He returned to New York where he embarked on a new stage of his life and became an actor. He soon got roles in films with top directors and it became clear that there was no turning back. His career really took off when he starred in *The Lord of the Rings*. At about the same time, Mortensen's life took a new direction when he founded a publishing company.

7B Listening exercises 1 & 2 💿 2.4

A: Jeff, tell us about the change you've made to your life.

B: Well, last year, I decided to give up my job and stay at home to look after my little boy, Ben.

A: Why did you decide to leave your job?

B: My wife went back to work after her maternity leave, so we had to put Ben into a nursery all day. It was really expensive and after a while we realized that after tax and travel expenses, we were paying more money in childcare than I was earning. It didn't make much sense! My wife earns almost twice as much as me, so it was easy to decide who should stay at home and look after Ben.

A: So basically, it was a financial decision …

B: … and a personal decision, too. We felt really guilty about leaving him for so many hours every day. He was changing and learning so much and we were missing out on it all. And then when he took his first steps at the nursery and neither of us was there to see it – that almost broke our hearts and I decided that some things in life were more important than work.

A: So how long have you been looking after Ben?

B: I've been looking after him for about six months now. Since his first birthday – and his first steps!

A: How has it changed your life?

B: Oh, completely. Totally. No more travelling, no more arguments with the boss. I no longer have to travel 40 minutes every morning to get into the office, I don't have to argue with my boss or waste time with difficult clients. Generally, I've been feeling much more relaxed since I gave up my job and although looking after a small child can be absolutely exhausting, I don't get as stressed as I did at work.

A: So, you enjoy being a stay at home dad?

B: Yes, I do. From the outside it can seem like a very boring life. The days are full of what appear to be boring jobs: shopping, cleaning, nappy changing! But with a little toddler around, it all turns into a game. And he's great fun to be with – he's been learning to talk for the last two or three months, and it's absolutely fascinating watching him pick up new words.

A: Don't you miss adult company at times?

B: Oh yes, definitely! It can be really tiring being with a small child, but there are plenty of playgroups and toddlers clubs. The kids get on with their activities and the mums and dads – much more mums than dads, of course – get a chance to sit down and have a cup of coffee, catch up on some adult conversation … I've been going to one club for about a month, and I've made some really good friends there.

A: It can't all be good. What about the bad times?

B: Well, Ben can be difficult at times – when he decides that he wants something, it's very, very difficult to change his mind. And there are times when it can be very stressful – when he's ill, for example. And it's very difficult to get time to myself during the day. Most days Ben sleeps for an hour or so after lunch – and that's great. But there are days when he doesn't and he has ten times more energy than me. On those days I'm exhausted by the time my wife gets home and I feel like I've really been working hard – much harder than I ever did at the office! And I suppose that, yes, I do miss my job. I'd really like to do more work from home. The last couple of weeks I've been doing some consultancy work in the evenings and at the weekends, and I've really been enjoying it.

A: So do you think you'll go back to work once Ben starts school?

B: I imagine that once Ben starts school I'll want to do something. But I can't imagine going back to a full-time nine to five office job again. I want to be there when Ben gets home from school I don't want to miss out on his childhood. I hardly ever saw my father when I was a child. I don't want it to be the same for Ben.

7D Listening exercises 1 & 2
2.5

L = Lynn   C = Carl

L: Thanks for coming, Carl. I really needed someone to talk to.

C: That's all right. It's about your promotion, I suppose.

L: How did you know about that?

C: Well, I knew you'd applied. The boss was smiling at you all day. So, it didn't take much to put two and two together.

L: No, I suppose you're right.

C: Well, anyway, congratulations, eh?

L: Erm, the thing is, I haven't decided if I'm going to take it yet.

C: What! Oh, come on, Lynn. You've got to be joking.

L: I know I wanted the promotion and all that, but I'm worried about what Tony will say. You know what he's like.

C: So what! I think you should take it! I mean, obviously!

L: Well, yes, maybe, but … it's not so easy, you know. The first trip they want me to go on is the same day as our wedding. And they say it can't be changed.

C: So, why don't you change the date of the wedding?

L: Oh no, I couldn't. He'll go ballistic!

C: No, he won't. Not if you break the news in a nice way. What you need to do is explain to him how important this is to you. You know, nice and gently.

L: I suppose I could give it a go.

C: Hmm, I tell you what. Have you thought about speaking to his parents first? Get them on your side – that won't be difficult. And then, when both you and Tony are with his parents at the weekend, mention it then.

L: Oh, yeah. I hadn't thought of that. What a good idea!

C: You know how he always agrees with his father. So. There you go. Problem sorted. And if I were you, I'd call them right now.

L: Now?

C: Yes, why not. No time like the present.

L: Yes, of course, you're right. But not right now, OK. In a bit.

C: Yeah, OK. Hey, you know what? I've just had another idea. Have you told the boss about the date of your wedding? I mean, maybe, just maybe, they could change the dates for that trip.

L: No. I didn't tell him. It's not his problem, is it?

C: Well, maybe it is. I mean, there's no harm in telling him, is there? He is human.

L: Do you really think that's a good idea? It doesn't sound very professional, does it?

C: Of course it's a good idea! You don't get married every day of your life! Tell him! Why not go and see him in the morning?

L: Oh no, I wouldn't want to do that. In the morning? Definitely not a good idea. You know what he's like in the morning.

C: Yeah, maybe you're right. But after he's had a few coffees, then.

L: All right, you've talked me into it. I'll give it a go.

7D Pronunciation exercise 1
2.6

L = Lynn   C = Carl

L: Erm, the thing is, I haven't decided if I'm going to take it yet.

C: What! Oh, come on, Lynn. You've got to be joking.

7D Pronunciation exercise 2
2.7

1   hello   2   right   3   yes

8A Listening exercises 1 & 2
2.8

R = Radio presenter   C = Colin Ashley

R: This week in the studio, we're pleased to welcome Colin Ashley whose latest book, *World Bank Robbers*, was published earlier this week. Colin, welcome to the programme.

C: Thank you.

R: Perhaps you could begin by explaining to us the title of your new book.

C: Yeah, sure. The book is about the World Bank. In theory, the job of the World Bank is to improve the living standards of people in the developing world. Unfortunately, most of the time it does the complete opposite.

R: That's a little exaggerated, isn't it?

C: Not a bit of it. And I'm not the first person to say it. A lot of the ideas in the book come from a professor at the Columbia Business School called Joseph E Stiglitz. Stiglitz won the Nobel Prize for Economics in 2001. He has taught at Princeton, Stanford, MIT and the University of Oxford, and from 1997 to 2000, he was Chief Economist and Senior Vice President of the World Bank. He wrote a bestseller called *Globalization and Its Discontents* and this inspired me to do more research.

R: And?

C: What interests me is how the World Bank and the International Monetary Fund are doing things in developing countries that is simply not helping those countries. But it is helping some of the big banks and the big engineering companies. A lot of what the World Bank does is good for Wall Street, but not for anybody else.

R: Your book has been described as an attack on America and American values. Would you say that's fair?

C: No, I wouldn't say that. I'm not anti-American. Although I'm Australian, my wife is American and my children are American. I would say that there's a very big difference between ordinary American people and big business America.

R: Your last book was about the connections between American industry and the Pentagon, the military. The one before that I think I'm right in saying, was about the operations of international oil companies in West Africa. You certainly choose some very powerful enemies.

C: I don't think of them as enemies. I see my job as telling people the truth.

R: But you probably wouldn't be very popular at a cocktail party on Wall Street.

C: No. But you'd be surprised – a lot of people in the business world are very happy to talk to me. I have a lot of friends there.

R: Colin, I understand that you're making a TV documentary based on your book. Do you have plans to do any more TV work after that?

C: I'd love to do more. It would be great to have more money, too, but it's difficult working for TV. They want the story too fast. They work to very tight schedules.

You just don't get enough time. You need to work on the story and some of these stories need time, a lot of time. You know, so I'd never work for some cable channels – just not enough time. You just don't get the time to do the story properly. So yes, I'd like to do more, but I'm waiting for the right opportunity to come along.

R: Do you have any advice for people who are thinking of becoming an investigative journalist?

C: I'd say that an investigative journalist needs two things. You need patience, you need to be able to keep at it, not give up. Sometimes it takes a long time to get the information you are looking for and you need to have a good nose, you need to be able to smell a good story when it comes your way.

R: Colin Ashley, thank you very much for joining us on this programme today.

8A Grammar exercise 3 🔘 2.9

A: Would you like to be a journalist?
B: I wouldn't mind, but I'd prefer to be a photographer.
A: What? A news photographer?
B: Yes, I'd love that.
A: You mean working for one of the big newspapers?
B: Yes, that would be really nice.
A: Personally, I'd hate it! Being away from home all the time, travelling to countries at war, ...
B: Oh, I'd love to. It would be really interesting.

8B Pronunciation exercise 2 🔘 2.10

/ʊ/(S): book; foot; good; pull; put; stood; took; would
/uː/(L): choose; few; food; group; moved; suit; true; two; whose

8B Pronunciation exercise 4 🔘 2.11

A man who was called Robin Hood
Went on demos whenever he could.
He hadn't a clue
What he wanted to do,
But he felt it was doing him good.

8D Listening exercises 2 & 3 🔘 2.12–2.13

1   D = driver   P = pedestrian
D: Excuse me. Sorry. I've er, do you know anything about cars?
P: Yes, a bit! What's the problem? Do you want me to have a look? I'll give you a hand.
D: Oh, thanks, yes, that would be great! There's a little light that started flashing, it was the oil light, so I thought I'd better stop. I mean, perhaps it's something serious. You never know.
P: The oil, eh? Well, shall I check it for you?
D: If you wouldn't mind.
P: It'll only take a second. Here. I'll have a look. Yes, you need some more oil, that's all. But, er, no great hurry.
D: So it's not too serious, then?
P: No, nothing to lose sleep over. But I'd

sort it out today, if I were you. Listen, there's a petrol station just round the corner. I'll come with you, if you like.
D: No, I'll manage, thanks. But thanks for the offer.

2   P = police officer
P2 = 2nd police officer   D = driver
P: Can I do anything for you, madam?
D: Yes. That's very kind of you. I'm trying to find my way out of town. I want to get on the motorway to London.
P: Yeah, no problem. Straight down here, turn right at the end, all the way down, and you'll see the signs, the motorway signs, a couple of hundred yards further on, OK?
D: Sorry? I didn't quite follow you.
P2: Here, let me explain, all right?
P: OK, thanks. Well, go on then.
P2: Right. So. Go straight on, OK.
D: Straight?
P2: Yeah, straight on. At the end, turn right. Right. Then, after two, three hundred yards, metres, you'll see a sign, a motorway sign. London. Motorway. A big sign. You can't miss it.
D: Thank you. Thank you very much.
P2: You've got that? Would you like me to repeat it?
D: No, that's OK, thank you. Turn right and then the motorway sign.
P: Yup, you've got it.
D: OK, thanks, bye.

9A Pronunciation exercises 1 & 2 🔘 2.14

A = Ann   B = Ben
A: Hi, where are you?
B: In the supermarket. I forgot the list – again! I can remember some of the stuff, but not all of it.
A: Oh, so what have you got so far?
B: OK, I've got some bottles of beer ...
A: Yeah ...
B: And a can of carrot soup ...
A: Aha ...
B: A carton of cranberry juice and a jar of jam and some packets of crisps ...
A: No, it wasn't crisps, it was peanuts. A couple of packets of peanuts.
B: Oh, right. And what else was there?
A: Er, let's see: some bottles of beer, a can of carrot soup, a carton of cranberry juice, a jar of jam, some peanuts and a tin of tuna.
B: OK, peanuts and tuna – got it! Thanks! See you later.
A: See you!

9A Pronunciation exercise 3 🔘 2.15

1   some bottles of beer
2   a can of carrot soup
3   a carton of cranberry juice
4   a jar of jam
5   a couple of packets of peanuts
6   a tin of tuna

9A Grammar exercise 3 🔘 2.16

A: Do you ever buy any traditional British food items?
B: No, I don't think I know any traditional British foods.

A: Oh, come on. A packet of English tea bags? A jar of marmalade? Some crackers?
B: Crackers?
A: Yes, the biscuits that we eat with cheese. Or some Cadbury's chocolate?
B: Sorry, I've never bought any of these things.
A: You should. Some British food is really nice.

9B Listening exercises 1 & 2 🔘 2.17

I = Interviewer   K = Katy
I: So, Katy, you say you're a shopaholic, what exactly does that mean to you?
K: Well, it's not me that says it, so much as most of ... or maybe I should say all the people who know me! All of them seem to agree that I'm a shopaholic. I enjoy shopping – any kind of shopping – I find it relaxing and satisfying and I don't think there's anything wrong with that ... but I do know that my family and many of my good friends think I'm an addict!
I: And are you really an addict?
K: I don't know, but when I miss out on a shopping opportunity, I get pretty frustrated and I suppose that most of the time I do go out of my way to make sure that I can visit the shops wherever I am. And I hate seeing an interesting shop and not being able to go in ...
I: Could you live without it?
K: Probably not!
I: When do you usually go shopping?
K: Whenever I can! At weekends, during my lunch breaks. when I'm on holiday ...
I: And is there an ideal time to go shopping?
K: If the shops are open, any time is a good time to go shopping!
I: And where do you most like shopping?
K: Well, I love shopping malls. I know some people complain that they're boring, that all the shops look alike, that the shops are always the same, you know, once you've seen one mall you've seen them all, but I don't agree. I think they're a great invention! It doesn't matter what the weather's like, you don't have to cut your shopping trip short to go and find something to eat ... they're perfect! But I also love exploring the little shops in old town centres – especially when I'm travelling.
I: Do you travel a lot?
K: Yes, I do, with my work, and I try to make sure I have time to do some shopping on most of my trips away from home!
I: What's your favourite country for shopping?
K: All of the countries I've ever visited! No, seriously, er, most countries are good for something. Let's see ... well, France is great for food, and no country I know is better than Italy for clothes, but I think Japan must be the best. I spent an absolute fortune in Tokyo on all sorts of electronic goods.
I: What do you most enjoy shopping for?

K: I love clothes shopping, of course, and I love buying presents for other people, but of all the things I buy, I think the one thing I most enjoy buying is stationery.

I: Stationery?

K: Yes, you know, pens, pencils, notebooks … I can spend hours in a stationery shop. I love handmade paper. That was another thing I spent loads of money on in Japan …

I: When did you last go shopping?

K: This morning – on my way to the office!

I: And what did you buy?

K: A pair of shoes, a T-shirt and a set of coloured pens. Would you like to see them?

I: Katy, thank you very much for being with us this evening. So, let's see what you bought then …

9B Grammar exercise 2 🔊 2.18

1 My brother spends most of his money on presents for his new girlfriend.
2 All my friends prefer shopping to doing sport.
3 None of them actually enjoys going shopping.
4 My mum spends most of her free time on the Internet finding new shopping sites.
5 Last week I spent all my money on a really expensive bottle of champagne for my boss.
6 My boyfriend never likes any of the clothes I buy for him.
7 Some of the best shops in town are down the little side streets.

9D Listening & functional language exercises 1 & 2 🔊 2.19–2.20

1

W: Customer service department. Can I help you?

M: Oh, hello. Er, I've got a problem with my phone. It's a KX 6700.

W: I'm sorry, sir. What seems to be the matter?

M: Well, I'm not too sure. I think there's something wrong with the battery. The light doesn't come on.

W: You haven't dropped it, have you? You know, by accident?

M: No, I haven't. Look, I'm sorry, I'm in a hurry because I'm calling from work. I just want to know where I can get it repaired.

W: Yes, sir. If you just go to the 'Services' menu on your phone, and then 'Help', the nearest repair shop will come up on your screen.

M: Yes. But I can't do that because the phone doesn't work.

W: Oh, yes, of course. I'm sorry. But I'm afraid we don't have the addresses of the repair shops on file here.

M: Right. Um, listen, I'm sorry, but this is totally unacceptable. I only bought the phone the other day. Could I speak to the manager, please?

W: Yes, sir. Can I tell him what it's about?

M: Yes, It's about my phone that doesn't work. I've had enough. I want a refund, I want my money back.

W: OK, hang on, I'll try to put you through. I'm sorry, sir, there's no reply. Could you call back later?

M: No, you call me. My number is …

2

M: Hello. How can I help you?

W: Hello. I've come in about my phone bill. I switched over to a new account with you last month, and now I've got the bill and it's twice what I normally pay.

M: Isn't there an explanation on the bill?

W: Not really, and I'm having problems understanding it. I don't know what half these numbers mean.

M: Could I have a look?

W: Yes, sure.

M: Well, I'm not sure. It's not a normal bill, is it? I'm not sure I can help you, I'm afraid. The best thing would be to call the number here where it says 'billing'.

W: I've tried that. About ten times, and there's never any answer. That's why I came back here.

M: Well, I'm not sure what to suggest …

W: Could you get someone else to have a look? Your colleague over there, for instance?

M: Well, he's only a trainee. But the manager's back from holiday next week.

W: Next week? I'm afraid that's not good enough. I don't want to wait a week!

M: But, as you can see, we're in a mess right now. There's only me and the trainee, I'm afraid.

W: Can't you telephone your head office? There must be someone there who can help.

M: Oh, that's a thought. Yes, OK, well, I'll see to it this afternoon after lunch, and I'll call you back, OK?

W: There's no way you could do it now, could you?

M: As you can see, we're a bit busy. But I'll do it later. For sure. OK?

W: I don't really have any choice, do I?

9D Vocabulary exercise 1 🔊 2.21

1 Have you ever telephoned the wrong number by mistake?
2 Do you switch off your telephone in class?
3 How many telephone numbers do you know by heart?
4 Have you ever been in trouble for using your phone?
5 How much do you spend on average per month on your phone?
6 Do you write words in full when you text?
7 How many people do you regularly keep in touch with by phone?
8 Do you look at your telephone bill in detail?

10A Pronunciation exercise 1 🔊 2.22

1 The show might be fun.
2 The show might be fun.

10A Pronunciation exercise 2 🔊 2.23

1 I might be able to help you.
2 They may be very busy later.
3 I'll answer the phone – it could be for me.
4 You must be very tired.
5 You can't be serious!

10B Listening exercises 2 & 3 🔊 2.24

P = Presenter   D = David
G = Gary   A = Amanda   Me = Megan
Mi = Michael

P: … and next up, we turn our attention to *The Da Vinci Code*. The novel by Dan Brown has now sold over 80 million copies and has been translated into over 40 languages, making it the top-selling book of the 21st century. The reviews have been mostly negative, but the book continues to attract huge attention. The question that people are asking is – how much of it is true? So, callers, over to you. Our first caller is on the line and it's David Sinclair from Edinburgh. David – *The Da Vinci Code* – fact or fiction?

D: Yeah, Mary, hi. I'd just like to say that the, I mean, the secret society in *The Da Vinci Code*, it's definitely a fact. It's an organization that has been around for nearly a thousand years and I've read quite a few books about it.

M: And you think that this organization is keeping a secret that could change the world?

D: Well, we don't really know, but it's definitely a possibility. You know, that they may be waiting for the right moment before revealing the secret.

M: OK, David. Thank you. Let's see if our other callers agree with you. We've got Gary Hunt from Blackburn on the line. Gary – do you think that David has a point?

G: Hi. I don't know if David's right or not, but I definitely think the secret society in the book is based on fact. I saw something on the internet the other day that said there's a secret organization that controls the world's banks, and the CIA is probably connected to it in some way. If you think about it, the CIA and the secret organization in *The Da Vinci Code* are probably the same thing. It's just logical.

M: OK, Gary. Many thanks. Over to Amanda Hussey from Bristol. Amanda? Do you agree?

A: I'm sorry, Mary, but I think this is all complete nonsense, I mean, it's just a story, isn't it? I think Gary must be spending too much time in front of the TV.

M: Er, could you say a little more?

A: Yes. The book says that there's some sort of secret society and they have this secret about Jesus having children.

M: Amanda, you've just given away the secret of the book!

A: Oh, sorry. But I don't think it matters, does it? This big secret – that Jesus had children – is just crazy. First of all, we know that Jesus was not married. And secondly, secondly, for a secret society, they can't be doing a very good job. I mean, it's not a secret any more. If you've read the book, it's not a secret, is it? And there are more than one hundred million people around the world who've read the book.

M: You've got a point. Thank you. Our next caller is Megan Todd. Megan.

Me: Yes, hi, Mary. We know that there are secret societies of bankers and so on. I read a book about the Freemasons, and how powerful they are, and I think a lot of the Freemasons are bankers, aren't they? Anyway, in this book, it said that the Freemasons had some connection with Jesus.

M: So, you think it could be true? The story of *The Da Vinci Code*?

Me: I don't see why not. I mean, anything's possible, isn't it?

M: Right, I think we've got time for just one more call on this subject. It's Michael Sheng from Leeds.

Mi: Thank you, Mary. Yes, I read *The Da Vinci Code* and I thought it was very good, but I can't understand why everyone's talking about it. You shouldn't take it seriously. It's just a novel. Why does everyone want to believe it? It's mad!

M: And with that, let's turn to ...

10C Grammar exercise 4
💿 2.26–2.29

A   Politician's clothes found on beach

It is not unusual for people to leave their clothes on the beach when they want other people to think they have died. But in 1967, Harold Holt, the prime minister of Australia, went swimming from the beach near Melbourne. Holt, who was 59, dived into the water and was never seen again. Many people believed that Holt did not die. Some thought he escaped because he wanted to live with his lover, and one journalist claimed that he was a secret agent who worked for the Chinese. But most people now accept that Harold Holt's death on the beach was an accident.

B   Police find box of snakes on highway

In May 2004, the police in Little Rock, Arkansas, found a box that contained four dangerous African snakes on the side of the road. A few days before that, the police also found a dead man in a car at Little Rock airport. The cause of death was a snake bite. Before his death, the man had bought the snakes from a snake shop in Florida, but the police cannot explain why the snakes were in a box on the road.

C   Alien attacks teacher

Kara Blanc, a teacher from Los Angeles, was the victim of an American TV show called *Scare Tactics*. Kara thought that aliens were attacking her, but in reality it was an actor who was wearing alien clothes. Kara did not find the joke funny and she took the makers of the programme to court.

D   Six people see monster in Chinese mountains

In recent years, hundreds of people claim that they have seen a large animal, which is half-man and half-ape, in the mountains south-west of Beijing. In the 1980s and 1990s, scientists tried to find the animal, but they had no success. Many people believe that a similar animal, called Bigfoot, lives in the forests of North America.

10D Listening exercises 1 & 2
💿 2.30

S = Senior manager (woman)
D = Dylan   P = Peter

S: Thanks for coming along bright and early. Let's get cracking, shall we? Dylan, Peter, what have you got for us?

D: Er, yep, we've been looking at the tracking software that can tell us what people are doing online, what sites they go to, how long they spend there, that sort of thing. Er, it seems that quite a lot of companies are using this kind of thing these days.

S: And?

D: Well, I think it's a possibility, but I think we should talk about it a bit more before we come to any decision.

S: Why? Is it expensive?

D: No, it's not that. It's just that, well, you know, I think we should think a little more about the pros and cons. I mean, the benefits of this are pretty obvious, but I think there may be one or two hidden drawbacks.

S: OK, tell me more.

P: Well, the good thing about this system ...

D: Er, do you mind?

P: Oh, sorry. I thought you'd finished. Sorry, you go first.

D: No, after you.

P: No, no, after you.

S: Come on, stop wasting time. Peter, say what you want to say and get to the point.

P: Yes, sorry. Er, yes, what I was saying was, er, the good thing about this system is that it stops time-wasting. We don't really know how much time people are wasting when they should be working, but probably a lot. I've seen people doing their shopping, and the other day, I even saw someone who had one of those online casinos on screen.

S: What? You saw someone gambling at work?

P: I think that's what he was doing.

D: I think we need to be a bit careful here. If someone wants to do that during their break, it's none of our business, really, is it?

S: I think it is, Dylan.

P: There's also a technical issue here, isn't there? The trouble is that every time they visit one of these sites – gambling sites, or whatever ... the trouble is that our computer system is open to viruses.

D: Sorry, can I say something here? You don't get more viruses with online casinos than anywhere else.

S: All right. We're talking about a number of different things here. Dylan, I think you said you were worried about some of the disadvantages of doing this?

P: Sorry, there's just one more thing that I wanted to mention. You were saying that you want people to understand how we need to improve efficiency so if we

use this program and we tell everyone what we're doing, then they'll all know how serious it is. You know, they'll see that we're doing something about the efficiency question. I can't see any point in waiting.

D: People are not going to go around saying 'Oh, what a good idea', I mean, hearing that your bosses are going to spy on you isn't exactly the high point of your day, is it? I've been reading an article about this in other companies. The experience there is that this kind of thing is very unpopular. If people think that the company is spying on them, well, they feel negative about it and they work less. You know, they start dragging their feet, extra five minutes break here, five minutes there.

S: Hmm, yes, I'd thought of that.

D: I think the other problem with this is, you know, the whole question of confidentiality. I mean, do we really have the right to spy on people like this? I don't think we do.

S: Dylan, you were saying that this may also cost us money.

D: Yes, I think it's possible. The programme itself isn't too expensive, but it needs someone to look at the information afterwards, and then to speak to people, and so on. So, in the long term, I think it will cost us money.

S: So what do you suggest?

P: I think we should go for it.

S: Dylan?

D: No, I don't think so. Not yet. I thought that maybe we could tell the staff that we're thinking of using this software and explaining why, and asking them what they think. I think we should play it safe. Make people a bit more involved. I think there's a lot to be gained.

S: OK. I'll need to think a bit before I make any decision. We'll meet again tomorrow morning to decide where we go from here.

11A Speaking & vocabulary exercise 3   💿 2.31

It's very complicated to explain. Basically, you have to catch a ball and run with it to the other end of the field. You can pass it to the other players, but you can't throw it forwards. Oh, and you can kick it sometimes. I think you kick it if you have a penalty, but I don't really understand the rules of that.

11B Reading & listening exercises 2 & 3   💿 2.32

I = interviewer   J = Jan

I: In today's *Sport in Depth* feature we'll be talking to child psychologist Dr Jan Freeman about child sports stars. Jan, is it true that sports stars are getting younger?

J: Yes, it certainly is. In a lot of sports the average age of the competitors is getting lower and lower, and many of the new names and new champions are still young enough to be at school. Look at tennis stars these days. If they haven't won their first big competition before they turn sixteen, they might as well give up. And they start training from a very young age. I know one player whose parents bought him his first tennis racquet at the age of two!

I: And of course there are the others who are following in their parents' footsteps ...

J: Yes, the father/coach figure is a fairly common figure.

I: Serena and Venus Williams, for example ...

J: Yes, their parents taught them the basics of tennis at a very young age.

I: So when did this child star phenomenon first appear?

J: It started in the 1970s with gymnasts like Nadia Comaneci who won four Olympic® gold medals. She was only fourteen years old and she looked even younger.

I: I remember the judges gave her ten for most of her performances – it made Olympic history. No gymnast had been given ten before. Wasn't she also the youngest gymnast ever to win a gold medal?

J: Yes, that's right. At the time she was an exception, but now it seems to be the rule. Younger girls are lighter and more agile. And they're easier to control and discipline.

I: But is it good for girls so young to be pushed so hard?

J: Basically, no. From both a physical and psychological point of view. Gymnasts need to be small and slim and many of them suffer from anorexia as they try to keep their weight down. And the pressure to win is incredible. These young athletes are working eight hours a day, seven days a week in the gym. They are never given any time for themselves. Nothing else matters. Only winning.

I: That kind of pressure is difficult enough for an adult. I imagine it must be a 100 times more difficult for a child.

J: Mmm, exactly! These girls are not children, they are medal-winning machines. Some start training from the age of three or four, when they are far too young to have a choice. Their parents choose the sport and if the coach sees real talent, then he or she will push them to their limits in order to win that all important gold medal.

I: And maybe the coach is also the one who's taking all the glory as well?

J: Yes, quite often. And the parents promise the kids all sorts of rewards if they win, but it's really the parents who are getting all the money!
And not only in gymnastics. It's just that gymnastics is such an extreme example.

I: Well, thank you Jan for being with us today ... Next, we'll be taking a look at ...

11c Pronunciation exercise 1
 2.33

ear   air

11c Pronunciation exercise 3
2.34

If you have a moment to spare on Christmas morning, go down to the beach near Brighton town centre where you can see a British sporting tradition. Every year, a group of about fifty people go for a swim in the sea. With a water temperature that is rarely more than seven degrees and an air temperature that is close to zero, most people keep their swim very short. More experienced swimmers stay in the water for nearly twenty minutes. The idea began in 1860 and there are similar events in other parts of the country.

11d Listening exercises 1 & 2
2.35–2.39

1   D = Dan   C = Claire

D: Er, sorry, Miss Ridley? Have you got a second?

C: Dan. Come in. But I think we can use first names, can't we? Call me Claire.

D: Oh, yeah, sorry, er, Miss Ridley.

C: It's about the photocopying machine again, isn't it?

D: No, no, it's fixed. Sorted. Er, it's something completely different.

C: Well?

D: It's, um, I'm doing a cycle ride from London to Brighton at the weekend. On Saturday. And er, I wondered if you'd like to sponsor me? It's for Sport Relief. For children in Africa.

C: Hmm, yes, fine. Shall we say £20?

D: Oh, great. Would you er, mind filling in the form?

C: Sure.

D: Great. Thanks.

C: Just one thing, Dan. You're not taking any time off work for this, are you?

D: No, no.

C: Mm, just wanted to check, that was all. Well, best of luck, Dan.

D: Thanks, Miss Ridley.

2   D = Dan   A = Annabel

D: Hello, Annabel. Er, have you got a second?

A: Not now, Dan. I've got to do these accounts.

D: It'll only take a second. I'm doing the London to Brighton cycle ride for Sport Relief. I wondered if you'd like to make a donation.

A: Oh! You said something about that last week, didn't you?

D: Yeah, it's this Saturday.

A: Well, you can put me down for £2.

D: Oh, can you fill in the form?

A: Do it for me, will you, Dan? There's so much I have to do.

D: Yeah, OK. It was, er, just £2, wasn't it?

A: Yeah.

D: Thanks, Annabel. Oh, by the way, is Donald in his office?

A: Yes, but he's making a call – something important, I think. Give him five minutes, all right?

D: OK.

3   Do = Donald   D = Dan

Do: Dan. Come in.

D: You look happy, Donald. Good news? That job you were applying for? You've got it, haven't you? Oh, well done, Donald, well done. We'll miss you, you know.

Do: Er, keep this between you and me, Dan.

D: Of course.

Do: Is that the sponsorship form?

D: Yeah, you er, want to make a little contribution?

Do: Definitely. Pass it over, I see you've already asked Miss Ridley. She hasn't given much, has she?

D: Twenty's not too bad.

Do: With her salary?

D: 50! Thanks. Listen, I'll catch you later, all right. I want to ask a few more people before lunch.

Do: Dan? Could you do me a favour? On your way out, ask Annabel to make me a cup of tea.

D: Will do. See you later.

4   D = Dan   L = Lucy

D: Hi there, Lucy. All right?

L: Yeah, all right. I've got to do these accounts all over again. Annabel's made a real mess of them. She's made mistakes on almost every page. I get so fed up doing her work all the time.

D: Yeah, know what you mean. Anyway, you'll sponsor me for the cycle ride, won't you?

L: 'Course I will. £5, OK? I have to do the shopping later and I'm a bit short of cash.

D: Oh, you don't have to pay me now. Next week's fine. Here, do you want to fill this in?

L: Where do I put my name?

5   P = Philip   G = Guy

P: Guy, did you give any money to Dan for his sponsored cycle ride?

G: Yeah, I put myself down for £30.

P: £30? You must be mad. I wish I had £30 to throw around like that.

G: No. I'll never give him the money, will I? There's no way he's going to do 54 miles on a bicycle without having a heart attack. He's never done any sport in his life, has he?

P: You're right. Five miles, maybe. And then he'll get the train or something. Your money's safe.

12b Listening exercises 1 & 2
2.40

M = Man   E = Elaine

M: Right, moving on to the next point on the agenda. Elaine and Kate are going to talk us through the results of our recent market survey into young people's attitudes to money. Elaine ...

E: Hi, as you know, we've got the results to the survey and you should all have a copy of the report on the table in front of you ... Greg, there's a spare copy over there ... got it? ... Right, so there's a summary of the results on page 13. I think you'll find that they're quite interesting.

Now, as Bob pointed out, the whole point of the survey was to find out more about young people's attitudes to money. As we all know, we aren't attracting as many young customers as we'd like to, and we hope this survey will help us improve our advertising campaign.

So, on to the details … Right … We interviewed a total of 1,200 young people between the ages of eighteen and 25. The interviews took place mainly in shopping centres, university student unions and multiplex cinemas. You can see a copy of the survey at the back of the report. The first two questions were very open and there were no surprises in the answers. When we asked if money was important to them, of course most people said that it was, but that it wasn't the only important thing.

So, as I said, no surprises there. I imagine we'd get the same answer from any group of people no matter how young or old. And the second question was pretty predictable as well. When we asked them if they worried about money most of the people we questioned said yes. So far so good.

But there were some surprises in the next question. When we asked them what they did with their money, there was no surprise when they said they liked to spend it on enjoying themselves, but we were surprised to see that a large number, over 30%, said that they regularly donated money to charity, but whilst only 2% said that they saved or invested it. This is something we really need to remember because at the moment our advertising campaign places far too much emphasis on investments and savings.

And the next question is quite an important one as well. When we asked what the main source of their income was, it was interesting to see that the majority said that it was their family, even though almost half of the people we talked to had a job. Which means that a lot of parents are still helping their children out financially when they first start to work. And, more importantly for our purposes, most of the people we questioned were still living at home. We really need to make sure we reflect this situation in any future advertising campaigns. We need to show more young people living at home with their parents. At the moment most of our ads show them sharing a flat with friends.

But even though they felt that they were still dependent on their families as far as for money's concerned, they didn't seem to turn to their parents for advice on money matters. In the answer given to the question of who influenced them most in their money decisions, more than 60% said that the TV, internet and newspapers influenced their decisions more than their own family and friends. This can only be good news for us!

Oh yes, and in case we're thinking of running another competition, the vast majority, that's almost 80%, wanted to win the limited edition Smart™ car!

Which brings us to the next part of our presentation. How do these results help us in planning our next advertising campaign. I'd like to hand over now to my colleague, Kate, who's going to outline a possible plan of action …

12D Pronunciation exercise 1 2.41

M = Man   W = Woman

M: Hello.
W: Hello.
M: How do you do?
W: How do you do?
M: How are you?
W: How are you?

12D Functional language exercise 2 2.42

1
A: Bad news, I'm afraid. I didn't get the job.
B: Oh, what a shame. That's really bad luck.

2
A: Excuse me, would you mind taking a photo of us?
B: Of course. Are you ready? Say 'cheese'.

3
A: Good luck for the big day tomorrow.
B: The same to you. I'll keep my fingers crossed.

4
A: Guess what! We've decided to get married.
B: Excellent news! Congratulations!

5
A: I'm afraid I can't come out for dinner this evening.
B: Oh, well, never mind. Another day, maybe?

6
A: Thank you so much. It was really kind of you.
B: Not at all. My pleasure.

7
A: We'll really miss you.
B: We'll miss you, too. Keep in touch, OK?

8
A: Well, I must be going. The plane leaves in half an hour.
B: OK. Have a safe journey and all the best.

12D Listening exercises 2 & 3 2.43–2.44

1   K = Karen   F = father
F: Hello?
K: Dad, hi. It's Karen here.
F: Hello, honey. All well?
K: Well, I'm fine, but I'm afraid we can't come round for dinner this evening. Magnus isn't feeling too well.
F: Oh, what a shame. Nothing serious, I hope.
K: Just a little stomach bug or something like that. But, listen, we were going to tell you this evening …
F: Yes?

K: Guess what?
F: What?
K: We've decided to get married.
F: Ah, Karen, excellent news. Congratulations! I'm very happy for you. Mind you, you took your time! Have you fixed the big day?
K: Not yet. It all depends how well the interview goes tomorrow.
F: Oh, yes, I'd forgotten that was tomorrow. Good luck with that. I'll keep my fingers crossed for you.
K: Thanks. 'Cos, you see, if I get the job, you know, all being well, they'll probably want me to work in the Stockholm office, and you know how Magnus wants to go back to Sweden, so we'll probably have the wedding over there.
F: You mean, not here, in Manchester?
K: Well, no, it can't be helped, really, can it? I mean, if we're living over there. Anyway, look, I must be going. I've got loads to do to get ready for tomorrow. We'll have a proper chat tomorrow, all right?

2   J = Jeff   G = grandmother
G: Jeff?
J: Hello?
G: Hello, Jeff, it's your gran here.
J: Oh, hello, Gran. How are things?
G: Oh, we're fine. Can't complain. I was just calling to say thank you for the present, the clock that you sent us for our anniversary. It was very sweet of you.
J: Not at all. My pleasure. I'm sorry I couldn't make it to the party last Saturday. You know how it is.
G: Well, we know how busy you are. And you know how proud we both are of you for winning the university scholarship. When are you off? In a couple of days, didn't you say?
J: It's tomorrow, actually. The flight's tomorrow morning.
G: We'll miss you, you know. You will keep in touch?
J: I will. I promise. But I'll be back for Christmas.
G: Look after yourself over there.
J: I will.
G: Your grandfather has put some money in your account for you. Just a little something. You know.
J: Oh, thanks, Gran. You shouldn't have. But, thanks, eh.
G: Well, have a safe journey. And look after yourself.
J: Yes, thanks, the same to you. Take care. Give my love to Grandpa.
G: I will. All the best, Jeff.
J: Thanks, Gran. I'll be in touch, OK?

IRREGULAR VERB LIST

Infinitive	Past simple	Past participle
be	was/were	been
beat	beat	beaten
become	became	become
begin	began	begun
bend	bent	bent
bite	bit	bitten
blow	blew	blown
break	broke	broken
bring	brought	brought
build	built	built
burn	burned/burnt	burned/burnt
burst	burst	burst
buy	bought	bought
can	could	been able
catch	caught	caught
choose	chose	chosen
come	came	come
cost	cost	cost
cut	cut	cut
deal	dealt	dealt
do	did	done
draw	drew	drawn
dream	dreamt	dreamt
drink	drank	drunk
drive	drove	driven
eat	ate	eaten
fall	fell	fallen
feed	fed	fed
feel	felt	felt
fight	fought	fought
find	found	found
fly	flew	flown
forget	forgot	forgotten
forgive	forgave	forgiven
freeze	froze	frozen
get	got	got
give	gave	given
go	went	gone
grow	grew	grown
hang	hanged/hung	hanged/hung
have	had	had
hear	heard	heard
hide	hid	hidden
hit	hit	hit
hold	held	held
hurt	hurt	hurt
keep	kept	kept
kneel	knelt	knelt
know	knew	known
lead	led	led
learn	learned/learnt	learned/learnt
leave	left	left
lend	lent	lent
let	let	let
light	lit	lit
lose	lost	lost
make	made	made
mean	meant	meant
meet	met	met
must	had to	had to
pay	paid	paid
put	put	put
read /riːd/	read /red/	read /red/
ride	rode	ridden
ring	rang	rung
rise	rose	risen
run	ran	run
say	said	said
see	saw	seen
sell	sold	sold
send	sent	sent
set	set	set
shake	shook	shaken
shine	shone	shone
shoot	shot	shot
show	showed	shown
shrink	shrunk	shrunk
shut	shut	shut
sing	sang	sung
sit	sat	sat
slide	slid	slid
sleep	slept	slept
smell	smelled/smelt	smelled/smelt
speak	spoke	spoken
spell	spelt/spelled	spelt/spelled
spend	spent	spent
spill	spilled/spilt	spilled/spilt
spread	spread	spread
stand	stood	stood
steal	stole	stolen
stick	stuck	stuck
swear	swore	sworn
swim	swam	swum
take	took	taken
teach	taught	taught
tear	tore	torn
tell	told	told
think	thought	thought
throw	threw	thrown
understand	understood	understood
wake	woke	woken
wear	wore	worn
win	won	won
write	wrote	written

1 | Review

1 Correct the mistakes in the dialogue.

A: Paul, hi, it's me. Listen, are you wanting to come out for a meal this evening?

B: Yes, sure, of course. But aren't you spending your birthday with Scott?

A: No, he's busy. He's doing something else.

B: What? On your birthday?

A: Yes, he's working late at the office today.

B: He's seeming to have a lot of work these days.

A: Yes, maybe. But I'm not believing him.

B: What? You're meaning that he's lying?

A: Well, I'm knowing that he's not telling me the whole truth.

B: Are you thinking that he's seeing someone else?

A: Maybe. He's behaving a bit strangely at the moment.

B: How terrible! Poor you.

2 Complete the postcard below. Put the verbs in brackets into the present simple or the present continuous.

3 Read the short text and complete the comprehension questions for these answers.

The Church of England decided that women could be priests in 1992. Two years later, 32 women became the first female priests in the country. At the time, some male priests complained. They thought that it was the end of the church.

1 Who _____? The Church of England.
2 When _____? In 1992.
3 When _____? Two years later.
4 How many women _____? 32.
5 Who _____? Some male priests.
6 What _____? That it was the end of the church.

4 Complete the questions with a word from the box.

    as   of   to

1 Do most people see you _____ an approachable person?
2 Do you consider yourself _____ be very patriotic?
3 Do you think _____ yourself as right-wing or left-wing?
4 How many people would you describe _____ very good friends?
5 Do you think you are lucky _____ live in the 21st century?
6 Which is more important _____ you – friends or family?

5 Work in pairs. Ask and answer the questions in exercise 4.

6 Complete the missing letters in the words.

1 He has a very p _ _ _ _ _ _ t nose, like a big carrot.
2 He looks ill and has a very unhealthy c _ _ _ _ _ _ _ n.
3 He prefers to have grey hair than to be b _ _ d.
4 He's got a very m _ _ _ _ _ _ r build – he must spend hours in the gym.
5 Her eyes look very n _ _ _ _ w in her new glasses.
6 He looks as if he's just got out of bed – his hair's a mess and he hasn't s _ _ _ _ d.
7 She looks very t _ _ _ _ d, but I think it's fake – some sort of cream.
8 Sometimes her hair is straight and sometimes it's w _ _ y.

I arrived in London yesterday and I (1) _____ (have) a good time already. At the moment, I (2) _____ (watch) a cricket match. Tom (3) _____ (play) cricket every Sunday afternoon and today his team (4) _____ (play) in Kew – near the famous gardens. I (5) _____ (not / understand) the rules, but it (6) _____ (not / matter) – it's good fun anyway. It (7) _____ (look) as if it's going to rain later (typical England!), but for the moment, the sun (8) _____ (shine). We (9) _____ (drink) warm beer and I (10) _____ (eat) a cheese and cucumber sandwich. England is everything I imagined! You'd love it!

Love

Claire XXX

Lauren Thompson

457 S. Monica Blvd.

Venice

CA

US

2 | Review

1 Choose the correct time expression to complete the questions.

1 Did you do anything special *last weekend / over the last few weeks*?
2 Have you booked your next holiday *yesterday / yet*?
3 Have you made many friends *during your time at this school / when you were at primary school*?
4 Have you seen any good films *one month ago / recently*?
5 How many times did you take a taxi *during the last year / last year*?
6 How often have you been ill *in the last six months / last month*?

2 Work in pairs. Ask and answer the questions in exercise 1.

3 Complete the article. Put the verbs in brackets into the past simple or the present perfect.

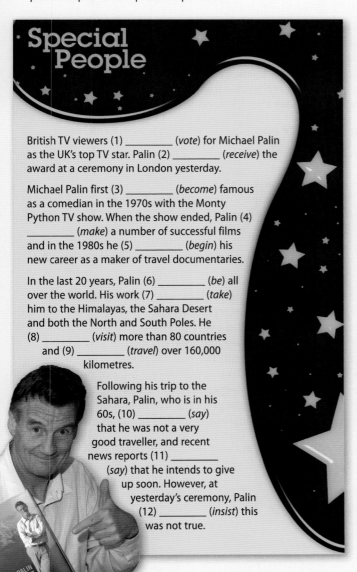

Special People

British TV viewers (1) _____ (*vote*) for Michael Palin as the UK's top TV star. Palin (2) _____ (*receive*) the award at a ceremony in London yesterday.

Michael Palin first (3) _____ (*become*) famous as a comedian in the 1970s with the Monty Python TV show. When the show ended, Palin (4) _____ (*make*) a number of successful films and in the 1980s he (5) _____ (*begin*) his new career as a maker of travel documentaries.

In the last 20 years, Palin (6) _____ (*be*) all over the world. His work (7) _____ (*take*) him to the Himalayas, the Sahara Desert and both the North and South Poles. He (8) _____ (*visit*) more than 80 countries and (9) _____ (*travel*) over 160,000 kilometres.

Following his trip to the Sahara, Palin, who is in his 60s, (10) _____ (*say*) that he was not a very good traveller, and recent news reports (11) _____ (*say*) that he intends to give up soon. However, at yesterday's ceremony, Palin (12) _____ (*insist*) this was not true.

4 Complete the sentences 1–8 with the phrases a–h.

1 A brown bear looks
2 He always drops
3 He often picks
4 I was surfing the net last night and came
5 It often takes a long time to get
6 She decided to give
7 She needs some help to sort
8 They've gone to see

a across a good site for hitchhikers.
b after her cubs for about two and a half years.
c off the kids at school on his way to work.
d off their friends at the airport.
e out a problem with a virus on her computer.
f over a serious illness like that.
g up hitchhikers in his truck.
h up the sport after her latest injury.

5 Rearrange the words to make sentences.

1 across before come him I never 've .
2 after her I if 'll like look you .
3 are picking them time up what you ?
4 came me nobody off see to .
5 could drop here me off please you ?
6 get it 'll over soon you .
7 give he it should up .
8 have it out soon sort to we .

6 Complete the dialogue with verbs from the box. More than one answer is sometimes possible.

| catch   get   get off   get on   miss   run |
| take   walk |

A: Excuse me, can you tell me how I can _____ to City Airport from here?
B: Yes, of course. The best way is to _____ a train to Stratford.
A: Thanks. How often do the trains _____?
B: Every ten minutes, so if you _____ one, you don't have to wait long. Platform 4.
A: Platform 4. OK. How long does it _____? Half an hour?
B: Oh no, only about fifteen minutes. You _____ the train at the last stop.
A: The end of the line. OK. And can I _____ to the airport from there?
B: No, you'll need to _____ the airport bus. It will be right outside the station.

7 Work in pairs. Practise the dialogue in exercise 6.

3 | Review

1 Choose the best explanation for the signs.

1
> **Free car park**
> for residents only

a) Everybody has to pay to park here.
b) Nobody has to pay to park here.
c) Residents do not have to pay to park here.

2
> Last check out
> **12.00**

a) You don't have to check out before 12.00.
b) You must check out before 12.00.
c) You must not check out before 12.00.

3
> ⊘ **No guests in rooms**

a) Guests are not allowed in the rooms.
b) Guests must not leave their rooms.
c) You can take guests to your room.

4

a) You are allowed to bring a dog with you.
b) You don't need to bring a dog with you.
c) You have to bring a dog with you.

5
> **Restaurant**
> non-residents welcome

a) Non-residents can't eat here.
b) You don't need to be a resident to eat here.
c) You must be a resident to eat here.

6
> **Swimming pool**
> **opening hours**
> **08.00–20.00**

a) Swimming is not allowed between 08.00 and 20.00.
b) You can swim between 08.00 and 20.00.
c) You mustn't swim between 08.00 and 20.00.

2 Complete the second sentence so that it has a similar meaning to the first.

1 In the Middle Ages, the church made most people give them one tenth of their money.
In the Middle Ages, most people _had to give_ one tenth of their money to the church.

2 Only important people could wear purple clothes in 16th-century England.
Only important people were _____ purple clothes in 16th-century England.

3 Between 1919 and 1932, Finnish people were not allowed to buy alcoholic drinks.
Between 1919 and 1932, the Finnish government _____ its people buy alcoholic drinks.

4 Before 1963, American law let employers pay a man more than a woman for the same job.
Before 1963, American employers _____ pay a man more than a woman for the same job.

5 The Soviet Union did not let some writers publish their work.
Some writers _____ publish their work in the Soviet Union.

3 Correct the mistakes in the sentences.

1 Could you possibly leaving your dog outside?
2 Do you mind if I opening the window?
3 Do you think could you pick us up at eight o'clock?
4 I wonder if could I invite a few friends for dinner.
5 Is it all right when I leave work early tomorrow?
6 Would you mind to pass the mayonnaise?

4 Choose an appropriate response for the requests in exercise 3.

1 *Yes, go ahead. / Yes, of course.*
2 *No, not at all. / Yes, sure.*
3 *No, that's OK. / Yes, no problem at all.*
4 *I'm sorry, but I'm busy tonight. / I'm afraid you can't.*
5 *No, that's fine. / Yes, that's fine.*
6 *Yes, here you are. / Certainly not.*

5 Complete the questions in column A with a phrase from column B.

A		B	
1	Can you get to	a	alarm clock when you're on holiday?
2	Do you always make the	b	asleep at school?
3	Do you ever set your	c	bed every day?
4	Have you ever fallen	d	nap and then decided to stay in bed until the next morning?
5	Have you ever had a	e	sleep when there's a lot of noise?
6	How often do you wake	f	sleeper that you know?
7	What time do you begin to feel	g	sleepy in the evening?
8	Who is the heaviest	h	up in the middle of the night?

6 Work in pairs. Ask and answer the questions in exercise 5.

4 | Review

1 Choose the correct verb forms to complete the text.

Coincidences

Post reply reply/quote email delete edit

The other day I (1) *thought / was thinking* of a song, and when I (2) *turned / was turning* on the radio, what (3) *did I hear / was I hearing*? The same song, of course.
Earlier this morning, I (4) *needed / was needing* to call a friend. I (5) *looked / was looking* for her number in the phone book when the telephone (6) *rang / was ringing*. Guess who?
A few years ago, I (7) *met / was meeting* a woman when I (8) *flew / was flying* to New York on business. Later that day, I (9) *saw / was seeing* her again when I (10) *had / was having* dinner in the hotel restaurant. She (11) *stayed / was staying* in the same hotel!

Post new topic

2 Complete the text. Put the verbs in brackets into the past simple, the past continuous or the past perfect.

Post reply reply/quote email delete edit

Last night I (1) _____ (*want*) to watch a film on TV, but my sister (2) _____ (*watch*) a quiz show. I (3) _____ (*agree*) to wait until the end of her show. The contestant (4) _____ (*sit*) in a big black chair. She (5) _____ (*answer*) nine questions correctly and she (6) _____ (*have*) one more question to get right for the jackpot. Her name (7) _____ (*be*) Emily – the same as me – and she (8) _____ (*wear*) exactly the same clothes as me! She (9) _____ (*have*) to give the name of the river in Budapest. I (10) _____ (*come*) back from a trip to Hungary only last week!

Submitted by Emily

3 Decide if the pairs of sentences below have the same (S) or different (D) meanings.

1   The fire started while he was at the petrol station.
    When he was at the petrol station, the fire started.
2   She bought a new house when she won the lottery.
    She won the lottery after she'd bought a new house.
3   She screamed the moment she saw him.
    As soon as she saw him, she screamed.
4   By the time we arrived, they had already left.
    They left before we arrived.
5   They called for help as soon as their car broke down.
    Their car broke down as soon as they called for help.
6   He had an accident while he was playing on the balcony.
    When he was playing on the balcony, he had an accident.

4 In four of the sentences below, one word is missing. Insert the missing words.

1   Both them like a bit of a gamble.
2   Neither my friends my family think it's against the odds.
3   Neither us feel like giving it a go.
4   We both want to try our luck.
5   There's a lot at stake for both the company the workers.
6   They both think it's a lottery.

5 Match the sentences 1–6 to the short responses a–f.

1   I bought a _____ last week.
2   I can't _____.
3   I like _____.
4   I wasn't _____ yesterday.
5   I'm going to _____ tomorrow.
6   I've never been to _____.

a   Neither can I.
b   Neither have I.
c   Neither was I.
d   So am I.
e   So did I.
f   So do I.

6 Complete sentences 1–6 in exercise 5 so that they are true for you.

Work in pairs. Read your sentences to your partner. Your partner must respond to your sentences truthfully.

7 Complete the sentences with a word from the box.

| ankle | black | bleeding | bruise |
| scratch | shock | sprained | unconscious |

1   He _____ his wrist playing squash.
2   He wouldn't explain how he got a _____ eye.
3   Her finger is _____ after she cut it with a knife.
4   Many people were suffering from _____ after the explosion.
5   She's got a _____ on her arm where the ball hit her.
6   The cat was frightened and tried to _____ me.
7   The doctors think he may remain _____ for a few hours.
8   The parachutist twisted her _____ when she landed.

5 | Review

1 Look at the information in the table and say if the sentences 1–8 are true (T) or false (F). Correct the false sentences.

A quick guide to local furniture stores			
Alum & Key	range of goods	price	staff
	(beds images)	£££	☺
Bettabeds	(beds images)	££	☺ ☺ ☺
Home Comforts	(beds images)	£	☺ ☺ ☺ ☺

1 Bettabeds is the least expensive of the three stores.
2 Home Comforts is slightly cheaper than Bettabeds.
3 Alum & Key is less friendly than the other shops.
4 The nicest staff are at Home Comforts.
5 Alum & Key has the biggest range of furniture.
6 It's easier to find what you want at Bettabeds than at Home Comforts.
7 On the whole, Bettabeds is better than Home Comforts.
8 Alum & Key is the worst place to go for good service.

2 Complete the sentences with a word from the box.

> as   from   not   the   to

1 The prices in superstores are similar _____ the prices in local shops.
2 Local shops are _____ as convenient as superstores.
3 The staff in superstores are _____ friendly as in local shops.
4 Opening hours at local shops are different _____ superstores.
5 One superstore is _____ same as another.

Work with a partner. Decide if you agree with the sentences in exercise 2.

3 Choose the best word to complete the sentences.

1 He gets the *fewest / more* complaints.
2 He has the *least / less* experience of all of them.
3 I have a lot *fewer / less* energy than him.
4 I've taken *fewer / least* holidays this year.
5 She has *less / more* projects than the others.
6 She probably has the *fewest / most* work to do.

4 Complete the dialogues with an appropriate phrase.

A: Hello. Could I (1) _____, please?
B: I'm afraid that Mrs Robinson isn't at home right now. Can I (2) _____?
A: Yes, please. This is Benjamin here.
B: I'm sorry. Could you (3) _____?
A: Yes. Benjamin. B-E-N-J-A-M-I-N. Could you (4) _____?
B: Yes, of course. I'll ask her to call you as soon as she gets back.

C: Sales and marketing. Can I (5) _____?
D: Yes, hello. Could I speak to Thomas, please?
C: I'm sorry, but Thomas isn't at his desk right now. I think he's at lunch.
D: Oh, right. Can I (6) _____? In about an hour?
C: Yes, I'm sure that he'll be back then. Could I (7) _____?
D: Yes, it's Mrs Laurence.
C: OK, Mrs Laurence. I'll tell him you called.

Work in pairs. Practise the dialogues.

5 Complete the sentences with a positive or negative form of the adjectives in the box.

> comfortable   correct   delicious
> polite   popular   satisfied

1 It was a very _____ restaurant so they had to book in advance.
2 It was a very stylish place, but the chairs were very _____.
3 Last time they went, the food was _____, but this time it was not so good.
4 In addition, they didn't enjoy the meal because the waiter was extremely _____.
5 The bill was _____ so they asked for it to be changed.
6 They were _____ with the service so they decided to complain to the manager.

6 Four of the sentences below are strange or illogical. Put a cross next to these sentences.

1 He made a few corrections with his pencil sharpener.
2 He ordered a couple of note pads from the stationery department.
3 Her secretary used a highlighter to show all the important information.
4 I need a new ink cartridge for my stapler.
5 She spent the day working in the filing cabinet.
6 She wrote an important biro to the new clients.
7 The photocopies were attached with a paper clip.
8 There are loads of reports in my in tray that I have to look at.

6 | Review

1 Choose the best verb forms to complete the dialogue.

A: (1) *Are you going to do / Will you do* anything interesting this weekend?

B: Probably not. (2) *We're staying / We'll stay* at home, I guess. And you?

A: Yes, (3) *we're visiting / we'll visit* some friends at the coast. But according to the weather forecast, (4) *it's going to rain / it will rain*, unfortunately.

B: Well, I'm sure (5) *you're having / you'll have* a nice time anyway.

A: Yes, it doesn't matter too much. We're more worried about the traffic. It's a holiday weekend, so there (6) *are going to be / will be* a lot of cars on the road.

B: If you leave early, (7) *you're going to be / you'll be* OK.

A: Yes, but we can't leave until after nine because (8) *we're going to do / we'll do* a bit of shopping first.

2 Look at the dialogue in exercise 1 again. Which examples of *going to* can you replace with the present continuous?

3 Complete the sentences. Put the verbs in brackets into the correct form.

1 We're going to look for a hotel as soon as we _____ (*arrive*).
2 After we've checked in, we _____ (*find*) somewhere to eat.
3 We'll go for a walk around the city when we _____ (*eat*).
4 If the weather _____ (*be*) bad, we'll go on a bus tour.
5 Once we know the city a bit better, we _____ (*visit*) a museum or two.
6 We'll visit the National Gallery before we _____ (*leave*).

4 Correct the mistakes in the questions.

1 Do you know what will your next film be?
2 Could you tell us which actor or actress would you really like to work with?
3 Can you tell us what do you like most about making films?
4 We'd all like to know how much did you earn for your last film.
5 Can you tell us if you ever do watch your own films?
6 Our viewers would like to know you're going out with anyone at the moment.

5 Work in pairs. Imagine that you are a journalist and a famous film star. Ask and answer the questions in exercise 4.

6 Complete the sentences with a word or phrase from the box.

arrive	book	check out	choose
do	find	pay	pick up

1 Don't forget the sunscreen when you _____ the packing.
2 Guests must _____ of the hotel before eleven.
3 Please _____ your excursions 24 hours in advance.
4 Signs in the town are written in English so it's easy to _____ your way around.
5 There will be a welcome party when you _____ at the hotel.
6 We have hundreds of exotic destinations to _____ from.
7 We kindly ask you to _____ a 5% deposit when you make your reservation.
8 You can _____ a brochure at our shop during normal shopping hours.

7 Complete the text with the best answers, a, b or c.

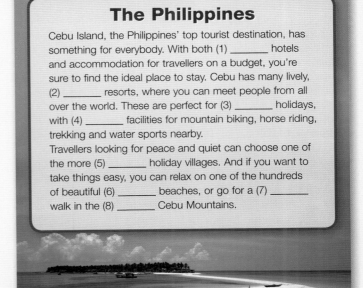

The Philippines

Cebu Island, the Philippines' top tourist destination, has something for everybody. With both (1) _____ hotels and accommodation for travellers on a budget, you're sure to find the ideal place to stay. Cebu has many lively, (2) _____ resorts, where you can meet people from all over the world. These are perfect for (3) _____ holidays, with (4) _____ facilities for mountain biking, horse riding, trekking and water sports nearby.

Travellers looking for peace and quiet can choose one of the more (5) _____ holiday villages. And if you want to take things easy, you can relax on one of the hundreds of beautiful (6) _____ beaches, or go for a (7) _____ walk in the (8) _____ Cebu Mountains.

1 a) dreadful   b) painful   c) upmarket
2 a) awful   b) cosmopolitan   c) guided
3 a) shy   b) gorgeous   c) action-packed
4 a) dramatic   b) laid-back   c) superb
5 a) horrible   b) secluded   c) talkative
6 a) exhausted   b) sandy   c) unbeatable
7 a) memorable   b) discreet   c) ancient
8 a) exclusive   b) picturesque   c) respectable

7 | Review

1 Choose the correct verb forms to complete the dialogue.

A: How long have you (1) *known / been knowing* him?
B: We've (2) *gone / been going* out for about three years.
A: Have you ever (3) *had / been having* any arguments?
B: Yes, a few, recently. I've (4) *worked / been working* late at the office and John doesn't like it.
A: He's jealous?
B: Yes, and I've (5) *thought / been thinking* that I'm not sure I want to get married to someone who gets jealous.
A: Have you (6) *spoken / been speaking* to him about it?
B: No, I've (7) *waited / been waiting* for the right moment.

2 Complete the text. Put the verbs in brackets into the present perfect simple or the present perfect continuous.

latest news

Royal wedding preparations nearly complete
(Filed: 09/04/05)

Staff at Windsor Castle (1) _____ (*be*) busy making the final preparations for the wedding of Prince Charles and Camilla Parker Bowles later today. Castle workers (2) _____ (*prepare*) St George's Hall, where the reception will take place. Four men (3) _____ (*build*) a small stage, from where the wedding speeches will be made. When they (4) _____ (*finish*), the stage will be covered in gold. Nearby, another group of servants (5) _____ (*polish*) champagne glasses. 35,000 yellow flowers (6) _____ (*arrive*) at the castle and eight flower arrangers (7) _____ (*work*) around the clock to decorate the hall. They expect to finish shortly before the arrival of the royal couple. Prince Charles (8) _____ (*return*) from Rome where he was attending the funeral of the Pope.

3 Complete the sentences with *for* or *since*.

1 A few people have been waiting outside the castle _____ yesterday evening.
2 One man has been there _____ two weeks to be sure of getting a good view.
3 He has been a fan of the royal family _____ he met Prince Charles in 1992.
4 He has been to three royal weddings _____ then.
5 Journalists have been interviewing people in the streets _____ the last few hours.
6 Charles and Camilla have known each other _____ 30 years.

4 Complete the sentences with one word.

1 Have you _____ about looking for a job as a film extra?
2 Have you _____ looking for work on local TV?
3 I think you _____ forget the idea.
4 If I _____ you, I'd just go to Hollywood.
5 There's no _____ in taking a few acting lessons.
6 What you _____ to do is get on a reality TV show.
7 _____ don't you send your photo to an agency?

5 Work in pairs. Which is the best advice in exercise 4 for someone who wants to become a film star?

6 Complete the dictionary definitions with the missing words.

1 **live** _____ _____ phrasal vb [T] [**live** _____ _____ **sth**] to be as good as what was expected or promised: *The beautiful scenery certainly lived _____ _____ expectations.*
2 **live** _____ phrasal vb [T] [**live** _____ **sth/sb**] to think that someone or something is so important that they are your main reason for living: *She lives _____ her work.*
3 **live** _____ phrasal vb [T] [**live** _____ **sth/sb**] to depend on someone or something for the money or food that you need: *He's 25 and still living _____ his parents.*
4 **live** _____ phrasal vb [T] [**live** _____ **sth**] to experience a dangerous or unpleasant situation and still be alive after it: *There are people who have lived _____ two world wars.*
5 **live** _____ phrasal vb [T] [**live** _____ **sth**] to have a particular amount of money to buy the things that you need to live: *They have to live _____ a pension of £350 a month.*

Extracts from Macmillan Essential Dictionary

7 Complete the sentences 1–6 with the phrases a–f.

1 Even when you're heartbroken, you have to move
2 It's when we're adolescents that we embark
3 It's quite common for couples to go
4 It's usually a good thing when our lives take
5 Most people's lives don't really take
6 When your life is at a

a an unexpected turn and we take a new direction.
b crossroads, it's best to ask an elderly relative for advice.
c off until they're middle-aged.
d on and find someone else.
e on the most important stage of our lives.
f their separate ways when they're in their early twenties.

8 Work in pairs. Do you agree with the statements in exercise 7?

8 | Review

1 Choose the best response.

1 Do you think it will rain?
I wouldn't say so. / Yes, I would.

2 Do you want to come for dinner this evening?
I'd love to. / I'd never do that.

3 How about spending the weekend in Paris?
I wouldn't know. / That would be great.

4 I don't think you should tell him.
No, he wouldn't understand. / Yes, I would think so.

5 Shall we stop for a break?
I wouldn't care. / I wouldn't mind.

6 Will we get a pay rise this year?
I'd never forgive myself. / I'd be very surprised.

2 Work in pairs. Think of at least two ways to complete the sentences below.

1 If I was the look-alike of someone famous, I …
2 If someone offered me a role in a movie, I …
3 If I had a private jet, I …
4 If I was the owner of a daily newspaper, I …
5 If I found a bomb in the street, I …

3 Rewrite the sentences beginning with the words given.

1 The nurses weren't happy with their salaries so they went on strike.
If the nurses _____.

2 The newspapers reported the demonstration because the protesters dressed as Elvis Presley.
If the protesters _____.

3 The police stopped him because he drove through a red light.
If he _____.

4 Stiglitz lost his job because he asked the wrong questions.
If Stiglitz _____.

5 He didn't do more TV work because he didn't have enough time.
If he _____.

4 Complete the sentences. Put the verbs in brackets in the correct form.

1 I _____ (not / need) to go to the launderette if I had a washing machine.

2 If it _____ (be) less left-wing, the paper would have better circulation figures.

3 If you _____ (study) engineering, you'd have found a better paid job.

4 They _____ (not / vote) for the government if they'd known about their plans for the war.

5 They wouldn't have gone in the fountain if they _____ (not / be) hot.

6 Would you walk naked down the street if I _____ (give) you £100?

5 Rearrange the words to make offers.

1 anything can do for I you ?
2 a give hand let me with that you .
3 if I'll do like the washing-up you .
4 a bottle champagne I of open shall ?
5 drive like me there to would you you ?
6 a coffee cup do make me of to want you ?

6 Cross out one noun in each group which cannot form a compound with the noun in bold.

1 credit / ID / rest **card**
2 face / safety / seat **belt**
3 mobile / pay / pie **phone**
4 police / strip / train **station**
5 speed / time / toy **limit**
6 money / street / traffic **lights**
7 driving / gun / war **licence**
8 bag / danger / no-parking **zone**

7 Match the headlines 1–5 to the beginnings of the news stories A–E.

1 **Journalist killer arrested**

2 **New bomb clue**

3 **Thieves get long sentence**

4 **Protesters not guilty**

5 **Witness disappears**

A A judge has sent two men to prison for fifteen years after a jury found them guilty of taking part in the Bettabeds Superstore robbery. The men had

B Dutch police have caught a man who fired a gun into the offices of a left-wing newspaper, resulting in the death of one member of staff. It is believed

C Three women who were arrested for violent behaviour at an anti-globalization demonstration have been found innocent. The judge said that the

D A woman who worked for Richie Preston failed to appear in court today to give evidence in the Cardiff gangster's trial. Police think that she may

E A Metropolitan Police spokesman announced earlier today that they have found new evidence in their investigation into last week's explosion at the

8 Work in pairs. Use your imagination to complete the unfinished sentences in exercise 7.

9 | Review

1 Complete the sentences with with *a/an*, *the* or Ø (zero article).

Have you ever had (1) _____ problem finding (2) _____ right birthday present for (3) _____ friends? Have you ever spent (4) _____ hours at (5) _____ shops only to return with (6) _____ empty bag and (7) _____ growing sense of (8) _____ frustration? If so, (9) _____ internet is (10) _____ only place to go.

2 Complete the sentences with *some* or *any*.

Type 'weird gifts' into (1) _____ search engine on the internet, and you'll find (2) _____ really original ideas. At (3) _____ sites, like stupid.com, you won't find (4) _____ normal ideas at all. But you will certainly find (5) _____ of the strangest gifts on the net. Even if your friend doesn't actually need (6) _____ of these things, they may find (7) _____ of them quite amusing.

3 Choose the best way to complete the text.

How about buying a piece of land on the moon? There are (1) *lots of / too much* online shops that have moon property on offer. It doesn't cost (2) *many / much* (about $15), and there are (3) *much / plenty of* people who are happy to pay.
Unfortunately, (4) *few / little* of them will ever get the chance to visit their property.
If you think that $15 is (5) *a few / too much* for something that you'll never see, there are (6) *many / much* other interesting ideas. If you only have (7) *a little / not enough* time, go to the 'weird stuff' section of Ebay. If you've got (8) *a lot of / many* money and (9) *not enough / a few* sense, you can buy a mystery brown box for $200. And if you really have (10) *few / too much* money, you can join (11) *a few / enough* other people and buy a bag of Iowa air for $1. What a bargain!

4 Put the dialogue in the correct order.

☐ A whole week? I'm afraid that's not good enough. I can't spend a week without one.
☐ Good morning. I think there's a problem with the watch I bought yesterday.
☐ Good morning, sir. How can I help you?
☐ And I'm sorry, but that's totally unacceptable. I'd like to speak to the manager.
☐ I see. Well, if you'd like to leave it with us, we'll look into it. Could you come back next Monday?
☐ I'm sorry, sir, but there's nothing else we can do.
☐ Oh yes? What seems to be the problem?
☐ There's something wrong with the alarm.

5 Work in pairs. Practise the dialogue in exercise 4.

6 Find four items on the shopping list that are in the wrong container.

1 bottle of red wine
1 large box of washing powder
2 cartons of organic marmalade
4 cans of diet cola
1 tin of pineapple slices
4 cartons of orange juice
1 jar of skin cream
2 small jars of beefburgers
1 packet of spaghetti
1 box of olive oil
3 tins of Italian tomatoes
1 small tin of fresh salad leaves
2.5 litre tub of vanilla ice cream

7 Complete the definitions 1–7 with the phrases a–g.

1 A discount is
2 A high street is
3 A shop assistant is
4 A shopaholic is
5 A shoplifter is
6 A shopping mall is
7 Window-shopping is

a a large building with a lot of shops, restaurants, and sometimes a cinema.
b a reduction in the price of something.
c someone who enjoys going to shops or buying things.
d someone who steals something from a shop.
e someone whose job is to serve people in a shop.
f the activity of looking at things in shop windows but not buying anything.
g the main street in a town or city, with a lot of businesses along it.

8 Complete the missing letters in the words.

1 I found the house in a real m _ _ _ when I got home.
2 I found the right answer totally by c _ _ _ _ _.
3 I have all your details on f _ _ _.
4 I met her ex-husband completely by a _ _ _ _ _ _ _.
5 I think we're in d _ _ _ _ _ of missing the last train.
6 I'd like the bill now, please. We're in a h _ _ _ _.
7 I'll be in t _ _ _ _ _ _ if Tom finds out about this.
8 I'm sorry, I took your keys by m _ _ _ _ _ _ last night.

10 | Review

1 Complete the dialogue with *must, might, could* or *can't*. Sometimes more than one answer is possible.

A: What's that noise? I think there (1) _____ be someone in the flat.

B: No, it (2) _____ be coming from our flat. The noise is too far away.

A: What do you think it (3) _____ be?

B: It (4) _____ be someone next door.

A: It (5) _____ be the neighbours. They've gone away.

B: If it's not the neighbours, it (6) _____ be a thief. Go and have a look.

A: I'm not going. They (7) _____ have a gun or something.

2 Rewrite the sentences beginning with the words given.

1 There's a chance you will meet someone through a dating agency.
You might _____.

2 That definitely wasn't an alien.
That can't _____.

3 I'm sure she's completely crazy.
She must _____.

4 Perhaps they buried the treasure.
They might _____.

5 I think she's spying on us.
She may _____.

6 He probably buried the murder weapon.
He may _____.

7 It's possible that he's working as a secret agent.
He could _____.

8 There's a possibility that it won't rain.
It might _____.

3 Work in pairs. Read the story. How many possible explanations can you think of?

It may have been a treasure map.

IN ABOUT 1890, the priest of Rennes-le-Château in the south of France discovered some very old, secret documents in his church. He could not understand the documents, so he took them to an expert in Paris. When the priest returned to his village, he was extremely rich. He never explained where the money came from and he took his secret with him to the grave.

4 Complete the sentences with a word from the box.

about	from	in	of	with

1 One of the good things _____ his job is he travels a lot.

2 The main problem _____ his work is that he can't tell anyone what he does.

3 Another drawback _____ his work is that he can't visit certain countries.

4 It also has the disadvantage _____ being very dangerous at times.

5 He works for the benefit _____ his country.

6 The trouble _____ working for the government is that the pay isn't very good.

7 There is a lot to be gained _____ carrying a gun in his job.

8 There is no point _____ asking him his name – he won't tell the truth.

5 Complete the text with words from the box.

audiences	magician	perform	pretended
revealed	stage	tricks	vanish

The world's greatest (1) _____ was probably Harry Houdini. When he first went on (2) _____, he did (3) _____ with playing cards and made women (4) _____ from magic boxes. He later became popular with (5) _____ around the world when he started to (6) _____ incredible escapes as part of his show. Houdini also (7) _____ the secrets of many people who (8) _____ to be able to communicate with the dead.

6 Replace the words in italics with a word from the box.

accused	admitted	claimed
pretended	refused	seemed	tried

1 He *acted as if* he was deaf.

2 He *said that it was true* that he had met an alien.

3 There was some vandalism in the school and the police *said it was* my brother.

4 One of the boys has *said that he was* bullying younger children.

5 She *made an effort* to calm down.

6 The casino *said they didn't intend* to pay.

7 They *appeared* to be using new tactics.

11 | Review

1 Rewrite the sentences beginning with the words given.

1 His tea is made by his secretary.
   His secretary _____.
2 You must do all the work before tomorrow.
   All the work _____.
3 When are your accounts going to be finished?
   When are you _____?
4 Someone's made a few mistakes with this.
   A few mistakes _____.
5 My car's being repaired at the moment.
   The garage _____.
6 They cancelled the marathon at the last moment.
   The marathon _____.
7 You haven't filled in your form.
   Your form _____.
8 They estimate the cost of the games to be more than $3 billion.
   The cost of the games _____.

2 Four of the sentences contain one unnecessary word. Cross out the unnecessary words.

1 I promised to my boyfriend a ticket for the cup final for his birthday.
2 A friend got the ticket for me on the black market.
3 I paid for her a fortune for it.
4 Then, my boyfriend was offered a well-paid job in Los Angeles on the day of the final.
5 So, I bought to him a pair of socks.
6 I found him a very nice pair with the English flag on them.
7 I gave them to him when he returned home.
8 As usual, he didn't bring for me anything from America.

3 Rearrange the words to make sentences.

1 am cut going hair have I my next to week .
2 bed breakfast had have I in never served .
3 delivered have house I my often pizzas to .
4 dyed hair have I my never would .
5 a car have I my once serviced year .
6 tested eyes have I must my soon .
7 all by clothes have I ironed mother my my .
8 decorated flat have I love my to would .

4 Work in pairs. Are the sentences in exercise 3 true (T) or false (F) for you?

5 Complete the question tags with an auxiliary verb.

1 You've been to Wimbledon, _____ you?
2 The weather's never good, _____ it?
3 The tickets are very expensive, _____ they?
4 British players never win, _____ they?
5 Wimbledon started over one hundred years ago, _____ it?
6 They play on grass, _____ they?
7 You can't park near Wimbledon, _____ you?
8 You haven't got an extra ticket, _____ you?

6 Complete the text with words from the box.

catch	championship	pass	penalty
players	run	team	throw

Netball is similar to basketball, and (1) _____ have to (2) _____ a ball in a net to score goals.
However, they cannot (3) _____ with the ball.
When they (4) _____ it, they must (5) _____ it to another member of their (6) _____.
If a player breaks a rule, the other team is given a (7) _____. The world netball (8) _____ is often won by Australia.

7 Choose the correct word to complete the sentences.

1 If you are *determination / determined* enough, you can usually get what you want.
2 It's better to have good looks than *intelligence / intelligent*.
3 Men don't usually like *ambition / ambitious* women.
4 Most people lose their *enthusiasm / enthusiastic* when they become adults.
5 People with natural *talent / talented* will always be successful.
6 Women have more mental *agility / agile* than men.
7 Women will always be less *power / powerful* than men.
8 You need to be absolutely *ruthlessness / ruthless* to succeed in the business world.

8 Work in pairs. Decide if you agree or disagree with the sentences in exercise 7.

12 | Review

1 Rewrite the quotations in reported speech.

1 I don't want money. It is only people who pay their bills who want that, and I never pay mine.
Oscar Wilde

2 A bank is a place that will lend you money if you can prove that you don't need it.
Bob Hope

3 The only reason I made a commercial for American Express was to pay for my American Express bill.
Peter Ustinov

2 Put the bank manager's questions in direct speech.

(1) The bank manager asked me what I would do with the money. (2) He wanted to know when I was going to pay the money back. (3) He asked how much I earned. (4) Then, he asked if I had any investments. (5) He wanted to know how much money I had saved last year. (6) He asked if I had ever had any credit card debts. (7) Finally, he asked me if I could give him the names of two referees.

1 'What will you do with the money?'
2 '_____?'
3 '_____?'
4 '_____?'
5 '_____?'
6 '_____?'
7 '_____?'

3 Work in pairs. Imagine that one of you wants to borrow £1,000 from the bank. Roleplay the interview between the bank manager and the customer.

Now work with a different partner. Tell him/her about the customer's answers to the bank manager's questions.

4 Complete the news story on the right at the top using a maximum of three words for each gap. Use sentences 1–6 to help you.

1 'You must appear in court.'
2 'We want the demonstrations to be stopped.'
3 'Could you limit the number of protesters to a maximum of ten?'
4 'Can you allow us to continue?'
5 'You can't go within 50 metres of the factory.'
6 'Stop making weapons!'

A group of protesters who demonstrated outside a weapons factory were in court in Brighton today. The anti-war protesters were told (1) _to appear_ in court after the factory asked the judge (2) _____ the demonstrations. The company's lawyer asked the judge (3) _____ the protesters to ten people on Thursday afternoons.

In reply, the protesters claimed they had a legal right to demonstrate and asked the judge (4) _____ them to continue. In his ruling, the judge told the protesters (5) _____ within 50 metres of the factory, but he did not agree to limitations on the number of people or the day of the week. It is believed that protests will continue. The protesters have told the factory (6) _____ making weapons if they want the demonstrations to stop.

5 Choose the best response for each exchange.

A: It's been nice meeting you. See you again soon, I hope.
B: (1) *Yes, another day, maybe. / Yes, keep in touch.*

A: I'm really sorry, but I've lost the pen you lent me.
B: (2) *Oh, never mind. / Oh well, all the best.*

A: It was really nice of you to show us around. Thanks.
B: (3) *Not at all. / The same to you.*

A: Katy's not feeling well, so she's decided to stay at home tonight.
B: (4) *Guess what? / What a shame!*

A: You've been so kind to me. I'll never forget it.
B: (5) *Congratulations! / My pleasure.*

A: I've got the interview for the new job tomorrow.
B: (6) *Have a safe journey. / I'll keep my fingers crossed.*

6 Complete sentences 1–8 with the phrases a–h.

1 He denied that he had made
2 I couldn't withdraw
3 I don't think I can pay
4 It's very easy to get into
5 She became very rich by investing in
6 We'll need to save
7 When I was little, my parents opened
8 You'll need to take out

a a mortgage to buy the house.
b a savings account for me.
c all my bills this month.
d any cash because the machine was out of order.
e debt when you lose your job.
f his money by selling heroin.
g some money before we can afford it.
h stocks and shares.

Macmillan Education
Between Towns Road, Oxford OX4 3PP
A division of Macmillan Publishers Limited

Companies and representatives throughout the world

ISBN 978-0-230-42324-4 Student's Book
ISBN 978-0-230-42447-0 Student's Book & website access

Text © Philip Kerr and Ceri Jones 2012
Design and illustration © Macmillan Publishers Limited 2012

This edition published 2012
First edition published 2006

This edition designed by eMC Design Ltd.
Original design by Oliver Design
Cover design by eMC Design Ltd.
Illustrated by Arlene Adams p70; Ross Cuthbert pp130, 133; Nigel Dobbyn pp126, 134; Javier Joaquin p41; Gary Kaye pp59; Roger Penwill pp40, 46,56, 120; Norbert Sipos pp32, 69, 90; Gary Wing p71.
Cover photograph by Corbis/Lois Ellen Frank, Getty Images/Doug Chinnery, Alamy/Robert Harding Picture Library Ltd, Corbis/Roger Tidman, Corbis/Gerolf Kalt, Alamy/Images & Stories
Picture research by Sally Cole

Authors' acknowledgements
The authors would like to thank Nicola Gardner for her sterling work as Content Editor. They would also like to express their debt of gratitude to Nicola Stewart, editor for the Intermediate level, the designers at eMc Design Limited, Sally Cole for picture research and James Richardson for the sound recording, who all played vital roles in the development of this new edition. Finally, they would like to thank Katy Wright and the late David Riley, the driving forces behind the first edition of Straightforward.

The publishers would like to thank all the teachers from around the world who provided invaluable comments, suggestions and feedback on the first edition. The publishers would also like to thank the following people for their help and contribution to the second edition:
Tatiana Baytimerova (Russia), Lenka Boehmová (Czech Republic), Dr. Manuel Padilla Cruz (Spain), Svetlana Elchaninova (Russia), Jennifer Díaz Green (Dublin), Elena Mokeeva (Romania), Lynn Thomson (freelance editor), Amany Shawkey (Macmillan Egypt), Maria Teresa Rius Villaplana (Spain), Natalia Vorobyeva (Russia).

The authors and publisher are grateful for permission to reprint the following copyright material:

Page 31: Extract from 'Bedrooms Through The Ages' by Richard Wood , copyright © Richard Wood 1999, first published in the UK by Wayland an imprint of Hachette Children's Books, 338 Euston Road, London NW1 3BH, reprinted by permission of the publisher;

Page 40: Extracts from 'World's luckiest man wins the lottery' 16.06.03; 'Toddler locked mum out on balcony' 15.10.03; 'Man fired after being stranded on mountain top' 04.11.03 and 'Fried egg cost teenager's mum £675.00' 04.11.03, all taken from Ananova.com.;

Page 68: Extract from 'The Lord of the Rings' by J.R.R.Tolkien, copyright © J.R.R.Tolkien 1954 (George Allen and Unwin, 1954), reprinted by permission of HarperCollins Publishers Limited;

Page 130: Extracts from 'Coin through elbow' and 'The self-tying handkerchief' both taken from www.conjuror.com.;

Dictionary extracts taken from the Macmillan Essential Dictionary, copyright © Macmillan Publishers Limited 2003, used with permission.

The authors and publishers would like to thank the following for permission to reproduce their photographs:
Alamy/A.F.Archive p68(bl), Alamy/J.Arnold Images Ltd pp57, 58(A), Alamy/Artpartner-image p122(m), Alamy/B.Bland p110(tr), Alamy/S.Belcher p46(D), Alamy/F1online digitale Bildagentur GmbH p62, Alamy/Blend Images p88(bl), Alamy/P.Bramhill p156(bl), Alamy/A.Bramwell p20-21(b), Alamy/J.Brooks p82(l), Alamy/N.Cannon p18(D), Alamy/M.Caruana p132(mr), Alamy/T.Cordoza p46(C), Alamy/D.Croucher p73, Alamy/Cultura Creative p67, Alamy/I.Dagnall p62(insert), Alamy/Gaertner p82(r), Alamy/T.Graham p11(tl), Alamy/Robert Harding Picture Library p61(br), Alamy/Ilian p92(tr), Alamy/R.Jahns p58(B), Alamy/Jinx Photography p122(tr), Alamy/Lemonlight Features p93, Alamy/Motoring Picture Library p18(E), Alamy/E.Nathan p83(mr), Alamy/One-image Photography p83(ml), Alamy/S.Outram p19(map), Alamy/PhotoEdit p76, Alamy/T.Simon p53, Alamy/D.Green Studio pp122(tl), Alamy/H.Sykes p11(tml), Alamy/TongRo Image Stock p46(B), Alamy/Vario Images GmbH & Co p18(B), Alamy/G.Vurtis p23(tr); **Alvaro Neil** the biciclown pp16(a),16(b); **Archive Photos** pp39, 43(m), 48(br); **AFP** p100(b), 108(a),108(b),108(c),123(mr); **Blend Images** p83(b); **Brand X** pp12(bl), 80(I); **Corbis**/Abode/Beateworks p31(br), Corbis/OTHK/Asia Images p161, Corbis/Blend Images p97(bl), Corbis/T.Brakefield p18(F), Corbis/R.Cousins p28(B), Corbis/Cultura p102(br), Corbis/Destinations p60, Corbis/H.Diltz p12(tr), Corbis/Construction Photography p28(tl), Corbis/E.Ghioldi p12(tml), Corbis/Imagmore Co. Ltd p28(ml), Corbis/ImageSource p12(tl), Corbis/Platform/Johner Images p12(tmr), Corbis/R.Klune p83(tl), Corbis/B.Lewis.In Pictures p20(mr), Corbis/M.Longhurst p28(C), Corbis/K.Maack/Nordicphotos p41(mr), Corbis/National Geographic Society p60(insert), Corbis/S.Neelman p110(tl), Corbis/C.Pizzello/Reuters p42(tl), Corbis/Pool Photograph p162, Corbis/H.Scheibe p42(br), Corbis/V.Streano p27(mr), Corbis/G.Thomas/Loop Images p28(F); **Digital Vision** p22(B); **Europic**/CEN p38(r); **Getty**/J.Frazier p83(tr),Getty/R.Kaufman /L.Hirshowitz p127(bl), Getty/M.Rochon p12(mr), Getty/K.Smeds p72(ml); **Getty Images Entertainment** p8(ml); **Getty Images News** pp78(tr), 100(tr), 100(mr); **Getty Images Publicity** pp106, 107(tl); **Getty Images Sport** p107(tr); **Tony Hawks** p17; **Hulton Archive** pp11(tr), 31(mr), 43(mr); **Iconica** p22(A); **Photodisc** p22(C); **Macmillan Publishers Ltd**/D.Ryan pp18(A), 51, 52, 87, 116(br), 134(oil), 134(tomatoes), 134(ice cream), 134(honey), 134(spaghetti), 134(juice, 134(chocolates, 134(cola), Macmillan Publishers Ltd/D.Tolley/R.Judges p19(money); Cover of The Secret Life of Walter Mitty reproduced with kind permission of **Penguin Books** p7; **Photoalto** p19(compass); **Photographers Choice** p36-37(b); **Photolibrary**/Britain on View p66-67(b), Photolibrary/J.A. Castellano p22(ml), Photolibrary/Corbis p18(C), Photolibrary/J.Curtis p112(b), Photolibrary/East Photo p19(sunglasses), Photolibrary/R.Edwards 28(A), Photolibrary/Evox Productions p118(tr), Photolibrary/Flight Images LLP p99, Photolibrary/FogStock p116(ml), Photolibrary/Food Collection p47(br), Photolibrary/D. & J. Heaton p89(br), Photolibrary/Imagebroker p20(m), Photolibrary/ImageSource pp10(l), 122(mr), Photolibrary/Image100 p20(ml), Photolibrary /D.Johnston p26-27(b), Photolibrary/S.Katzer p103(tl), Photolibrary/J.Klee p128(mr), Photolibrary/J.Osmond p28(E), Photolibrary/L.Pampalone p46(A), Photolibrary/Photo Equipe 153 p92(bl), Photolibrary/D.Gair Photographic p23(br), Photolibrary/Stockbrokerxtra Images p118(bl), Photolibrary/LWA/D.Tardif p123(bl), Photolibrary/J.West p103(tl); **Rex Features** /Action Press p33, Rex Features/Everett Collection p6(br), Rex Features F1 online p108(br), Rex Features/D.Hartley p157(bl), Rex Features/N.Jorgensen p28(D), Rex Features/Lehtikuva OY pp109(bl), 110(mr); **Ross Parry Syndication**/Collect pp70(t), 70(br); **Stockbyte** p118(tm); **Stockimage** p12(ml); **Stone** p81(tl); **Taxi** pp12(m), 68(mr); **The Bridgeman Art Library**/Portrait of Henry VIII (engraving), English School, (19th century) (after) / Private Collection / Ken Welsh p11(tmr), The Bridgeman Art Library/Louis XIV (1638-1715) receiving the Papal Legate at Fontainebleau on 29 July 1664 (colour litho), Le Brun, Charles (1619-90) (after) / Bibliothèque des Arts Decoratifs, Paris, France / Archives Charmet p31(ml), The Bridgeman Art Library/King Arthur, 1903 (oil on canvas), Butler, Charles Ernest (1864-c.1918) / Private Collection / © Christopher Wood Gallery, London, UK p99(br); **The Conservative Party** logo p9(mbr); **The Image Bank** p83; **The Labour Party** logo p9(br); **The Liberal Democrat Party** logo p9(tm); **The Ronald Grant Archive**/Columbia Pictures/Imagine Entertainment p98(tr), The Ronald Grant Archive/Warner Brothers p80(mb), **Topfoto**/Topham PA p78(br), Topfoto/Topham Picturepoint p80(tm); **Wire Image** pp77(br), 113(mr)

Printed and bound in Thailand
2016 2015 2014 2013
10 9 8 7 6 5 4 3 2